The *Spirit* of Holiness & Power

- An Anthology on the Holy Spirit -

The *Spirit* of Holiness & Power

- An Anthology on the Holy Spirit -

Ralph I. Tilley, Editor

LITS Books
PO Box 405
Sellersburg, Indiana 47172

The Spirit of Holiness & Power: An Anthology on the Holy Spirit
Copyright ©2020 Ralph I. Tilley

No part of this book may be reproduced in any form (except for brief quotations) without permission in writing from the author. All rights reserved.

Unless otherwise indicated, the editor's articles are taken from *The Holy Bible, English Standard Version®*, copyright ©2011 by Crossway, a publishing ministry of Good News Publishers. Used by permission. All rights reserved.

Scripture quotations marked (NASB) are taken from the *New American Standard Bible®*, Copyright ©1995 by The Lockman Foundation. Used by permission. www.Lockman.org.

Words italicized in Scripture quotations are the author's and added for emphasis.

ISBN: 978-1-7328087-3-7

This book is also available in Kindle.

For all books authored or edited by Ralph I. Tilley, go to litsjournal.org or amazon.com.

LITS Books is the publishing ministry of Life in the Spirit Ministries, a not-for-profit organization.

LITS Books
PO Box 405
Sellersburg, Indiana 47172

Dedicated to the memory of
Dr. Leslie D. Wilcox (1907-1991),
*my first New Testament Studies professor,
whose Christian character was unimpeachable
and classes unforgettable.*

Contents

Preface	ix
A Prayer for Heart-Holiness	x
Chapter 1 / The Spirit of Holiness & Power	1
Ralph I. Tilley	
Chapter 2 / The Spirit in the Life of Jesus' Followers	9
Gerald F. Hawthorne	
Chapter 3 / The Executive of the Godhead	18
Daniel Steele	
Chapter 4 / Union with Jesus	22
Samuel L. Brengle	
Chapter 5 / I Believe in the Holy Ghost	29
Maynard James	
Chapter 6 / The Holy Spirit and the Church	36
Charles H. Spurgeon	
Chapter 7 / The Enduement of the Spirit	39
A. J. Gordon	
Chapter 8 / The Spirit-Filled Christian Life	45
Fredrik Wisloff	
Chapter 9 / A Living Sacrifice	59
James Montgomery Boice	
Chapter 10 / Have You Given Him the Reins?	67
Ted S. Rendall	
Chapter 11 / The Pivot Point	76
Phillip Keller	
Chapter 12 / My Conversion and Empowerment	87
Duncan Campbell	
Chapter 13 / "Unless the Spirit …"	92
Vance Havner	

Chapter 14 / "Look Not to Your Own Interests" 96
    Dennis F. Kinlaw
Chapter 15 / Transfiguration of Character 103
    J. Sidlow Baxter
Chapter 16 / I Met a Man with a Shining Face 114
    Harry E. Jessop
Chapter 17 / The Story Behind *Streams in the Desert* 120
    Lettie Cowman & Ed Erny
Chapter 18 / Power from on High 130
    Leslie D. Wilcox
Chapter 19 / The Cost of Service 137
    John E. Hunter
Chapter 20 / The Minister with a Laughing Face 143
    Warren W. Wiersbe
Chapter 21 / How God Revived Me 148
    Barry Shoemake
Chapter 22 / Used of God 153
    Jonathan Goforth
Chapter 23 / Amy Carmichael: The Radiant Life 159
    V. Raymond Edman
Chapter 24 / The Irreducible Minimum 168
    D. Martyn Lloyd-Jones
Chapter 25 / Choked Channels 175
    S. D. Gordon
Chapter 26 / Step by Step 181
    J. Gregory Mantle
Chapter 27 / What to Do When You Stumble 186
    W. E. Sangster
Chapter 28 / Breathe on Me, Breath of God 193
    Ralph I. Tilley
  Books by Ralph I. Tilley 203

Preface

THIS BOOK is about holiness—about the power of the Holy Spirit, who both cleanses and enables Christians to live a life pleasing to God. God has called us to holiness: "As obedient children, do not be conformed to the passions of your former ignorance, but as he who called you is holy, you also be holy in all your conduct, since it is written, "You shall be holy, for I am holy" (1 Pet. 1:14-16).

As disciples of the Lord Jesus Christ, we always need our faith stimulated to live soberly, righteously, and godly in this present world. The following writings have been selected to serve as a vehicle in stirring up the reader to live a life wholly to the glory of God—from the inside out.

This volume is mostly a compilation of articles that appeared in *Life in the Spirit Journal*, of which I was the editor for some 20 years. The selected authors represent a wide range among evangelical scholars, preachers, and writers, whose ecclesiastical identities vary: Methodist, Lutheran, Nazarene, Presbyterian, Salvation Army, Baptist, Nondenominational, etc. Regardless of their respective church backgrounds, each of these writers evidenced a heart for God and a sincere desire to live a holy and godly life to the glory of God and the Lord Jesus Christ. These authors would not have necessarily agreed among themselves on some of the finer points of the doctrine of sanctification. However, each believed that God has called followers of Christ to live a holy life and to be continually filled with the Holy Spirit.

To those authors and publishers who granted permission for reprinting these writings when they appeared in *Life in the Spirit Journal*, we offer sincere gratitude (some of the articles are in the public domain). To these authors, most of whom have passed on to their eternal reward, I owe an immeasurable debt for contributing to my growth in the knowledge and grace of the Lord Jesus Christ.

Ralph I. Tilley
Soli Deo Gloria

I am a companion of all who fear you, of those who keep your precepts.
Psalm 119:63

THE SPIRIT OF HOLINESS & POWER

A Prayer for Heart-Holiness

O God, my Father, holy is your name! From all eternity the angelic hosts have cried out,

> *"Holy, holy, holy is the Lord God Almighty, who was, and is, and is to come."*

This very moment, the heavenly created beings are worshipfully singing,

> *"Holy, holy, holy."*

With the prophet of old, I painfully confess,

> *"Woe is me ... my eyes have seen the King, the LORD Almighty."*

With the trembling apostle, I humbly agree,

> *"Depart from me, for I am a sinful man, O Lord."*

O righteous Father, you sent your Son to break sin's tyranny and bondage over me and in me. Christ died to set me free from Satan's cruel yoke. Jesus came to destroy the works of Satan. Sin shall not be my master, for Jesus has set me free. "Blessed are the pure in heart, for they shall see God."

By the power of your Holy Spirit, penetrating my deepest need, be pleased to increasingly transform your unworthy servant into the likeness of your Son. According to your sovereign wisdom, use whatever is necessary to make me more holy: using trials, when trials are needed; using tests, when tests are warranted; using afflictions, when afflictions serve your higher purposes; use misunderstandings, hardships, and all manner of unfriendly providences—to shape your church and me to resemble the Lord Jesus Christ more perfectly.

Help me to say "yes" to you when I do not feel *like surrendering. Help me to say "no" to sin when I am inclined to enter temptation's door. By your grace abundantly working in me, enable me to always live under your loving control so that I may exercise the discipline of self-control at all times.*

> *Oh, to be like Thee! Oh, to be like Thee.*
> *Blessed Redeemer, pure as Thou art!*
> *Come in Thy sweetness, come in Thy fullness;*
> *Stamp Thine own image deep on my heart.* (Kirkpatrick)

In the mighty name of your Son, the Lord Jesus Christ. Amen.

Ralph I. Tilley

CHAPTER 1

The Spirit of Holiness & Power

Ralph I. Tilley

Ralph I. Tilley served as a pastor (38 years), professor of New Testament Studies, founding editor of *Life in the Spirit Journal* for 20 years, and continues to serve as the online editor of *Life in the Spirit*; he is presently engaged in writing, publishing, and teaching ministries. He holds degrees from God's Bible School & College (Th.B.), Andrews University (M.A.), and Trinity Theological Seminary (D.R.S.). Since 2008, Ralph has served as a visiting lecturer at West Africa Theological Seminary, Lagos, Nigeria.

Ralph and his wife Emily reside in Sellersburg, Indiana; they have two married daughters and three grandchildren.

THE ONLY PREREQUISITE for a seeking heart to be purified and filled—and continually purified and filled with the Holy Spirit—is a healthy appetite for God, a deep thirst for God. Remember, God forgives what we confess, he sanctifies what we offer, he fills what he sanctifies, and he uses what he fills—all through grace given to the God-thirsty soul.

The 120 who gathered for prayer ten days before the Pentecost outpouring of the Holy Spirit were thirsty-hearted followers of the crucified, risen, and ascended Lord Jesus Christ. These men and women had walked with Christ during his earthly sojourn; they were convinced he was the way, the truth, and the life. Their Lord had told them that apart from him, they could not do anything that God considered a success. They were to live their lives in total dependence upon Christ, always giving Christ the glory for anything he accomplished through them. The apostles were selected to serve as Christ's witnesses, going into all the world to preach the gospel, making disciples of all their converts. But there was one requirement that must first be met before they were prepared to serve Christ fully and effectively—they must be cleansed and filled—

cleansed and filled with power from on high.

The One Essential

The Lord Jesus, before his ascension into heaven, alerted the disciples to the one essential for fruitful ministry—the power of the Holy Spirit: "And behold, I am sending the promise of my Father upon you. But stay in the city until you are clothed with power from on high" (Lk. 24:49).[1]

To be filled with the Holy Spirit is to be filled with the Spirit's power—the power to live a life pleasing to God, the ability to accomplish God's purposes through us. Too much of the work of the church is self-generated and self-maintained. One can hear it in so much of the music, praying, and preaching. What pleases carnal hearers and what pleases our Father in Heaven are not to be confused.

Prior to the Pentecost event, Simon Peter was the personification of one who possessed good intentions but lacked the power to bring those intentions to successful fruition. Peter, along with the other disciples, experienced the power to cast out demons but lacked the ability of the Holy Spirit to control their passions and energize their respective ministries to the glory of God.

How we need the power of the Holy Spirit! How we need his strength to minister effectively and live obediently. Without the indwelling, filling power of the Holy Spirit, we cannot live a life in total consecration and surrender to the Lord Jesus.

The same Simon Peter who denied his Lord three times—but afterward repented—and was subsequently empowered with the Spirit at Pentecost, wrote a letter to the Christian Diaspora some 30 years later. In that letter (The First Epistle of Peter), this Spirit-filled, Spirit-empowered apostle of the Lord, called the letter's recipients to a *humanly impossible* lifestyle. Note the following selections from each of the five respective chapters.

As obedient children, do not be conformed to the passions of your former ignorance, but as he who called you is holy, you also be holy in all your conduct, since it is written, "You shall be holy, for I am holy" (1:14-16).

Servants, be subject to your masters with all respect, not only to the good and gentle but also to the unjust. For this is a gracious thing, when, mindful of God, one endures sorrows while suffering unjustly. For what credit is it if, when you sin and are beaten for it, you endure? But if when you do good and suffer for it you endure, this is a gracious thing in the sight of God (2:18-20).

Finally, all of you, have unity of mind, sympathy, brotherly love, a tender heart, and a humble mind (3:8).

Above all, keep loving one another earnestly since love covers a multitude of sins (4:8).

Clothe yourselves, all of you, with humility toward one another (5:5b).

Defective Christians

Don't you see the impossibility of living out these, or any other, biblical imperatives apart from the ever-present indwelling, filling, empowering Holy Spirit?

Christianity is a supernatural religion that is incapable of being lived-out without supernatural help. But the good news for Christians is that the Helper is available to all who invite him to take control. But that is the problem—we want to be in control, at least to control some areas of our life.

Transformed and empowered by the Spirit of God, Peter knew his readers could not possibly obey his apostolic injunctions. How could one not be conformed to sinful passions, treat an unjust master with respect, live in unity and brotherly love with all Christians, and walk in humility with fellow believers? Impossible!—impossible as long as we seek to live a self-directed life instead of a Spirit-controlled and Spirit-empowered life.

Here is where the church is failing miserably short. We are walking in the flesh instead of being controlled by the Spirit. Hence, the tensions and conflict, the disputes and arguments, the world-conformity instead of Christ-conformity, the man-pleasing spirit instead of a God-fearing spirit, pride instead of humility, self-assertion instead of self-abasement.

The average Christian stands in need of another conversion! Why? He is living without power, without the Spirit controlling his or her passions, temperament, desires, motives, choices, ambitions, thoughts, and pursuits. The church needs changed Christians, Spirit-filled, and Spirit-controlled followers of the Lord Jesus.

When our grandson Luke was six years of age, he was just learning to spell a bit and learn a few punctuation marks. One day he placed a little yellow note on my desk. Here's what he wrote: "I love you, God. ! ?" Period, exclamation point—then a question mark. Those three items could very well summarize Peter's walk with Christ—before the Pentecost event, as well as summarizing the walk of many of Christ's contemporary spasmodic disciples. They are living life without certainty, real purpose, and direction. Their hearts are divided.

They need a fresh cleansing and the definitive filling and empowering of the Holy Spirit.

What is the answer for such vacillating, powerless, joyless, divided hearts? What is the solution for these defeated Christians?

Separation and Cleansing

For those who are professing faith in Christ but living powerless lives, the first step one must take before he can enter into a life of fullness and power is to repent of his fleshly ways and receive a heart-cleansing—a cleansing from a self-centered ego. The specific things one needs to be cleansed from and repent of can only be suggested by the Holy Spirit; he will let us know.

One of the apostle Paul's most challenging churches he founded and tended was the Corinthian Church. This church excelled in spiritual gifts (though incorrectly understood at points), but they fell short of *agape* love; these brothers and sisters had been set apart by God to live a holy life, but they often failed miserably—demonstrating a sectarian spirit, jealousy, and were sometimes contentious, and lacked moral courage. When we fail on the outside, it is because we have a real need on the inside. These Corinthians had a real *inside* need. What were Paul's recommendations and solutions to the Corinthians' heart-need? Part of that solution is found in his second letter to the church.

> [14] *Do not be unequally yoked with unbelievers. For what partnership has righteousness with lawlessness? Or what fellowship has light with darkness?* [15] *What accord has Christ with Belial? Or what portion does a believer share with an unbeliever?* [16] *What agreement has the temple of God with idols? For we are the temple of the living God; as God said,*
>
> *"I will make my dwelling among them and walk among them,*
>   *and I will be their God,*
>   *and they shall be my people.*
> [17] *Therefore go out from their midst,*
>   *and be separate from them, says the Lord,*
> *and touch no unclean thing;*
>   *then I will welcome you,*
> [18] *and I will be a father to you,*
>   *and you shall be sons and daughters to me,*
> *says the Lord Almighty."*
>
> 7 [1] *Since we have these promises, beloved, let us cleanse ourselves from every defilement of body and spirit, bringing holiness to completion in the*

fear of God (2 Cor. 6:14-7:1).

What was Paul's solution to the heart-needs of these failing Christians? To remove from themselves every contaminant, everything that defiled body and spirit. Radical heart-surgery was required, separating themselves from every uncleanness identified by the Holy Spirit. Holiness of heart always precedes the Spirit's infilling and empowerment. J. C. Ryle (1816-1900), one of Anglicanism's foremost pastors and bishops of the 19th century, said it well on this subject: "A holy man will follow after purity of heart. He will dread all filthiness and uncleanness of spirit and seek to avoid all things that might draw him into it. He knows his heart is like tinder and will diligently keep clear of the sparks of temptation."[2]

The prophet Isaiah had ministered for some years before his transformative, cleansing experience. He said it happened in the year of King Uzziah's death. He saw the Lord that day in the temple as he had never encountered him before: "high and lifted up" (Isa. 6:1). The hovering seraphim were singing antiphonally: "Holy, holy, holy is the LORD of hosts; the whole earth is full of his glory" (Isa. 6:3). Immediately, Isaiah was convicted of his uncleanness and confesses: "Woe is me! For I am lost; for I am a man of unclean lips, and I dwell in the midst of a people of unclean lips; for my eyes have seen the King, the LORD of hosts!" (Isa. 6:5).

Isaiah had allowed the pressure of his culture to influence his life. It was only through the manifestation of God's revealed presence that the unclean prophet recognized his impurities.

How we need the convicting presence of God among us! Why is it that people can come and go from the church sanctuary week after week and live untouched, unchanged lives? Because God fails to show up! When God shows up, sinners and saints are convicted of their sins, their shortcomings, their lack, their powerless living. The conviction of the Holy Spirit is personal and pungent. He will press his finger deeply into our need. Conviction always precedes repentance; repentance always precedes cleansing; cleansing always precedes filling; filling always precedes ultimate usefulness to the glory of Christ.

We need to ask ourselves, "Are there areas of my life that need surrendering to the lordship of Christ? Are there attitudes, thoughts, or behaviors that need to be repented of? Do I need a fresh, radical heart-cleansing?" Can you identify with the cry of the pleading leper: "Lord, if you will, you can make me clean"? Will you feel the touch of the ever-living Christ just now and hear him say, "I will; be clean" (Matt. 8:1-4).

You may want to pray the words of Charles Naylor (1974-1950):

THE SPIRIT OF HOLINESS & POWER

Make me clean, make me clean,
Though defiled and so sinful I am;
Make me clean, make me clean,
Make me clean in the blood of the Lamb.[3]

The following words were written by J. Edwin Orr (1912-1987) while conducting revival services in Ngaruawahia, New Zealand, many years ago. They have become classic and used mightily by the Spirit in turning many hearts fully to the Lord:

Search me, O God, and know my heart today;
Try me, O Savior, know my thoughts, I pray.
See if there be some wicked way in me;
Cleanse me from every sin and set me free.[4]

I have never sung or read those words without the Spirit searchingly ministering to me. Even now, as I listened to them over the Internet, my heart was touched anew by the Spirit of God.

Cleansing always precedes fullness—cleansing from a self-centered ego, cleansing of a man-pleasing spirit, cleansing of every precious idol, cleansing of a self-managed life, cleansing of everything that vies for control of the throne of our heart. Our hearts need to be circumcised by the Spirit's surgical knife, with all uncleanness excised.

We are in need of a deep cleansing. And with a deep confession and repentance, there will follow a deep cleansing, accompanied by full assurance that we have been heard by our gracious God. After that we will continue to sing with J. Edwin Orr:

I praise Thee, Lord, for cleansing me from sin;
Fulfill Thy Word, and make me pure within.
Fill me with fire where once I burned with shame;
Grant my desire to magnify Thy Name.

Fullness and Power Follow Cleansing

The fullness and power of the Holy Spirit is the inevitable consequence of cleansing. Following the Pentecost outpouring of the Holy Spirit, the followers of the Lord Jesus were *full* men and women. Acts records that they were filled with the Holy Spirit (2:4; 6:3; 7:55; 11:24; 13:9, 52); filled with joy (13:52); and that some were filled with wisdom, grace, faith, power and good works (6:3, 5, 8; 9:36; 11:24).

How we need Spirit-filled churches! How we need Spirit-filled Christians!

A problem we face, however, is that too often we want to be filled but are unwilling to pay the price to be cleansed.

I think just now of the Evangelist Duncan Campbell (1898-1972), whom I heard preach in 1969. This Scottish preacher had spent many years in useful service to the Lord and then strangely entered a seventeen-year period of barrenness. In his own words: "Here I was—a lovely congregation, and now proud of the fact that I was being asked to address conventions. You see, I was Campbell of the Mid Argyll Revival.... Oh, this heart of mine began to swell."[5]

The Holy Spirit used both his daughter and a young minister to bring conviction to his proud heart. Listening to the young minister speaking, his heart was powerfully convicted of its need. Campbell said, "As he spoke, conviction deepened and gripped me until I felt utterly unworthy to hold the Bible in my hands. I said to my wife and daughter, 'I'm going to my study, and I do not wish to be disturbed. I want to face God with honesty and sincerity.'" Then Campbell said, "So I went to my study. I fell on my face and confessed my backsliding. I confessed how I had drifted into modernism. I confessed how the evil heart of unbelief had gripped me." The altar had been prepared; God responded with forgiveness, cleansing, and fullness. And the evangelist resumed an effective ministry for his remaining years.

Do you desire—really desire the Spirit's fullness and power in your life? What is the Spirit saying to you just now? Are you willing to pay the price? It matters not whether you are a layperson or one whom the Lord has consecrated to vocational ministry—God requires each of us to be holy from the inside out and to live a Spirit-anointed life.

Listen to the holy apostle exhorting first-century Christians:

> [13]*Therefore, preparing your minds for action, and being sober-minded, set your hope fully on the grace that will be brought to you at the revelation of Jesus Christ.* [14]*As obedient children, do not be conformed to the passions of your former ignorance,* [15]*but as he who called you is holy, you also be holy in all your conduct,* [16]*since it is written, "You shall be holy, for I am holy."* (1 Pet. 1:13-16).

And read once more what occurred on that glorious Pentecost Day when 120 people were gathered, praying and waiting for the promise of the Father:

> [1]*When the day of Pentecost arrived, they were all together in one place.* [2]*And suddenly there came from heaven a sound like a mighty rushing wind, and it filled the entire house where they were sitting.* [3]*And divided tongues as of fire appeared to them and rested on each one of*

them. *⁴And they were all filled with the Holy Spirit* ... (Acts 2:1-4a).

Are you thirsty?

---

1. Unless otherwise indicated, all Scripture quotations in this article are taken from *The Holy Bible, English Standard Version.*
2. J. C. Ryle, *Holiness*, p. 36.
3. Charles W. Naylor, "Make Me Clean."
4. J. Edwin Orr, "Search Me, O God."
5. Duncan Campbell, source unknown.

God of All Power, Truth, and Grace

God of all power, and truth, and grace,
Which shall from age to age endure,
Whose word, when Heaven and earth shall pass.
Remains, and stands forever sure.

Calmly to Thee my soul looks up,
And waits Thy promises to prove,
The object of my steadfast hope,
The seal of Thine eternal love.

That I Thy mercy may proclaim,
That all mankind Thy truth may see:
So hallow Thy great, glorious name,
And perfect holiness in me.

Thy sanctifying Spirit pour
To quench my thirst, and wash me clean:
Now, Father, let the gracious shower
Descend, and make me pure from sin.

Purge me from every sinful blot,
My idols all be cast aside,
Cleanse me from every evil thought,
From all the filth of self and pride.

O take this heart of stone away!
Thy sway it doth not, cannot own;
In me no longer let it stay;
O take away this heart of stone.

- Charles Wesley

CHAPTER 2

The Spirit in the Life of Jesus' Followers

Gerald F. Hawthorne

Gerald F. Hawthorne (1925-2010) served as a professor of New Testament Greek for 42 years at Wheaton College, Wheaton, Illinois. He was the editor, with Ralph P. Martin, of *Dictionary of Paul and His Letters* and the *Word Biblical Commentary: Philippians*. He served on the Committee of Translators for the *New International Version of the Bible*. Hawthorne received the B.A. and M.A. degrees from Wheaton College and the Ph.D. from the University of Chicago.

The following article is taken from *The Presence and the Power: The Significance of the Holy Spirit in the Life and Ministry of Jesus* by Gerald F. Hawthorne.

JESUS WAS A GENUINE HUMAN BEING in the fullest sense of this term, hemmed in by the limits of his humanity. But he was a human being filled with the Spirit, the Spirit who, on more than one occasion enabled Jesus to break through those human limits that bound him, so that the otherwise impossible became possible.

The Gift of the Spirit

Now what is of extraordinary importance to women and men today, people of all ages and from every country and social strata is this: The very first thing Jesus did immediately after he was resurrected from among the dead and reunited with his followers was to pass on to them, as a gift from his Father (cf. Acts 2:23), that same power by which he lived, triumphed, and broke the bands of his own human limitations. On the very day of his resurrection, he came to them locked in by their fears, "breathed" (*enephysēse*) on them and said, "Receive the Holy Spirit" (John 20:22).

Now there are several things of importance about this action of Jesus and about his word to those who were in that room, the nucleus of the church, that must be noticed:

1. The first thing to note is that the verb describing Jesus' action (*empysaiō*, "breathe on," or more literally, "breathe into") is wonderfully significant. It appears nowhere else in the New Testament, but it is the verb used in the Genesis description of the beginning of the human race. There it says that God "breathed" (*enephysēse*) into Adam's nostrils the breath of life, and he became a living person (Gen. 2:7). It is found also in that famous section of the Old Testament that contains the vision of the valley of very dry bones. Here the prophet is asked, "Can these bones live again?" And when he skeptically replies, "O Lord God, you know," the word of the Lord comes to him with a firm answer and a command: "Thus says the Lord God to these bones, 'Behold, I will cause breath to enter you that you may come to life.' [And to the prophet], 'Prophesy to the breath [wind/spirit/Spirit], prophesy, son of man, and say to the breath, Thus says the Lord God, Come from the four winds, O breath, and breathe (*emphysēson*) on these slain that they may live.'" When Ezekiel obeyed and prophesied as commanded, the breath (i.e., the Spirit) was breathed over those dry bones, and they came to life! (Ezek. 37:2-4, 9).[1]

It seems obvious, then, that the choice of this rare verb to tell of Jesus' first post-resurrection act was intentional. It seems that the writer of the Gospel of John intended to make it obvious to everybody that just as a lump of clay fashioned from the earth or a pile of bones bleaching in a valley were caused to spring to life by the breath of God then, so now the followers of Jesus are being given the opportunity to spring to life with a new spiritual vitality by that same breath of God. This, then, heralded the beginning of the new creation for human beings (2 Cor. 5:17), the fulfillment of Jesus' own words, "I have come that you may have life and have it in abundance" (John 10:10).

2. The second thing to note is the word of Jesus: "Receive (*labete*) the Holy Spirit" (John 20:22). Since Jesus breathed upon all those in that upper room, none being excluded, it is clear from this act that the gift of the Spirit was being freely offered by him to all. But the fact that it is to be received (*labete*, an imperative mood with its intrinsic appeal of will to will) "demands a responsive effort on the part of [the one] to whom it is offered."[2] This is to say, because the Spirit is the promised gift of the Father to the resurrected Jesus for him to pour out on others—the same Holy Spirit which had been abundantly poured out on him (cf. Luke 4:1; Acts 2:32-33)—Jesus has, in his act of breathing on his followers, done precisely that. Yet just as the Spirit never infringed upon the personal nature of Jesus' inward life and did not force him to

do what he might choose not to do, so Jesus does not impose the Holy Spirit on his followers; he does not infringe upon their freedom nor does he overpower their wills. He simply gives the gift to all. All, however, must receive the Holy Spirit on their own, by their own choice. It follows that just as Jesus remained master of his will and consciousness yet nevertheless deliberately chose to subject himself to the guiding influence of the Spirit throughout his life and thus lived powerfully and triumphantly, so his followers must do as he did if they would experience the same power and triumph in their own personal experiences. The choice is theirs—to receive the Spirit or not, to subject themselves to the Spirit's leading or not.

Some Implications

This truth of the gift of the Holy Spirit of God given freely for all the followers of Jesus to receive has some astounding implications:

1. Jesus was a real human being, but he was anointed by God with the Holy Spirit. Thus he became the Christ *par excellence* (cf. 1 Sam. 10:1, 6; 16:13 with Luke 3:21-22; 4:1), enabled by the Spirit to know the mind of God and authorized to carry out the work of God. In a similar way the followers of Jesus, who have received this gift of the Spirit, are thus anointed by God with that same Holy Spirit and so become God's contemporary "christs," so that they might know the mind of God and be authorized to carry out his will in this day and age (cf. 1 John 2:20, 27).

It is no accident, therefore, that Paul in writing to the Corinthian Christians places two key words side by side (unfortunately they go unnoticed in translation): "Now He who establishes us with you in Christ (*Christon*) and anointed (*chrisas*) us is God" (2 Cor. 1:21 NASB), i.e., "the one who establishes us in the Anointed One and anointed (*christon kai chrisas*) us is God." Thus just as it is recorded of Jesus that he said of himself, "The Spirit of the Lord is upon me, because he has anointed me" (Luke 4:18), and as Peter is reported as having said to Cornelius, "God anointed Jesus of Nazareth with the Holy Spirit and with power" (Acts 10:38), just so in this same way Christians are now spoken of as anointed ones because they, too, have received the Holy Spirit and are thus set apart to serve God, authorized to act in his behalf.

2. Jesus was a genuine human person. But he was filled with the Holy Spirit (Luke 4:1),[3] and it was this filling that made all the difference between an ordinary human being and one who was extraordinary. Luke calls attention to this filling at the threshold of Jesus' ministry (Luke 4:1), without necessarily meaning to say that Jesus had not been filled with the Spirit before that time (cf.

Luke 1:35). But by calling special attention to this action at this point in Jesus' life, the evangelist is saying that Jesus now, precisely because of this filling, was enabled to see through the most subtle of temptations and resist yielding to any of them. He was enabled to do his mighty works of healing the sick, opening the eyes of the blind, putting strength into the limbs of the lame, and exorcising demons. He was enabled to teach with authority, preach with power, stand for what was right, champion the cause of the oppressed, and proclaim Good News to the poor. He was enabled to free people from all kinds of bondage—self-inflicted or otherwise. The evangelist was saying that Jesus was endowed with supernatural power and that the Spirit was the giver of this power, even that the Spirit was this power (cf. Luke 7:22 with Isa. 61:1).

The Spirit for Today

And as it was true of Jesus, so it is true of his followers: "As the Father has sent me, even so I send you" (John 20:21b). As Jesus was filled and equipped by the Spirit, so those who belong to Jesus are filled and equipped by the Spirit (Acts 2:4), or at least potentially so (Eph. 5:18). Just as it was true that this filling of Jesus enabled him to be and do the extraordinary, so it is true of those who believe in him. The Acts of the Apostles (or "of the Holy Spirit"), to say the very least, was intended to show something of the nature of those things that God is able to do through people who yield themselves willingly to the influence of the Spirit. Through the Spirit, those people of the very early church were enabled to preach boldly, convincingly, and authoritatively (Acts 2:14-41), to face crises and surmount obstacles with a courage and resoluteness and power they never dreamed they had (4:29-31), to cheerfully face persecution and suffering, and even to accept death with a prayer of forgiveness (5:40-41; 7:55-60), to heal the sick and raise the dead (9:36-41; 28:8), to arbitrate differences and bring about peace (15:1-35), to know where to go and where not to go, what to do and what not to do (16:6-10; 21:10-11), and so on.

There is no reason whatsoever to believe that what was true of those earliest Christians is any less true of Christians in this century. Surely contemporary crises are no less great, the pains of the world are no less meliorated, the challenges to one's strength, wisdom, patience, and love are no less demanding of resources beyond human resources than they were in the first century, and followers of Jesus today are no more sufficient for all these in and of themselves than were his followers yesterday. Furthermore, God's program of enabling people to burst the bounds of their human limitations and achieve the impossible is still in place and still effective—that program that involves filling people with his Spirit, filling them with supernatural power.

In the spiritual as in the natural world, there is a law which teaches that the same cause will, under the same conditions, produce the same consequence. Hence, under the same conditions of surrender and dependence as in which our Lord lived His earthly life, the same cause—the Eternal Spirit—will produce the same consequence, and our lives can thus be like His life (in kind though not in degree), in the reality and beauty of holiness."[4]

What is Your Calling?

Are you a minister of the Gospel or a teacher, intelligent, educated, learned in the Scriptures? The life of Jesus teaches that intelligence and learning are not in themselves sufficient when it comes to making God's message meaningful to those who hear it. It is the Spirit of God within the minister that makes the word a living word, sharper than any two-edged sword (Acts 2:4, 14-37, especially vv. 33 and 37). It is equally important, however, to say that God frowns on neither intelligence nor education, nor on people continuously pushing themselves to go beyond the supposed limits of their abilities. What he is concerned about is that spiritual work never be done solely in a natural way, only with natural endowments. Rather he wishes by the power of his Holy Spirit present and available, as in the life of Jesus, to make it possible for the followers of Jesus to exceed the real limits of their humanness and thus speak to the hearts of people with a life-creating, life-transforming power. Recall, "the letter kills, but the Spirit gives life" (2 Cor. 3:6 NASB).

Are you among the healers of this world, those who through years of study, discipline, and unreasonably hard work have trained themselves to learn the art of healing those who are sick in body and mind? The life of Jesus teaches you that as a Spirit-filled person, whatever powers you possess, whatever skills you have developed, whatever diagnostic abilities you own, whatever faculty you enjoy of penetrating to the root of a problem and resolving it—any or all of these can be strengthened and lifted beyond the limits of your natural abilities by the Spirit of God. For the Holy Spirit stands with you against every destructive force at work in your world and only waits for you to yield to him, as did Jesus, the control of your life.

And in this connection, what is to be said of those followers of Jesus who claim to have the gift of healing yet who have never been certified by the accredited schools of medicine? In spite of one's own personal experience, which may be devoid of ever having seen a miracle of healing and which thus may cause one too easily to stand among the skeptics, the testimony of the New

Testament, nevertheless, is that certain people did have the ability to heal with a touch or with a word (Acts 9:34; 10:38; 28:8). And when Paul lists the gifts that were given by the resurrected Jesus to his church, the gift of healing is numbered among them (1 Cor. 12:9,28). There are no grounds for saying, therefore, other than one's own biases, that such a gift has been withdrawn from among the ranks of the followers of Jesus or has ceased to be in existence. But what is of importance for this study is to realize that such a gift is a gift of the Spirit (1 Cor. 12:1, 7-9). The earthly life of Jesus, a life that was filled with the Spirit, underscores this statement and makes it clear that if and when one person heals another person directly, immediately, instantaneously, it is by the power of the Spirit that that person does so.

Are you a creative person, an artisan, an artist, a teacher, a writer, a musician, a performer, a designer? Are you a person whose divine calling in life is to beautify the world, to create something new, to do what has never been done before? Are you a person gifted to make other people think or laugh or cry? Then know with full assurance that it is God's plan and pleasure to enhance your talents by the power of his Holy Spirit (cf. Exod. 31:3-4), to thus increase your skills, enhance your abilities, enlarge your knowledge, and deepen your insights so that you might be a better artisan, artist, teacher, writer, musician, performer, designer, so that you might more effectively serve your God in your world and, like Jesus, fulfill your God-given mission in life.

Are you a person whose life seems humdrum, consumed by the endless round of unexciting daily chores, by work that is often judged by others (and perhaps by yourself) as unfulfilling but that is nevertheless necessary if, for example, there is to be a home provided and a family fed and held together in wholeness, health, and contentment? Recall, then, that if the thrust of this [article] is correct, the Holy Spirit was present with and in Jesus, who was as truly human as you, for the purpose of strengthening him, enthusing him, aiding him to live meaningfully during the majority of the years of his life when his days, too, were filled with very menial, humdrum, repetitive, perhaps even boring tasks. But Jesus teaches by example that the Holy Spirit is here and available in the midst of just such tasks and that his power is a power to quicken, enliven, inspire so that one's life need never sink to the level of the inconsequential.

The Spirit's Adequacy

Are you one who truly wants to do the will of God, knowing that the will of God is good, pleasing, and perfect, and yet you are severely tempted at times to take things into your own hands, to go your own way, to do your own will? Are you a person whose lack of strength is amplified by important and worthwhile tasks you have accepted that seem vastly too big for you, and are you inclined to take the easy way out and quit? Are you overwhelmed with the problems of poverty and injustice for which there seem to be no solutions, and you wish to give up the struggle? If any of this is so, reflect again on the life of Jesus and the powerful resource of the Spirit of God that was always present with him. The Spirit within him, filling him, aiding him both to recognize real temptation when it came and helping overcome it, is your resource too. The Spirit within him that infused him with power, strengthened his weakness, and fortified him to such a degree that he could do the humanly impossible, is the Spirit that is in you. The Spirit that was in Jesus that drew him to the poor, the disenfranchised, the outcasts of society, that gave him the moral courage not to give up the task of being their spokesperson and their Savior—that same Spirit is also with you, in you, ready to infuse you with what it takes to finish the task to which God has called you.

Are you one of the many who faces death with dread, weeping in the face of your impending mortality? Jesus shares your grief and understands your anguish, for he, too, faced his own death with "horror and dismay" (Mark 14:33 NEB), and was heard to say to his disciples, "My heart is ready to break with grief" (Mark 14:34 NEB). But the Holy Spirit was present with Jesus in the hour of his death, strengthening him to accept death, to endure its pain, and by it to guarantee eternal salvation for all who wish to follow him. And it was the Holy Spirit, the power of God, that raised Jesus from the dead and gave him the victory over death and the grave. It is that same Holy Spirit who is present in you now even at the very moment of your dying. Hence, listen to the joyously exultant affirmation of the church: "If the Spirit of him who raised Jesus from the dead dwells within you, then the God who raised Christ Jesus from the dead will also give new life to your mortal bodies through his indwelling Spirit" (Rom. 8:11 NEB). And thus it is that Paul prays for you, "that your inward eyes may be illumined, so that you may know what is the hope to which [the Lord Jesus Christ] calls you," and that you may know how vast are the resources of his power to those who trust in him—resources measured by the strength and the might (i.e. the Spirit) of God "which he exerted in Christ when he raised him from the dead" (Eph. 1:18-20 NEB).

The significance of the Holy Spirit in the life of Jesus extends to his followers in all of the little and the big things of their existences. The Spirit that helped Jesus overcome temptations, that strengthened him in weakness, that aided him in the hard job of taking on himself the hurts of the hurting, that infused him with a power to accomplish the impossible, that enabled him to stay with and complete the task God had given him to do, that brought him through death and into resurrection, is the Spirit that the resurrected Jesus has freely and lavishly (note the force of the verb in Acts 2:33) given to those who would be his disciples today!

The Spirit Will Not Be Manipulated

It is worth closing ... with a warning, however. The Holy Spirit of God must never be thought of as a genie whose presence and power are available for personal enrichment or aggrandizement. When Jesus had been led into the desert, the arena of testing, by the Spirit and was tempted to use the power of the Spirit that was available to him to change stones into bread to satisfy his own real hunger, he refused to do so. Why? Because he knew that the power that filled him was power to do the Father's will, not his own will. It was power to equip him to triumphantly complete the mission God had given him to do, even if that involved hunger, not to prove to anyone, especially the devil, that he could perform the spectacular. Much later when Simon the magician saw the signs and great miracles performed by Philip and the other apostles through the power of the Spirit, he came with money in his hands, saying, "Give me also this power, that anyone on whom I lay my hands may receive the Holy Spirit." But he was sternly rebuffed by Peter for such an iniquitously selfish desire to manipulate the Spirit for his own gain (Acts 8:9-23).

The Holy Spirit is God present and active in the lives of Jesus' followers not to make life rich and comfortable for them, but to equip them to fulfill God's mission for them in the world. It is a mission of helping, serving, healing, restoring, giving, sharing, and loving, a mission of binding up the broken, of being just and striving for justice, of proclaiming the Good News that God is King, of taking the Gospel everywhere, preaching the message that God has acted to save the world and transform people in and through the life, death, and resurrection of his Son Jesus Christ.

> O Holy Spirit of God, visit now this soul of mine and tarry within it until [the] eventide [of life]. Inspire all my thoughts. Pervade all my imaginations. Suggest all my decisions. Lodge in my will's most inward citadel and order all my doings. Be with me in my silence and in my speech, in my haste and in my leisure, in company and in solitude, in the freshness of the morning and in the weariness of the evening, and give me grace at all times to rejoice in Thy mysterious companionship. Amen.[5]

1. Cf. also Wisdom 15:11, where it is said of the potter, who fashioned a false god from the same clay from which he came, that "he did not recognize by whom he himself was molded, or who it was that inspired (*empneusanta*) him with an active soul and breathed into (*emphysesanta*) him the breath of life" (NEB).
2. J. H. Bernard, *A Critical and Exegetical Commentary on the Gospel According to St. John* (Edinburgh, 1928), 2.678. Hear the other possibility to receiving, taking, accepting the gift of the Spirit in Jesus' words in John 14:17, where he speaks of "the Spirit of truth (i.e., the Holy Spirit) which the world is not able to receive."
3. This expression, "filled with the Spirit," is not to be taken literally as though the Spirit is some kind of liquid that may be poured into a person as into a container, but, metaphorically, meaning that the Holy Spirit to whom one must willingly accede is then totally present endowing that person with insights and powers beyond human limits.
4. J. S. Holden, *The Price of Power* (New York, 1908), 40.
5. J. Baillie, *A Diary of Private Prayer* (New York, 1949), 89.

Come Dearest, Lord

Come, dearest Lord, descend and dwell
By faith and love in every breast;
Then shall we know, and taste, and feel
The joys that cannot be expressed.

Come, fill our hearts with inward strength,
Make our enlargèd souls possess,
And learn the height, and breadth, and length
Of Thine unmeasurable grace.

Now to the God whose power can do
More than our thoughts or wishes know,
Be everlasting honors done
By all the Church, through Christ His Son.

- Isaac Watts

CHAPTER 3

The Executive of the Godhead

Daniel Steele

Dr. Daniel Steele (1824-1914) was a Methodist Episcopalian. He was born in Windham, New York, educated at Wesleyan University in Connecticut, where he also served as a tutor from 1848 to 1860. He then held pastorates of his denomination in various cities in Massachusetts until 1862, when he was appointed professor at Genesee College, Lima, New York, a position which he occupied until 1871. In 1872 he was elected the first president of Syracuse University, while from 1884 to 1893 (when he retired from active life), he was a professor in the School of Theology at Boston University. Steele wrote several books, including a *Commentary on Joshua, Love Enthroned, Milestone Papers*, and *The Gospel of the Comforter*, from which this article is taken. The book was first published in 1897.

FOR SEVERAL YEARS my mind has been laboring to invent some concise expression for the sum of all the offices of the Third Person of the Trinity in the transformation, sanctification and habitation of souls who fully believe in Christ Jesus. At last, Dr. Charles Hodge, President of Princeton Theological Seminary, has struck out with his die the very coin which our own mint has failed to stamp and contribute to the currency of Christian experience and theological discussion: "The Holy Spirit is the Executive of the Godhead."

This clear-cut conception and expression of the work of the Spirit is exceedingly beautiful because it is indisputably true. Law emanates from the Father, mercy and judgment are committed to the Son, while the executive of both Persons is the ever-blessed Spirit. Here we have the three departments of government—the legislative, the judicial and the executive.

Through the Holy Spirit, the Father and the Son operate on human souls, reproving, regenerating, witnessing, and sanctifying. We now see how a person may honor the Father, and in a measure, the Son, and yet fail to attain the highest spiritual grace through a failure to honor the Holy Spirit, the blessed

Comforter—just as a man may show all proper respect to the lawmaking and law-interpreting departments of our own government and secure their action, and then miss his purpose at last by ignoring the last link necessary to its realization—the executive officer, without whose agency statutes and courts are ineffective.

We fear there are many Christians who inadvertently fail in their tribute of respect, faith, and worship to the Holy Spirit, regarding him as an impersonal emanation or influence streaming from God, or as only another name for the Father, who can just as well without Him reach and transfigure their sin-stained souls through the blood of the Lamb that takes away the sins of the world.

To human reason, this looks very plausible. But Christian experience, especially in its advanced stages, has proved to be fallacious. We must believe in the Holy Spirit as an indispensable agent in the production of spiritual life both in its inception and in its fullness. There is a sense in which he is now the most important active factor in the production of Christian character. The work of the Father in the gift of the Son, and the work of the Son in pouring out His own blood as a sin offering are completed past acts. But the work of the Spirit in each individual believer is incomplete.

Bible scholars make a great mistake when they suppose that the Holy Spirit fully accomplished his mission to our world on the day of Pentecost, or at the most when he had inspired the last word of the New Testament, and that he then withdrew, leaving the Church under the reign of fixed spiritual laws. Such a creed as this chills the soul and deadens all the fires of faith and love.

Let the entire Church come to a full realization that the Comforter came to abide, and that He is now descending in personal Pentecosts as certainly and as demonstrably in the consciousness of every perfect believer as He did in the upper room in Jerusalem. When the Church truly believes this, then will the glory of the dispensation of the Spirit begin to be generally seen and "the Executive of the Godhead" receive fitting honor.

"To have faith in Christ and not to have faith in the Spirit seems to be a great contradiction, yet we submit it for the judgment of candid inquirers whether this very contradiction is not strikingly exhibited in the case of almost all who profess to be followers of Christ. To know the Father, we must know the Son; to know Christ, we must know the Spirit."[1] This is our privilege: "You shall know him ... He shall testify of me." (John 14:17; 15:26).

We suspect that much of the repugnance among good Christian people to an instantaneous holiness comes from a sort of a naturalistic view of the kingdom of grace left to the operation of fixed laws in the absence of the King. They forget that the King has left in his stead a personal Successor and Vicegerent clothed with omnipotent power.

The day of Pentecost was a pattern day; all the days of this dispensation should have been like it, or should have exceeded it. But alas! the Church has fallen down to the state in which it was before this blessing had been bestowed, and it is necessary for us to ask Christ to begin over again. We, of course, in respect to knowledge—intellectual knowledge of spiritual things—are far in advance of the point where the disciples were before the Pentecost. It should be borne in mind that when truths have once been fully revealed and made a part of orthodoxy, the holding of them does not necessarily imply any operation of the Spirit of God. We deceive ourselves, doubtless, in this way, imagining that because we have the whole Scriptures and are conversant with all its great truths, the Spirit of God is necessarily working in us. We need a baptism of the Spirit as much as the apostles did at the time of Christ's resurrection.[2]

That was not a mere dash of rhetoric which fell from the pen of John Fletcher when he spoke of the Pentecost as the opening of "the kingdom of the Holy Ghost." He has the signet ring of our glorified King Jesus, and reigns over the family on earth as the Son of man reigns over the family above. He has not shut Himself up as an impersonal force in the tomb of uniform law, but He walks through the earth a glorious personality, with the keys of divine power attached to His girdle and with the rod of empire in His right hand. He works miracles in the realm of Spirit, as did Immanuel in the realm of matter. The new Creator of the soul performs a greater work than the original Creator of man, inasmuch as the former works upon material, which is capable of an eternal resistance to His plastic touch, while in matter, there was no such antagonism.

In that sublime formula of worship, the *Te Deum Laudamus*, which has dropped from the lips of dying sires to living sons for fifteen centuries, there is found this sentence referring to the work of Christ in opening the dispensation of the Spirit. "When Thou hadst overcome the sharpness of death, Thou didst open the Kingdom of Heaven to all believers."

To make the Church realize the presence of "The Executive of the Godhead," there must be more praying in the Holy Ghost, more preaching with the demonstration of the Spirit, more singing with the spirit and testifying as the Spirit gives utterance; with the attesting fruits of the Spirit, love, joy, and peace. There must be more faith in the Holy Spirit as the greatest gift that men can wish or that heaven can send.

We belie His presence when in our fruitless lives, we present Him as a barren tree with no golden fruit to attract and feed hungry souls. This poor, blind world, which apprehends only sensible things, physical causes and effects, must be lifted up by the lever of sanctified character from the low plane of naturalism to apprehend the presence of the supernatural on earth, the standing miracle of Christianity—the Holy Spirit dwelling in human hearts and transfiguring human lives. How glorious will be that era when the brief credo, "I believe in the Holy Ghost," has descended from the head into the heart of the Church, or has ascended from an intellectual assent into assured knowledge (John 14:17). Then, and not till then, will Jesus, the glorified Bridegroom, have the entire heart of His bride, for then will the Spirit, the Bridegroom's looking-glass, fully reflect His loveliness to her eyes as the chief among ten thousand. "He shall glorify me; for he shall receive of mine, and shall show it unto you."

How cheering the thought that this period of intense spiritual illumination and power is not fixed by the decree of God in the distant future, but that it may be inaugurated in our own day by a simple, all-surrendering faith in Christ's promise of the Comforter. There are indications of the dawn of that returning day of Pentecost when the Spirit shall be poured out in His fullness upon all who "know the exceeding greatness of Christ's power to usward who believe" (Eph. 1:19).

The eastern sky has streaks of light betokening the sunrise of a day of power. Christians of every name, lone watchers on the mountain tops, now see the edge of the ascending disk and are shouting to the inhabitants of the dark valleys below to awake and arise and behold the splendors of the King of day.

Reader, the perfect restoration of the reign of the Spirit over the Church involves your personal cooperation, the entire consecration of your heart, your victory over the world, your crucifixion with Christ, the entire cleansing of your heart and the transformation of your body into "a temple of the Holy Ghost, the habitation of God through the Spirit." Are you ready to be nailed to the cross? By the "you" I mean the old self-life. You should be willing to enter into that state of conscious deadness to self in which the great German reformer was when he said, "If anyone knocks at the door of my breast and says, 'Who lives here?' I will answer, 'Not Martin Luther, but Jesus Christ.'"

---

1. George Bowen, *Love Revealed*.
2. Ibid.

CHAPTER 4

Union with Jesus

Samuel L. Brengle

Samuel L. Brengle (1860-1936) was converted as a child. At fifteen years of age, he became assistant Sunday School superintendent in his home church, and at seventeen he enrolled in DePauw University, where he proved to be a brilliant scholar and an eloquent orator. Political ambitions soon began to awaken in Brengle's heart, but these were short-circuited when God called him to be a preacher of the gospel. From DePauw, Brengle went to Boston Theological Seminary. It was there that he entered into a deeper union with the Lord Jesus Christ under the tutelage of Dr. Daniel Steele, a foremost Methodist scholar. Soon afterward, Brengle refused the flattering offer of the pastorate of a large, renowned Methodist church, choosing instead to join the Salvation Army, where he spent the rest of his life as a traveling evangelist, writer, and, eventually, commissioner. The following article is adapted from *Heart Talks on Holiness* by Samuel L. Brengle.

JESUS SAID, "I and My Father are one" (John 10:30), and it is His loving purpose that you and I shall be able to say that too and say it now in this present time, in the face of the devil and in holy, triumphant defiance of a frowning world and of shrinking, trembling flesh.

There is a union with Jesus as intimate as that of the branch and the vine, or as that of the various members of the body with the head, or as that between Jesus and the Father. This is shown by such Scriptures as that in which Jesus said, "I am the Vine, ye are the branches' (John 15:5), and in His great intercessory prayer, where He prays, "that they all may be one; as Thou, Father, art in Me, and I in Thee, that they also may be one in us' (John 17:21).

It is also shown in such passages as that in which Paul, speaking of Jesus, says that God "hath put all things under His feet, and gave Him to be the Head over all things to the Church, which is His body" (Eph. 1:22-23), and again that we "may grow up into Him in all things, which is the Head, even Christ" (Eph. 4:15), and again, "For both He that sanctifieth and they who are sanctified are all of one" (Heb. 2:11). It is also shown clearly in Paul's testimony, "I am crucified with Christ: nevertheless I live; yet not I, but Christ liveth in me' (Gal. 2: 20)....

Union with Jesus Illustrated

This spiritual union is mysterious and yet simple, and many of our everyday relationships partially illustrate it. Where two people have interests or purposes the same, they are, to that extent, one. A Republican or Democrat is one with every other man of his party throughout the whole country insofar as they hold similar principles. This is an imperfect sort of union. And yet it is union. Our General may be in any part of the world, pushing forward his mighty schemes of conquest for Jesus, and every other Salvationist [a term for Salvation Army officers], however humble he may be, just insofar as he has the same spirit and ideals as the General, is one with him. A husband and wife, or a boy and his mother, may be separated by continents and seas, and yet be one. For six months, three thousand miles of wild waves rolled between me and a little woman I rejoiced to call '"wife," but my heart was as absolutely true to her, and my confidence in her fidelity was as supreme as now when we sit side by side—and we were one.

But more perfect, more tender, more holy, and infinitely more self-consuming and ennobling and enduring is the union of the soul with Jesus than is any other possible relationship. It is like the union of the bay with the sea. It is a union of nature, a commingling of spirit, an eternal marriage of heart, and soul, and mind.

A Union of the Will

It is a union of will. Jesus said, "I came down from Heaven, not to do My own will, but the will of Him that sent Me" (John 6:38), and again, "My meat is to do the will of Him that sent Me" (John 4:34). And so it is with those who are one with Jesus. The Psalmist said, "I delight to do Thy will, O my God' (Ps. 40:8), and that is the testimony of everyone who has entered into this divine union. There may, and doubtless will be times when this will is hard for flesh and blood, but even then the soul says with its Lord, "Not my will, but Thine, be done' (Lk. 22:42), and prays always, "Thy will be done in earth, as it is in heaven" (Mt. 6:10).

In the very nature of things, there can be no union with Jesus without this union of will, for there is really very little of a man but his will. That is really all he can call his own. His mind, with all its splendid powers and possibilities, may be reduced to idiocy; he may be robbed of his property. His health and even his life may be taken away from him, but who can enter into the domain of his will and rob him of that?

I say it reverently, so far as we know, not even God Himself can compel a man's will. God wants to enter into a partnership, an infinitely tender and exalting fellowship, a spiritual marriage with the will of man. He approaches man with tremendous inducements and motives of infinite profit and loss, and yet the man may resist and utterly thwart the loving thought and purpose of God. He can refuse to surrender his will. But surrender he must, if there is to be a union between him and God, for God's will, based as it is on eternal righteousness, founded in infinite knowledge and wisdom and love, is unchangeable, and man's highest good is in a hearty and affectionate surrender to it and a union with it.

A Union of Faith

It is a union of faith—mutual confidence and esteem. God trusts him, and he trusts God. God can entrust him with the honour of His name and His holy character in the midst of a world of rebels. God can empower him and beautify him with His Spirit and adorn him with all heavenly graces, without any fear that the man will take the glory of these things to himself. God can heap upon him riches and treasures and honors without any fear that the man will use them for selfish ends or prostitute them to unholy purposes.

Again, the man trusts God. He trusts God when he cannot trace Him. He has confidence in the faithfulness and love of God in adversity as well as in prosperity. He does not have to be fed on sweetmeats and live in sunshine and sleep on roses in order to believe that God is for him. God can mingle bitter with all His sweets, and allow the thorns to prick him, and the storm clouds to roll all about him, and yet he will stubbornly trust on. Like Job, his property may be swept away in a day, and his children die about him, and yet with Job, he will say, "The Lord gave, and the Lord hath taken away; blessed be the name of the Lord" (Job. 1:21), and still, trust on.

His own life may be menaced and be filled with weariness and pain, and his faithless wife bid him curse God and die, and yet he will say, "What? shall we receive good at the hand of God, and shall we not receive evil?' (Job. 2:10), and still trust on.

His friends may gather about him and attack his Christian integrity and character and foolishly assault the foundations of his faith by assuring him that if he were right with God, these calamities could never befall him. Yet he will look up from his ash heap and out of his utter wreck and ruin and desolation, cry, "Though He slay me, yet will I trust in Him." (Job 13:15). And though communities or nations conspire against him, he will say with David, "The Lord is my light and my salvation; whom shall I fear? The Lord is the strength of my life; of whom shall I be afraid?" "Though an host should encamp against me, my heart shall not fear: though war should rise against me, in this will I be confident" (Ps. 27:1, 3).

A woman said to me the other day, "I dread to think of the end of the world. It makes me afraid." But though worlds, like drunken men, tumble from their orbits, and though the universe crash into ruin, the child-like confidence of the man who trusts God will enable him to sing with the Psalmist, "God is our refuge and strength, a very present help in trouble. Therefore will not we fear, though the earth be removed, and though the mountains be carried into the midst of the sea; though the waters thereof roar and be troubled, though the mountains shake with the swelling thereof" (Ps. 46:1-3).

God can be familiar with such a man. He can take all sorts of liberties with his property, his reputation, his position, his friends, his health, his life, and allow devils and men to taunt him; but the man unchangeably fixed in his estimate of God's holy character and everlasting love, will still triumphantly trust on.

A Union of Suffering

It is a union of suffering, of sympathy. Once when I was passing through what seemed to me a perfect hell of spiritual temptation and sufferings, the Lord supported me with this text, "In all their affliction He was afflicted" (Isa. 63:9). The prophet refers in these words to the afflictions of the children of Israel in Egypt and in the wilderness after their escape from the hard bondage of Pharaoh, and he says in all their sufferings, Jesus suffered with them.

Let her child be racked with pain and scorched with fever and choked with croup, but the mother suffers more than the child, and so let the people of God be sorely tempted and tried, and Jesus agonizes with them. He is the world's great Sufferer. His passion is forever. He once tasted death for every man. He suffers still with every man. There is not a cry of anguish, nor a heartache, nor a pang of spiritual pain in all the world that does not reach His ear and touch His heart and stir all His mighty sympathies. But especially does He suffer and sympathize with His own believing children. And in turn, the man who is one with Jesus suffers and sympathizes with Jesus.

Any injury to the cause of Christ causes him more pain than any personal loss. He mourns over the desolations of Zion more than over the loss of his property. The lukewarmness of Christians cuts him to the heart. The cry of the heathen for the gospel of salvation is to him the cry of the travail, the agony of Jesus Himself. He gladly says, with David, "The reproaches of them that reproached Thee have fallen upon me" (Ps. 69:9). He esteems the reproach of Christ greater treasure than all the pleasure and power and profits of this world combined. As the true wife gladly suffers privation and shame and reproach with her husband whom she knows to be righteous and honorable, so he who is one with Jesus rejoices that he is "counted worthy to suffer shame for His name" (Acts v.41)....

A Union of Purpose

It is a union of purpose. The great mass of men serve God for a reward; they do not want to go to Hell; they want to go to Heaven. And that is right. But it is not the highest motive. There is a union with Jesus in which the soul is not so anxious to escape Hell as it is to be free from sin, and in which Heaven is not so desirable as holiness. The soul in this state thinks very little about its reward. His smile of approval is its Heaven. The housekeeper wants wages, but the wife never thinks of such a thing. She serves for very love. She is one in purpose with her husband. His triumphs are hers. His losses are hers. All he has is hers, and she is his. And, as the Apostle says, "For all things are yours, ... and ye are Christ's" (1 Cor. 3:21, 23). The will of God is the supreme good of this man. Someone has said that if two angels were sent into this world, one of whom was to rule it, and the other was to sweep street crossings, that the sweeper would be so satisfied with his Heavenly Father's will that he would not exchange places with the ruler.

The purpose of Jesus is to save the world and uphold the honor of God and establish truth in the lives, the hearts, the laws, the customs of men, and this is the purpose of this man. In order to do this, Jesus sacrificed every earthly prospect and laid down His life, and this man does the same. He does not stand in the presence of the world's great crying need and hesitate and wonder if the Lord really wants him to give a few cents or dollars for the salvation of the heathen. He does not quibble as to whether God really requires him to make the sacrifice and leave his dog kennel and chicken coop and barn and house furnished a little below the standard of beauty and luxury set by his ungodly neighbors. He does not struggle and kick against the pricks when he feels God would have him forsake business and preach the gospel. He would loathe himself to have such mean thoughts. He does not say, "If I were rich," but out of the abundance of his poverty, he pours into the lap of the world's need, and like the widow, he gladly gives all his living to save the world.

When God looks about for a man to stand up for His honour and warn a wicked world and offers terms of peace to sinners, this man does not say, "If I were only educated or gifted I would go," but with a heart flaming with love for Jesus and the world He has bought with His Blood, cries out, "Here am I, send me." It can be said of him as it was of his Lord, "The zeal of Thine house hath eaten me up' (John 2: 17).

A young carpenter in New England, whose name was unknown, came every few months to the [Salvation Army] Divisional Headquarters and gave a hundred or more dollars for the work of God in India, or some other portion of the world. He was one with Jesus in His purpose to save the world.

On a bitter wintry day, a poor woman came to John Wesley's apartment at Oxford University. She was shivering with cold. Wesley asked her why she did not dress more warmly. She replied that she had no warmer garments. When she was gone, Wesley looked at the pictures on his walls, and said to himself in substance, "If my Lord should come, would He be pleased to see these on my walls when His poor are suffering with cold?" Then he sold the pictures and gave to the poor. And in this way began that mighty and lifelong beneficence and almost matchless self-sacrifice that has led to the blessing of millions upon millions of men.

O my God, that Thy people might see what union with Thee really means. Do you ask, "How can I enter into this union?"

1. Read God's promises until you see that it is possible. Especially read and ponder over the fifteenth and seventeenth chapters of The Gospel According to John.

2. Read and ponder over the commandments until you see that it is necessary. Without this union here, there will be no union in eternity.

3. Make the sacrifice that is necessary in order to become one with Jesus.

The woman who will be the true wife of a man must be prepared to give up all other lovers, leave her home, and forsake father, mother, brothers and sisters, change her name, and utterly identify herself her prospects for life, her all, with the man she loves. And so must you be prepared to identify yourself utterly with Christ, to be hated, despised, rejected, crucified of men, but armed, baptized with the Holy Ghost, and crowned of God.

Does your heart consent to this? If so, make a perpetual covenant with your Lord just now. Do it intelligently. Do it with a true heart, in full assurance of faith, and God will seal you for His own. Do not waver. Do not doubt. Do not cast away your confidence because of your feelings or lack of feelings, but stand by your facts. Walk by faith, and God will soon prove His ownership in you in a way that will be altogether satisfactory to both your head and your heart, and convincing to men and devils.

Christ Himself

More than a way out of my darkness,
  more than joy in my distress;
More than a remedy for sickness—
  I need Christ himself!

More than relief from a bad conscience,
  more than smiling Providence;
More than a signal of his presence—
  I need Christ himself!

More than mere feelings without measure,
  more than blessings I treasure;
More than passing sentient pleasure—
  I need Christ himself!

More than titillating sensation,
  more than a revelation;
More than a brilliant visitation—
  I need Christ himself!

All of these gifts absent the Giver,
  leave the heart like a pauper;
Let me trust in only the Savior—
  then I'll have Christ himself!

- Ralph I. Tilley

CHAPTER 5

I Believe in the Holy Ghost

Maynard James

Maynard James (1902-1988) was born in Bargoed, South Wales. In 1927 he became a student at the well-known Methodist training school, Cliff College, England, where he studied under the renowned Samuel Chadwick and was soon nicknamed "Holiness James." It was while at Cliff College that James founded the Trekkers, a group of young men who traveled from town to town and village to village preaching the gospel. His span of ministry included church administration, evangelism, pastoring, and publishing. He ministered alongside evangelists Leonard Ravenhill, Duncan Campbell, and Jack Ford for several years. He served for nearly 50 years as the editor of *The Flame* magazine (now defunct), from which this article is taken.

IT WAS AT A CONVENTION in Cornwall. After preaching on the text John 7:38-39, I went into the counseling room where an intelligent youth was seeking earnestly to be filled with the Holy Spirit. Almost tearfully, he told me that about twelve months previously, he had asked the Lord for the Holy Spirit. "But," he said, "I have only a trickle." He longed for the "rivers of living water" that Jesus had promised to those who believe on Him. He belonged to that host of Christians who say to the Lord:

"Rivers" is Thy promise,
This shall be our plea,
Less than this can never
Meet our cry for Thee:

Tired of lukewarm service,
And the loss it brings,
We would live entirely
For eternal things.

Most of Christ's important statements about the Holy Spirit are found in

John's Gospel. None is more vivid than His promise in chapter 7, verses 38 and 39: "He that believeth in me, as the scripture hath said from within him [his innermost being] shall flow rivers of living water. But this spake he of the Spirit, which they that believed on him were to receive."

It was on the final day of the Feast of Tabernacles that Jesus uttered such stirring words. This festival lasted for seven days, although an eighth day was added as a time of "holy convocation."

Every morning, for seven days, a procession headed by a priest and accompanied with music went from the Temple of Jerusalem to the Pool of Siloam. There the priest filled a golden vase with water and carried it to the Temple amid the joyful shouts of the people. Then he poured the water upon the western side of the altar of burnt offerings. At the same time, another priest poured a drink offering of wine upon the eastern side of the altar. During this act, the congregation chanted the words of the "Hallel" (Psalms 113 to 119).

This symbolism was undoubtedly connected with the gift of the latter rain, which was at that season. It spoke also of the gift of water, which was so vital in the East. The Jews at the Feast of Tabernacles must have recalled that time when, as their fathers thirsted in the wilderness, the life-giving waters gushed from the rock smitten by Moses.

It was on the last great day of the feast, probably the eighth, that Jesus stood up and made His dramatic announcement. It was all the more dramatic because (as some Bible scholars believe), no water was carried from the Pool of Siloam on the eighth day. It was a waterless day.

In His revolutionary statement Jesus spoke of the promise, purpose, and pathway of the Holy Spirit's fullness in the human heart.

The Promise of the Spirit's Fullness

No promise in the Old Testament is more important than the coming of the Holy Spirit to indwell and empower the soul of man. Ever since Adam, through the Fall in Eden, had lost the grace and indwelling of the Holy Spirit, men had groaned in their bondage and longed for their forfeited inheritance. But in their own strength, they were powerless to regain what, in Adam, they had lost. However, the darkened sky had been lightened by God's gracious promise that one day the Holy Spirit would return in plentitude to indwell the sons of men. Through Isaiah, Ezekiel and Joel, that promise was reiterated (Isa. 44:3; Ezek. 36:26, 27; Joel 2:28, 29).

When Jesus came, He confirmed and clarified what He termed "the promise of the Father." By His atoning death, resurrection, and ascension, He made possible the fulfillment of that promise. Being exalted to the throne of God, He received of the Father the promise of the Holy Ghost, that He might "pour" Him upon obedient hearts (Acts 2:33).

It is vital to note that Christ's promise of the fullness of the Spirit was not made to sinners. It was for His disciples, for those who believe on Him. Elsewhere (John 14:17), Jesus plainly said that the world could not receive the Comforter.

The Purpose of the Spirit's Fullness

How significant is the emphasis Jesus placed upon the penetration of the Holy Spirit in a believer's heart: "Out of his *innermost being* shall flow rivers of living water."

The Greek word *koilia* (translated "belly" in the A. V.) speaks of the very foundation of human personality, or as the mystics might render it, "the central depths" of the soul. This teaches us that before there can be the *outflow* of divine power from our lives, there must be the *incoming* of the Holy Spirit to possess the deepest recesses of our being.

Over 90 times in Scripture, the adjective "holy" is used of the Spirit. He is the Spirit of holiness, and so it is inconceivable that any indwelling sin can remain in the heart when He has penetrated into and fully possessed the *koilia* of our personality. The Holy Spirit comes to give us, as it were, a spiritual "spring cleaning." He enters not only into the upper stories and ground floor of our being; He possesses also the basement of our personality. The subconscious is cleansed by His all-pervasive efficacy. There are plenty of Christians who long for power and yet are unwilling for the deep, inward cleansing of their nature.

I had a big surprise when preaching in a church in California some years ago. A young lady was seeking the Spirit's fullness and seemed to be in earnest. But when I told her that inner purity preceded the outflow of divine power, she exclaimed: "Cannot I be filled with the Holy Spirit without having a pure heart?" I replied: "No, you cannot." Realizing the true purpose of the Holy Spirit for her life, she refused to obey the light from heaven and left the counseling room sadder than when she had entered it.

How illuminating is Ezekiel's vision of the life-giving, healing waters that flowed from under the altar in the house of God. Those waters are clearly a picture of the Spirit-filled life from which issue the streams of divine grace and power, bringing blessing and healing to needy humanity. But it is significant that the living waters did not begin to flow until the altar had been thoroughly purged and purified (43:26). So it is with the Christian life. The altar of the heart must be entirely sanctified by the Holy Spirit before the coveted power can flow out. This is always the divine order.

Samuel Chadwick made a revealing confession when he said: "The blessing I sought was power. The blessing God had for me began further in and deeper down. Power was conditioned. The truth that sanctifies begins with a cleansing of heart and motive, a life surrendered to the divine will, and a personality possessed by and filled with the Holy Spirit."

If purity of heart can be termed the negative side of Pentecost, then the positive side of the blessing is surely power for effective service.

The Holy Ghost does not possess us simply that we might have inward rapture. He comes right into the heart so that He might flow out from us to thirsty souls around. The waters in Ezekiel's vision flowed toward the desert. God, the Holy Ghost, will never enter any sphere which has no outlet. As William Luff has put it:

God fills the soul that it may pour
The fullness on another heart:
Not that the filled with good may store
The good God giveth to impart.

Jesus illustrated this life of power by the figure of rivers of living water flowing from the inner depths of the sanctified Christian.

In the Holy Spirit is power that is abundant, spontaneous, irresistible, and life-giving. Not a well, or a spring, or even a single river—but "rivers." What a picture of abundance is this! Pentecost always speaks of overflowing fullness—enough and to spare.

The feast of Pentecost was during the wheat harvest in Palestine, at the time of the ripening of the summer fruits. God had promised such abundant crops to an obedient Israel that when Pentecost came, the farmers were to leave the corners of their fields, along with the gleanings, for the benefit of the poor.

Not only is this power of the Spirit in abundant supply, it is also spontaneous. The rivers of living water *flow* (they are not forced) from the inner depths of the purified heart. We have to pump water from a well or else let down a bucket to get a supply. But rivers flow spontaneously.

How tragic is the spectacle of Christian leaders trying to *organize* faith, or prayer, or love. It simply cannot be done. It is just like forcing an unwilling horse to the water trough but unable to make him drink!

We may be able to attract a crowd to a well-advertised service; we may put on an extremely clever and interesting program. But by human endeavor we can never make people intercessors and soul-winners. Only God, the Holy Ghost, can do that. It is only when the Spirit himself is poured forth into the heart that the Christian can truly say: "There is a love constraining me to go and seek the lost."

When Peter and John were commanded by the Sanhedrin to stop preaching and teaching about Jesus, they exclaimed: "We cannot but speak the things which we have seen and heard" (Acts 4:20).

The Spirit-anointed John Bunyan confessed: "I preached what I *felt,* what I smartingly did *feel."* There will be no lack of happy, eager witnesses for Christ in our churches when believers are filled with the Holy Spirit. The reluctant "Must I?" will be changed to the joyous "May I?"

Irresistible power

How comforting to the weak, handicapped Christian is the guarantee of the Lord himself that rivers of living water *shall* flow from him when the Holy Ghost takes possession. His power is irresistible; no demons or wicked man can stay its flow. Try to dam up mighty rivers and see what happens! They must have an outlet; a channel must be made for them.

So with the Spirit-filled life. God has promised not only to dwell in us but also to "walk about" in us (2 Cor. 6:16). Not only God in residence in the human soul but the almighty God in action in a humble believer!

Whatever be our circumstances, however difficult our lot, life in the Holy Ghost will make us irresistible for God. Satan may be allowed to cast us into the fiery furnace, but he is powerless to stop the "Form of the Fourth" from stepping into the furnace along with us.

With the bride in the Song of Solomon, the Spirit-possessed Christian exclaims: "Awake O north wind; and come thou south; blow upon my garden, that the spices thereof may flow out." The biting north wind of adversity or the pleasant south wind of prosperity—all will have the same effect upon the entirely sanctified heart. The sweet spices will flow out for the benefit of others.

The Pathway of the Spirit's Fullness

How assuring are the words of Scripture: "This spake he of the Spirit, which they that *believe* [put their trust] in him should receive."

The language of many Christian hearts is this:

My soul crieth out for the Spirit,
I'm hungering and thirsting to know

The fullness of blessing He giveth;
Now fill me while humbly I bow.

In praying for our Pentecost, we must realize that the Holy Ghost does not come according to men's preconceived ideas and plans. He travels along a divinely appointed pathway. It is via the risen and exalted Christ. It is Christ who baptizes with the Holy Ghost. It is He who has received of the Father the promise of the Spirit so that He might pour Him forth unto men. By the Holy Spirit, we are baptized into the mystic body of Christ at our conversion. But it is Jesus alone who baptizes His own people *with* the Holy Spirit.

So Jesus declared: "If any man thirst, let him come unto *me* and drink." In order to be filled with the Holy Spirit, the seeking soul must do three things:

1. Go to Christ directly and ask Him for the coveted blessing. Look away from all else: fix the gaze on the spotless Lamb of God.

2. Go to Him with a *thirsty* heart, longing more than anything else on earth to be filled with the Holy Spirit. It is only those who hunger and thirst after righteousness who are filled. Only the fully consecrated believer can obtain Christ's coronation gift—the gift of the Holy Spirit's fullness.

3. Ask in simple, childlike faith. The Day of Pentecost has fully come. There is no longer any need to wait ten days in an upper room. The command to every Christian is to "be filled [*now*] with the Spirit." This word in Ephesians 5:18 is in the present tense. If God commands His children to be filled *now* with the Holy Spirit, then no Christian has the right to remain unfilled one hour after receiving the divine imperative. That being so, then (and we speak reverently) God has no right to withhold from the trusting soul for a single moment what He has commanded it to receive *now*.

In Galatians 3:14, we have the golden key that unlocks the gate into blessing. It reads: "That we might receive the promise of the Spirit through *faith.*" God is sovereign, and He has the exclusive right to give whatever outward manifestation of the Spirit is pleasing to Him. "There are diversities of gifts, but the same Spirit. There are diversities of operations, but it is the same God which worketh all in all.... But all these worketh that one and the self-same Spirit, dividing to every man severally as he will" (1 Cor. 12:4, 6, 11).

Then follow the inevitable questions: "Are all workers of miracles? Have all the gifts of healing? Do all speak with tongues? Do all interpret?" (1 Cor. 12:29, 30).

There is but one answer to these questions. It is "No."

Let us leave the outward manifestations to the ordering of a wise God. What we *can* claim, without the slightest fear of being denied, is the incoming of the Holy Spirit himself in response to simple faith. And that is all that really matters: that the blessed Comforter should come into the trusting heart as president—forever afterwards guiding, keeping, and empowering, and revealing to the soul the transcendent beauty of Jesus Christ the Lord.

Then, and then only, will the Christian be fully satisfied. It may well be that just now some reader is earnestly praying:

Less than Thyself O do not give,
In might Thyself within me live,
Come, all Thou hast and art!

Then let that seeking soul take the next decisive step and, resting on the sure promises of God, cry out:

Holy Ghost, I now receive Thee!
I accept Thy mighty power:
And by faith, I claim Thy promise,
In this solemn, sacred hour.

Come, Holy Ghost, Our Souls Inspire

Come, Holy Ghost, our souls inspire,
And lighten with celestial fire;
Thou the anointing Spirit art,
Who dost Thy sev'nfold gifts impart.

Thy blessèd unction from above
Is comfort, life, and fire of love;
Enable with perpetual light
The dullness of our blinded sight.

Anoint and cheer our soilèd face
With the abundance of Thy grace;
Keep far our foes, give peace at home;
Where Thou art Guide, no ill can come.

Teach us to know the Father, Son,
And Thee, of both, to be but One;
That through the ages all along
This, this may be our endless song.

- Rhabanus Maurus

CHAPTER 6

The Holy Spirit and the Church

Charles H. Spurgeon

Charles Haddon Spurgeon (1834-1892) was England's best-known preacher for most of the second half of the nineteenth century. In 1854, just four years after his conversion, Spurgeon, then only 20 years of age, became pastor of London's famed New Park Street Church. The congregation quickly outgrew their building, moved to Exeter Hall, then to Surrey Music Hall. In these venues, Spurgeon frequently preached to audiences numbering more than 10,000—all in the days before electronic amplification. In 1861 the congregation moved permanently to the newly constructed Metropolitan Tabernacle. Spurgeon's printed works are voluminous.

The following selections are excerpts from *Spurgeon's Expository Encyclopedia*, Vol. IX, published by Baker Books, 1951.

I BELIEVE, BRETHREN, that whenever the church of God declines, one of the most effectual ways of reviving her is to preach much truth concerning the Holy Spirit. After all, he is the very breath of the church. Where the Spirit of God is, there is power. If the Spirit be withdrawn, then the vitality of godliness begins to decline, and the energy thereof is near to dying out. (p. 10)

• If we have not lived in the light, can we marvel that we are in great part dark? If we have not fed upon the bread of heaven, can we wonder that we are faint? Let us return unto the Lord. Let us seek again to be baptized into the Holy Ghost and into fire, and we shall yet again behold the wonderful works of the Lord. (p. 15)

• Must it not be confessed by us that we think far less of the Holy Spirit than we should? I am sure we do not exalt the Saviour too much, nor is he too often the subject of our meditations; but at the same time, we give to the Holy Spirit a very disproportionate place, even as compared with the Redeemer. (p. 21)

• If there be this day any power in the church of God, it is because the Holy

Spirit is in the midst of her. If she be able to work any spiritual miracle, it is through the might of his indwelling. If there be any light in her instruction, if there be any life in her ministry, if there be any glory gotten to God, if there be any good wrought among the sons of men, it is entirely because the Holy Spirit of God is still with her. (p. 23)

- You are called to preaching, but you feel you cannot; you are dull, and your talk will be flat, stale, unprofitable; bring the Holy Spirit into it, and if he fire you, you shall find even the slender materials you have collected will set the people on a blaze. (p. 32)

- A sermon of Christ, even a single word of Christ, set in the light of the Holy Spirit, shines like a diamond; nay, like a fixed star, with light that is never dim. (p.60)

- If it is not distinctly my aim to glorify Christ, I am not in accord with the aim of the Holy Ghost, and I cannot expect his help. We shall not be pulling the same way, and therefore I will have nothing of which I cannot say that I am saying it simply, sincerely, and only that I may glorify Christ. (p. 90)

- Now that we have the Holy Spirit from Christ as our inner life and quickening he also comes upon us with the intent to use us in blessing others, and this is the manner of his visitation—he comes as the wind, which wafts the words we speak, and as fire which burns away for the truth we utter. Our words are now full of life and flame; they are borne by the breath of the Spirit, and they fall like fire-flakes and set the souls of men blazing with desire after God. (p. 97)

- If the Spirit of God shall give us once again a full and fiery ministry we shall hear it clearly proclaimed, "Ye must be born again," and we shall see a people forthcoming which are born, not of blood, nor of the will of the flesh, but of the will of God, and by the energy which cometh from heaven. A Holy Ghost ministry cannot be silent about the Holy Ghost and his sacred operations upon the heart. (p. 101)

- Pray mightily that the Spirit of God may rest upon all who speak in God's name, for then they will create deep feeling in their hearts. (p. 102)

- O Spirit of God, if thou wilt rest upon me, even me, men shall not hear and go their way and forget what they have heard! They will arise and seek the Father and taste his love. If thou wouldst rest upon the brotherhood that publish thy word, men would not merely weep while they hear and be affected while the discourse lasts, but they would go their way to ask, "What must we do to be saved?" (p. 102)

• But where the Spirit of God is really at work, the converts will stand: they are well-rooted and grounded, and hence they are not carried about by every wind of doctrine, but they continue steadfast in the apostolic faith. (p. 103)

• O Spirit of God, thou art ready to work with us today even as thou didst [at Pentecost]. Stay not, we beseech thee, but work at once. Break down every barrier that hinders the incomings of thy might. Overturn, overturn, O sacred wind! Consume all obstacles, O heavenly fire, and give us now both hearts of flame and tongues of fire to preach thy reconciling word, for Jesus' sake. Amen. (104)

• The influences of the Holy Ghost at times pass through the soul like winds through an Eolian harp, creating and inspiring sweet notes of gratitude and tones of desire, to which we should have been strangers if it had not been for his divine visitation. He knows how to create in our spirit, hunger, and thirst for good things. He can arouse us from our spiritual lethargy, he can warm us out of our lukewarmness, he can enable us when we are on our knees to rise above the ordinary routine of prayer into that victorious importunity against which nothing can stand. He can lay certain desires so pressingly upon our hearts that we can never rest till they are fulfilled. He can make the zeal for God's house to eat us up and the passion for God's glory to be like a fire within our bones, and this is one part of that process by which in inspiring our prayers, he helps our infirmity. (pp. 108-109)

• Prayers, which are the offspring of great desires, sublime aspirations, and elevated designs, are surely the work of the Holy Spirit, and their power within a man is frequently so great that he cannot find expression for them. Words fail, and even the sighs which try to embody them cannot be uttered. (p. 112)

• We admire the condescension of Jesus in leaving heaven to dwell upon earth; but do we equally admire the condescension of the Holy Spirit in coming to dwell in such poor hearts as ours? Jesus dwelt with sinners, but the Holy Ghost dwells in us. If it were possible for the condescension of the incarnation to be outdone, it would be in the indwelling of the Holy Ghost in the hearts of men. (p.120)

CHAPTER 7

The Enduement of the Spirit

A. J. Gordon

Adoniram Judson Gordon (1836-1895) was born in New Hampshire to devout Christian parents. At about age fifteen, he was converted; one year later, he expressed his desire to prepare for the ministry. In 1856 he attended Brown University, and in 1860 entered Newton Theological Seminary. Upon graduation in 1863, he accepted a pastorate at Jamaica Plain, New Boston. After six successful years there, he accepted a call to pastor Clarendon Street Baptist Church in Boston, which was in a poor spiritual condition. In 1877, evangelist Dwight Moody came to Boston. When Moody, as Henry Drummond said, "laid one hand on America and one on Britain, and moved them toward God," he more than moved A. J. Gordon and his church. Dr. Gordon remained there for more than 25years, seeing the church completely transformed into one of the most spiritual and aggressive churches in America. Gordon's Spirit-filled life and deeply spiritual books have had a powerful influence around the world. The following article is taken from *The Ministry of the Spirit* by A. J. Gordon, first published in 1896 by the American Baptist Publication Society.

Editor: I consider *The Ministry of the Spirit* by Gordon to be one of the finest expositions on the work of the Holy Spirit, and should be read and pondered by all of God's people, especially ministers.

WE HAVE MAINTAINED ... that the baptism of the Holy Spirit was given once for all on the day of Pentecost when the Paraclete came in person to make his abode in the church. It does not follow, therefore, that every believer has received this baptism. God's gift is one thing; our appropriation of that gift is quite another thing.

Our relation to the second and third persons of the Godhead is exactly parallel in this respect. "God so loved the world that he gave his only begotten Son" (John 3:16). "But as many as received him to them gave he the right to become the children of God, even to them that believe on his name" (John 1:12). Here are the two sides of salvation, the divine and the human, which are absolutely co-essential.

There is a doctrine somewhat in vogue, not inappropriately denominated redemption by incarnation, which maintains that since God gave his Son to the world, all the world has the Son, consciously or unconsciously, and that therefore all the world will be saved. It need not be said that a true evangelical teaching must reject this theory as utterly untenable since it ignores the necessity of individual faith in Christ. But some orthodox writers have urged an almost identical view with respect to the Holy Spirit. They have contended that the enduement of the Spirit is "not any special or more advanced experience, but simply the condition of everyone who is a child of God"; that "believers converted after Pentecost, and living in other localities, are just as really endowed with the indwelling Spirit as those who actually partook of the Pentecostal blessing at Jerusalem."[1]

Every Believer's Privilege

On the contrary, it seems clear from the Scriptures that it is still the duty and privilege of believers to receive the Holy Spirit by a conscious, definite act of appropriating faith, just as they received Jesus Christ. We base this conclusion on several grounds. Presumably, if the Paraclete is a person, coming down at a certain definite time to make his abode in the church, for guiding, teaching, and sanctifying the body of Christ, there is the same reason for our accepting him for his special ministry as for accepting the Lord Jesus for his special ministry. To say that in receiving Christ we necessarily received in the same act the gift of the Spirit, seems to confound what the Scriptures make distinct.[2] For it is as sinners that we accept Christ for our justification, but it is as sons that we accept the Spirit for our sanctification: "And because ye are sons, God hath sent forth the Spirit of his Son into your hearts, crying Abba, Father" (Gal. 4:6).

Thus, when Peter preached his first sermon to the multitude after the Spirit had been given, he said: "Repent and be baptized, every one of you, in the name of Jesus Christ, for the remission of sins, and you shall receive the gift of the Holy Spirit" (Acts 2:38). This passage shows that logically and chronologically, the gift of the Spirit is subsequent to repentance. Whether it follows as a necessary and inseparable consequence, as might seem, we shall consider later. Suffice that this point is clear, so clear that one of the most conservative as well as ablest writers on this subject, in commenting on this text in Acts, says:

> Therefore it is evident that the reception of the Holy Spirit, as here spoken of, has nothing whatever to do with bringing men to believe and repent. It is a subsequent operation; it is an additional and separate blessing; it is a privilege founded on faith already actively working in the heart.... I do not

mean to deny that the gift of the Holy Spirit may be practically on the same occasion, but never in the same moment. The reason is quite simple too. The gift of the Holy Spirit is grounded on the fact that we are sons by faith in Christ, believers resting on redemption in him. Plainly, therefore, it appears that the Spirit of God has already regenerated us.[3]

Examining the Scriptures

Now, as we examine the Scriptures on this point, we shall see that we are required to appropriate the Spirit as sons, in the same way that we appropriated Christ as sinners. "As many as received him, even to them that believe on his name," is the condition of becoming sons, as we have already seen, receiving and believing being used as equivalent terms. In a kind of foretaste of Pentecost, the risen Christ, standing in the midst of his disciples, "breathed on them and said, 'Receive the Holy Spirit.'" "The verb is not passive, as our English version might lead us to suppose, but has here as generally an active signification just as in the familiar passage in Revelation: "Whosoever will, let him take the water of life freely."

Twice in the Epistle to the Galatians, the possession of the Holy Spirit is put on the same grounds of active appropriation through faith: "Did you receive the Spirit by the works of the law or by the hearing of faith ?" (3:2). "That you might receive the promise of the Spirit through faith" (3:14). These texts seem to imply that just as there is a "faith toward our Lord Jesus Christ" for salvation, there is a faith toward the Holy Spirit for power and consecration.

If we turn from New Testament teaching to New Testament example, we are strongly confirmed in this impression. We begin with that striking incident in the nineteenth chapter of Acts. Paul, having found certain disciples at Ephesus, said unto them: "Did you receive the Holy Spirit when ye believed? And they said unto him, 'No, we did not so much as hear whether there is a Holy Spirit.'"

This passage seems decisive as showing that one may be a disciple without having entered into possession of the Spirit as God's gift to believers. Some admit this, who yet deny any possible application of the incident to our own times, alleging that it is the miraculous gifts of the Spirit which are here under consideration, since, after recording that when Paul had laid his hands upon them and "the Holy Spirit came upon them," it is added "that they spoke with tongues and prophesied." All that need be said upon this point is simply that these Ephesian disciples, by the reception of the Spirit, came into the same condition with the upper room disciples who received him some twenty years before, and of whom it is written that "they were all filled with the Holy Spirit and began to speak with other tongues as the Spirit gave them utterance." In other words, these Ephesian disciples on receiving the Holy Spirit exhibited the traits of the Spirit common to the other disciples of the apostolic age.

Whether those traits—the speaking of tongues and the working of miracles—were intended to be perpetual or not, we do not here discuss. But that the presence of the personal Holy Spirit in the church was intended to be perpetual, there can be no question. And whatever relations believers held to that Spirit in the beginning, they have a right to claim today.

We must withhold our consent from the inconsistent exegesis, which would make the water baptism of the apostolic times still rigidly binding but would relegate the baptism in the Spirit to a bygone dispensation. We hold indeed that Pentecost was once for all, but equally that the appropriation of the Spirit by believers is always for all, and that the shutting up of certain great blessings of the Holy Spirit within that ideal realm called "the apostolic age," however convenient it may be as an escape from fancied difficulties, may be the means of robbing believers of some of their most precious covenant rights.[4]

Application

Let us transfer this incident of the Ephesian Christians to our own times. We need not bring forward an imaginary case, for, by the testimony of many experienced witnesses, the same condition is constantly encountered. Not only individual Christians, but whole communities of disciples are found who have been so imperfectly instructed that they have never known that there is a Holy Spirit, except as an influence, an impersonal something to be vaguely recognized. Of the Holy Spirit as a Divine Person, dwelling in the church, to be honored and invoked and obeyed and implicitly trusted, they know nothing. Is it conceivable that there could be any deep spiritual life or any real sanctified energy for service in a community like this?

And what should a well-instructed teacher or evangelist do on discovering a church or an individual Christian in such a condition? Let us turn to another passage of the Acts for an answer:

> Now when the apostles which were at Jerusalem heard that Samaria had received the word of God they sent unto them Peter and John, who when they were come down prayed for them that they might receive the Holy Spirit; for as yet he had fallen upon none of them; only they were baptized in the name of the Lord Jesus. Then laid they their hands on them and they received the Holy Spirit (Acts 8:14-17).

Here were believers who had been baptized in water. But this was not enough. The baptism in the Spirit, already bestowed at Pentecost, must be appropriated. Hear the prayer of the apostles "that they might receive the Holy Spirit." Such prayer we deem eminently proper for those who today may be ignorant of the Comforter. And yet such prayer should be followed by an act of believing acceptance on the part of the willing disciple: "O Holy Spirit, I yield to You now in humble surrender. I receive You as my Teacher, my Comforter, my Sanctifier, and my Guide." Do not testimonies abound on every hand of new lives resulting from such an act of consecration as this, lives full of peace and power and victory among those who before had received the forgiveness of sins but not the enduement of power?

Christ our Pattern

We conceive that the great end for which the enduement of the Spirit is bestowed is our qualification for the highest and most effective service in the church of Christ. Other effects will certainly attend the blessing: a fixed assurance of our acceptance in Christ, and a holy separateness from the world. But these results will be conducive to the greatest and supreme end, our consecrated usefulness.

Let us observe that Christ, who is our example in this as in all things, did not enter upon his ministry till he had received the Holy Spirit. Not only so, but we see that all his service from his baptism to his ascension was wrought in the Spirit. Ask concerning his miracles, and we hear him saying: "I by the Spirit of God cast out devils" (Mt. 12:28). Ask concerning that death which he accomplished at Jerusalem, and we read "that he through the eternal Spirit offered himself without spot unto God" (Heb. 9:14). Ask concerning the giving of the great commission, and we read that he was received up "after that he through the Holy Spirit had given commandments unto the apostles" (Acts 1:2). Thus, though he was the Son of God, he acted ever in supreme reliance upon him, who has been called the "Executive of the Godhead."

Plainly we see how Christ was our pattern and exemplar in his relation to the Holy Spirit. He had been begotten of the Holy Spirit in the womb of the virgin and had lived that holy and obedient life which this divine nativity would imply. But when he would enter upon his public ministry, he waited for the Spirit to come upon him, as he had hitherto been in him. For this anointing, we find him praying: "Jesus also being baptized and praying, the heaven was opened, and the Holy Spirit descended in a bodily shape like a dove upon him" (Luke 3:22). Had he any "promise of the Father" to plead, as he now asked for the anointing of the Spirit, if as we may believe this was the subject of his prayer? Yes; it had been written in the prophets concerning the rod out of the stem of Jesse: "And the Spirit of the Lord shall rest upon him; the spirit of wisdom and understanding, the spirit of counsel and might, the spirit of knowledge and of the fear of the Lord" (Isa. 11:2). "The promise of the sevenfold Spirit," the Jewish commentators call it. Certainly, it was literally fulfilled upon the Son of God at the Jordan, when God gave him the Spirit without measure. For he who was now baptized was in turn to be baptizer: "Upon whom you shall see the Spirit descending, and remaining on him, the same is he which baptizes with the Holy Spirit" (John 1:33). "I indeed baptize you in water unto repentance: but he that comes after me is mightier than I ... he shall baptize you in the Holy Spirit and with fire" (Mt. 3:11). And now being at the right hand exalted, and having "the seven spirits of God" (Rev. 3:1), the fullness of the Holy Spirit, he will shed forth his power upon those who pray for it, even as the Father shed it forth upon himself.

---

1. Rev. E. Boys, *Filled with the Spirit*, p. 87.
2. It is assumed by some that because those that walked with Christ of old received the baptism of the Holy Ghost and fire at Pentecost, more than eighteen hundred years ago, therefore all believers now have received the same. As well might the apostles, when first called, have concluded that because of his baptism, the Spirit like a dove rested upon Christ; therefore, they had equally received the same blessing. Surely the Spirit has been given, and the work in Christ wrought for all; but to enter into possession, to be enlightened and made partakers of the Holy Spirit, there must be a personal application to the Lord, etc.—Andrew Jukes, *The New Man*.
3. William Kelly, *Lectures on the New Testament Doctrine of the Holy Spirit*, p. 161.
4. It is a great mistake into which some have fallen, to suppose that the results of Pentecost were chiefly miraculous and temporary. The effect of such a view is to keep spiritual influences out of sight; and it will be well ever to hold fast the assurance that a wide, deep, and perpetual spiritual blessing in the church is that which above all things else was secured by the descent of the Spirit after Christ was glorified. —Dr. J. Elder Cumming, *Through the Eternal Spirit*.

CHAPTER 8

The Spirit-Filled Christian Life

Carl Fredrik Wisloff

In the middle of the 18th century, an unusual spiritual awakening came to the country of Norway. It began in the city of Oslo. In this fresh move of the Spirit, God used a man by the name of Gisle Johnson (1822-1894), a member of the theological faculty of the local university. He was invited by one of Oslo's pastors to give some Bible studies on a week-day evening. The Spirit that pervaded the meetings was so penetrating that men and women were gripped by the Spirit of God and led to a personal experience of salvation. The impact of the awakening soon began to be felt in other places, with the result that what started as an unpretentious series of devotional Bible studies grew till it became a movement that spread to the far corners of the country. The Inner Mission Society was one of several organizations which grew out of this new movement; it prepared hundreds of lay preachers in its service.

Lutheran Pastor Carl Fredrik Wisloff (1908-2004), after graduating from seminary, served a parish in Norway and then set sail for America. During the academic year 1929-30, he taught at Augsburg Seminary in Minneapolis. The following year he was associate pastor of Trinity Congregation in Brooklyn, New York. In 1931, he returned to Norway on a call from the Inner Mission Society to become a teacher at its Bible School. In 1935 he became its president, a position which he held till the year 1946. His deep roots in Lutheran piety are witnessed to by the many choice quotations from Arndt, Scriver, and others. This article is taken from *I Believe in the Holy Spirit* by Carl Fredrik Wisloff, translated into English by Ingvald Daehlin and published by Augsburg Publishing House © 1946, and is adapted.

IF THE FULLNESS OF THE SPIRIT is the crown of the Christian life, we can readily understand that the enemy of souls will do his utmost to destroy this life and to replace it with something else, something that looks like the fullness of the Spirit but which is false spirituality, a condition of soul wrought in man without the Holy Spirit.

We are, therefore, now going to see what, according to the Scriptures, the characteristics are of the right and true fullness of the Spirit.

1. ***The Spirit-filled person is humble and poor in spirit. No one hungers and thirsts more for the Spirit than the Spirit-filled person.*** For to be filled means ever anew to become filled. The day that a Christian no longer hungers and thirsts, he is no longer blessed (Matt. 5:3; Luke 6:25; Phil. 3:12).

The Spirit-filled person does not feel that he is all right. The same illustration can be used about the fullness of the Spirit as Scriver uses about humility: "Fullness of the Spirit resembles the eye: it sees everything except itself." No one admires his fullness of the Spirit less than the person who is filled with the Spirit. The constant prayer of the Spirit-filled person is: Lord, give me more.

Deep groaning belongs in the Christian life, and therefore the groaning is deepest where this life is lived most richly. "He who has the Spirit of God is [chastened] for even the most secret corruption such as coldness, self-love, and neglect, and therefore he must always live only in Christ" (Rosenius).

If you are chastened for the weakness of your sinful flesh and the deep-seated, inward sin of your heart, that is no proof that you are not on the way of the fullness of Spirit; but if you are not chastened for such sins, that is a proof that your "fullness of the Spirit" is false. Even the smallest little sinful desire causes Christian suffering. The suffering is greatest in the heart that is purest and most sanctified. "Heart-suffering because of sin is the best proof that the Holy Spirit dwells in your heart" (Arndt).

Outwardly toward men, too, it is humility that characterizes Spirit-filled persons. Precisely by their humility, they are able to open and enter through locked heart-doors; and their quiet, humble mind has the effect of making all evil forces dread them more than all other Christians. "The devil sees nothing more abominable than a truly humble Christian, for he is just the opposite of his own image" (Hauge). The Spirit-filled person carries the image of Jesus in his soul; He said of Himself: "I am meek and lowly in heart" (Matt. 11:29).

The Spirit-filled Christian does not look with contempt on the Christianity of others. He does not feel that he is on a higher plane. On the contrary, he feels his own insignificance, and every day he continues to marvel that the grace of God still is sufficient. Therefore "each counts others better than himself." "Do not think that you have made progress in the Spirit unless you feel inferior to all others" (Thomas à Kempis).

The type of Christianity that makes bad blood between Christians by criticism, contempt, and intolerance, should be the last to lay claim to the stamp of the Holy Spirit. Where the fullness of the Spirit is found, there are the fruits of the Spirit in great richness, and among them are love, peace, longsuffering, kindness, goodness, meekness, and faithfulness (Gal. 5:22). Where any one of these is lacking or has had to yield to its opposite, such a factiousness, adverse criticism, self-importance, and a condescending, perhaps somewhat indulgent view of other Christians—there one must no longer speak of the fruit of the Spirit; for in spite of a strong spiritual appearance, this is only disguised carnality.

The Spirit-filled person is not eager to speak about his fullness of Spirit. Humility makes him always dissatisfied with himself, and ever hungering for more grace. He is not much occupied with his own experiences but is always near to Him, whom he has experienced—Christ. Scriver compares certain Christians with a hen. "When she has laid an egg, she cackles and makes a great ado about it."

A man who had been through a powerful religious experience, later said in his testimony: "I see now that my fault up to this time in my Christian life was that I was too much occupied with myself." Later a friend said to him: "That is true, and it is well that you discovered it. But a thing that you do not see is that you have never been as occupied with yourself as you are now. It is only that you are occupied with yourself in a different manner."

The enemy of souls makes use of the steady circling about one's own religious experiences to destroy many Christians. When Christian arrived at "the Delectable Mountains," he sat down and began looking at and admiring his shining armor. Then he fell asleep, and that sleep might have cost him his life (Bunyan).

When Paul was in the act of exalting himself by reason of the exceeding greatness of the revelations, God found it necessary to humiliate him greatly so he might learn to know his own weakness, and not forget that the ground of salvation is grace and not religious experiences of any kind.

The fateful misfortune of many Christians is that they build on their experiences instead of building on Christ. And so that which was unto life was found to be unto death. Consciously or unconsciously, their own ego is growing by what they experience; and while they themselves are talking about the death of the ego, their old man is rejoicing because the ego is there present, very much alive, disguised in a garb so spiritual that one does not recognize him. We must not forget that where God should win His mightiest victories, there Satan appears with his greatest cunning and power.

The distinguishing marks of true fullness of the Spirit are that he who has experienced this fullness continues to keep close to Christ; his own ego is drowned in a deep and earnest worship of Him.

2. *The Spirit-filled person has found life's deep and inexhaustible fountain*

in Christ.

Here too, we see that life is richer than thought. While the Spirit-filled person feels poor in spirit, and is conscious of a deep longing for more, and has an unceasing pain in his heart, he can still continue to draw from the fountain that sends forth joy, peace, and power, and that never goes dry no matter how much he drinks. We cannot understand that pain and joy, poverty and riches, hunger, and power can dwell in the same heart at the same time. Still, nevertheless that is the continual experience of the Spirit-filled person, and also the teaching of Scripture: It is he who is poor in spirit who possesses the kingdom of heaven (Matt. 5:3).

It is he who hungers and thirsts that the Lord calls blessed. Real hunger surely is no pleasant feeling, and yet the Lord says that the person who hungers already has tasted the heavenly joy. The Spirit filled person lives his life under this word: "As sorrowful, yet always rejoicing; as poor, yet making many rich; as having nothing, and yet possessing all things" (2 Cor. 6:10).

The Spirit-filled Christian lives under the discipline of the Spirit. No one feels the least little sin as suffering as much as he does, but it is just this that drives him to Christ, and that makes Christ's finished work so unspeakably precious to him. No one is as dependent as he on unmerited grace, and no one rejoices more in the daily forgiveness of sins. Grace never becomes a matter of course; the Spirit-filled person lives daily in the miracle of grace.

The insight of every Christian into the glory of the atonement is according to the light of the Spirit that he has received. The Spirit-filled Christian gazes down into this mysterious deep in the piercing light of the Spirit. He never gets tired of meditating on it. To no one is the blood of Jesus so precious. To no one is the glory of Christ so great as just to him. His mind and thought dwell with tender eagerness on the cross of Christ, for the Spirit does nothing for Himself; all His work is to glorify Christ. Therefore the Crucified One is never so precious and glorious to anyone else as He is to the person in whom the Spirit dwells in fullness.

It is not true that the Spirit-filled person is never assaulted by doubt and temptation. All living faith is acquainted with the struggle for life. "Faith lives only so long as it continues to fight" (Luther). "Great temptations and anxieties make their hardest attacks against the best souls, the most tender consciences, and the most God-fearing hearts" (Scriver). It is precisely the God-fearing person on whom Satan especially has his eye. Therefore the Lord said to Satan before Job was to endure his afflictions: "Hast thou considered my servant Job? for there is none like him in the earth" (Job 1:8). The reason that Satan was to have his eye on Job was because of his godliness.

That a Christian experiences temptations, spiritual depression, and the designs of Satan against him is no proof that he is not filled by the Spirit of God. On the contrary, the Spirit-filled person will know these to a greater degree than anyone else. But in the midst of these struggles, he receives the hidden power that brings him victory. In the storms of spiritual depression, he always has the wisdom to seek the quiet central point at the cross of Christ. "In the midst of the greatest misery, the sorely tried child of God is a vessel unto honor" (Scriver).

Everything must change for the good for him, who has the fullness of the Spirit. The struggle against temptation increases his strength. Therefore it can be said that he is more than conqueror (Rom. 8:37). The darkness of spiritual depression must give place to a still clearer understanding of the glory of Christ. All tribulations are transformed into rungs on his ladder to heaven. Affliction works for him more and more exceedingly an eternal weight of glory (2 Cor. 4:17). Things that seemed to be heavy weights dragging him down are altered by the Spirit of God into wings that lift him up. He now becomes master over sinful habits to which he formerly succumbed, and there is a strain of victory over his whole life. "Thanks be to God, who giveth us the victory through our Lord Jesus Christ" (1 Cor. 15:57). "Thanks be unto God, who always leadeth us in triumph in Christ" (2 Cor. 2:14).

The Spirit-filled person has in his life moved into a new and rich world. He need not live on crumbs and drops but can always help himself out of the inexhaustible storerooms of God. "God is able to make all grace abound unto you; that ye, having always all sufficiency in everything, may abound unto every good work" (2 Cor. 9:8).

For the Spirit-filled person, it is as though he were walking in the mountains in the great kingdom of God's grace. At every mountain top, new and glorious views are unfurled before him. He walks and does not become faint (Isa. 40:31). He waits for the Lord and receives new strength, and as he goes on, something new and glorious is always awaiting him. He is acquainted in the prayer world, but there are always new surprises, for God "is able to do exceeding abundantly above all that we ask or think" (Eph. 3:20). He can testify to the truth of God because he daily experiences its truth. But he can never get through sinking himself down farther into the deep of God's promises.

The hidden power of the fullness of the Spirit is seen in the many tasks of everyday life. In our daily work, the power of the fullness of the Spirit is transformed into holy faithfulness to duty with the joyous mind of Christ. The

Spirit-filled person is not caught up into a higher sphere, there to live his life in the Spirit. No, he is placed with both feet on the ground in the midst of all tasks, large and small, and there he lives his everyday life with a mind conformed to the will of God. For him, who really is filled with the Spirit, the workshop is a sanctuary and his working clothes a ministerial robe. The person whose eyes the Spirit keeps open sees eternal values in the little things of every day; for him, nothing is small that belongs to Christian duty.

He who has experienced the true fullness of the Spirit does not shut himself in his private room while duties and tasks wait in vain outside. For him, the kingdom of God consists of a holy life active in the fulfillment of duty, and therefore he seeks to attend to that first. In everything that the Spirit-filled person does, the fullness of the Spirit makes its impress.

When the temple of the Lord was to be built, every single thing was to be made accurately and carefully, the little things too. They were "to devise skillful works," and also work in the cutting of stones "and in carving of wood, to work in all manner of skillful workmanship." But to do all this, God appointed men who were filled with the Spirit of God (Ex. 31:1-6; 35:30-33). A man's fullness of the Spirit is seen even in the smallest and most insignificant little piece of work; for to him, everything is great because it is done for the Lord.

"And the God of peace himself sanctify you wholly" (1 Thess. 5:23). The Greek word which is translated "wholly" has been translated in a variety of ways into different languages. Perhaps the best translation is the one by Luther: "through and through." The Spirit-filled person does not only perform holy deeds; he is holy. The Spirit has leavened his whole being; he is sanctified clear through.

"Be not drunken with wine, wherein is riot, but be filled with the Spirit" (Eph. 5:18). The point of comparison is this: The person who is drunken with wine bears the stamp of it through and through. His walk, his gestures, and his whole being testify to it. The case is similar to the person who is filled with the Spirit. He bears the stamp of the Spirit. His behavior, words, dress, train of ideas, interests, everything that he does, says, and is, bear the stamp of God. The Spirit-filled person is a realization of God's plan for men.

Gustav Jensen offers this prayer: "Give me holy power and perseverance to form my headstrong nature according to the law of my mind, so that the new man who is to live forever, more and more may shine through my words and deeds, and sanctify also my body to be a sacrifice acceptable to God."

To be a Christian is to be a man. To be a Spirit-filled Christian is to live a harmonious human life—fully. Because he himself is pure, he can rejoice in everything that is pure. The sensual person hears something lewd in connection with every slip of the tongue and sees something foul in all that he observes. The holy person sees that which is pure and beautiful about him and rejoices in that. He who has looked at Christ a great deal will observe something heavenly in all that he sees after that. No one else can say with as much right as he: "Even the pure little moss rose is heaven's chapel."

The fullness of the Spirit is not a uniform that makes men alike and blots out their distinctive characteristics. On the contrary, the fullness of the Spirit brings out the individual qualities: strengthens what is weak, hallows and straightens that which is crooked and bungled, and God-given natural gifts are developed and permitted to grow freely under the discipline and light of the Spirit.

You must not believe that a man is not filled with the Spirit of God if his interests, behavior, and temperament are not identical to yours. Everything in man's life must be put under God's sanctifying power, for He desires to sanctify you wholly; but God's sanctifying power does not operate directly contrary to God's creative power. Such as He created us He wills to sanctify us. God desires to make all men equally holy, but not all holy men alike. God sanctifies your temperament; He does not do away with it. He cuts away the excrescences, develops, and sanctifies that which is your strength. Neither will He blot out your character; a Spirit-filled person is a Christian character.

Therefore God's Spirit desires to permeate man through and through. The fountainhead itself must be cleansed. God desires to make His dwelling in man's inmost self, and from thence to sanctify and put His stamp on all of that man's life. God is permitted to reach the mainspring of the character, the inmost chamber of the heart of the Spirit-filled man, and for that reason, the whole personality and being of the Spirit-filled man bears the stamp and seal of God. "There is an inner fountainhead for every character; let yours be Christ. Every act has its special keynote; let Christ strike the keynote in you" (H. Drummond).

The Spirit-filled person lives the harmonious human life; therefore, the dominant tone in his life is peace and joy.

We have already noted that the Spirit-filled person is by no means spared from struggle, temptation, and spiritual depression and that groans and pains are marks of the life lived closest to God. And just here we find the paradox of the fullness of the Spirit: In the midst of the struggle, he has peace; in the midst of his groaning, he feels rejoicing.

Peace and joy are fruits of the Spirit; in the Spirit-filled life, the fruits of peace and joy are picked the year around, throughout life, always in abundance and richness. In Isaiah 48:18, we read of "peace as a river," so deep and strong, so quiet and smooth, not unstable and changeable like the babbling brook, which in the rainless season quite dries up, but reliable and deep like a mighty stream. Nothing can stop its calm course toward the ocean. In storm or calm, in the rainy season and in the dry season, through fertile land and barren steppes, everywhere this stream makes its way onward, deeper and deeper until it reaches the sea. The only unrest in the stream is its quiet course toward its goal, the great and mighty ocean.

The Christian's peace can be like that if God is permitted to dwell fully in his heart. In sickness and pains, in disappointments and blasted hopes, in difficulties and opposition, in temptations and trials, in struggles and hard times for the cause of the kingdom of God, when despondency is trying to seep in, when boldness is beginning to fail, in all circumstances and all conditions there is a peace so deep and calm, as mighty and unbroken as the deep waters of the river. The only unrest found in this peace is the Christian's longing for eternity.

Such is the peace that "passeth all understanding" (Phil. 4:7). "For the mountains may depart, and the hills be removed; but my lovingkindness shall not depart from thee, neither shall my covenant of peace be removed, saith the LORD that hath mercy on thee" (Isa. 54:10).

As deep as the river, as secure as the mountain—such is the Christian peace. "In peace will I both lay me down and sleep; For thou, LORD, alone makest me dwell in safety" (Psalm 4:8).

Such is the life in which God Himself has become the center, and thousands of people can testify that this is true. In life's most burdensome circumstances and severest afflictions, they have had this deep peace in their hearts. God Himself is called "the God of peace" (2 Thess. 5:23). And about Christ, we read: "He is our peace" (Eph. 2:14). "Now the Lord of peace himself give you peace at all times in all ways" (2 Thess. 3:16). Because peace is the harmony of the Christian life, joy becomes the dominant tone when the strings are struck. "The kingdom of God is ... righteousness and peace and joy in the Holy Spirit" (Rom. 14:17). The Christian is always sorrowful, yet always rejoicing. The Christian joy is God's answer to the longing of all times for happiness. The fullness of the Spirit is the true and pure joy of human life; it is the blessedness of heaven enjoyed in advance. "Rejoice in the Lord always: again I will say, Rejoice" (Phil. 4:4).

Christ Himself is the ground of joy; so long as the soul possesses Him, it also possesses joy. The gospel is the good news. It was only with Christianity that the "great joy" came to the world. Where Christianity is not found, this true and deep joy is not found either.

Every day the Christian encounters strong gusts of wind that would extinguish the flame of his joy, but as long as he is in Christ, he is also in the joy.

> *Wherein ye greatly rejoice, though now for a little while, if need be, ye have been put to grief in manifold trials, that the proof of your faith ... may be found unto praise and glory and honor at the revelation of Jesus Christ: whom not having seen ye love; on whom, though now ye see him not, yet believing, ye rejoice greatly with joy unspeakable and full of glory: receiving the end of your faith, even the salvation of your souls* (1 Pet. 1:6-9).

He who is filled with God can, in the midst of deepest sorrows and during the severest trials, rejoice with joy unspeakable and full of glory, while he always longs for the day when he shall taste the eternal joy unmixed when he shall never be sorrowful, but always rejoicing.

3. The Spirit-filled person lives the abundant life which issues forth with blessings for all those that meet him.

God does not want the Christian to live a life in spiritual poverty. He shall indeed, as we have seen, always be poor in spirit, but just when he has nothing, he possesses all things. When he is weak, then he is strong (Matt. 5:3; 2 Cor. 6:10; 12:10). The Lord "is rich unto all that call upon Him" (Rom. 10:12). "God is able to make all grace abound unto you" (2 Cor. 9:8).

God has not promised His children only victory, but He says that they shall be "more than conquerors" (Rom. 8:37). They shall not only have life, but they shall have it abundantly (John 10:10). God does not pour His blessings sparingly and stingily into the cup of salvation—barely enough so that a man may know that he is saved. No, "My cup runneth over" (Psalm 23:5).

Hence, the Spirit-filled Christian life is a life not only in riches but also in abundance. And this abundance is to flow out and be a blessing to other people. "He that believeth on me, as the scripture hath said, from within him shall flow rivers of living water" (John 7:38). John explains in these words what Jesus means: "But this spake he of the Spirit, which they that believe on him were to receive" (v. 39).

To the Samaritan woman, Jesus said: "The water that I shall give him shall become in him a well of water springing up unto eternal life" (John 4:14). From every true Christian, some of the blessings of this living water flow out to other people. Merely by his existence, a Christian becomes a blessing, provided he lives in the light. However, the blessing that flows out from many

Christians is very slight. It often seems that the lives of many hardly leave a trace.

The lives of other Christians are like a fountain running over with blessings. Wherever they go, some light shines forth from God Himself. That which was wrong and crooked before is righted and set in order when these people arrive; this seems to happen almost of itself. They create an atmosphere of joy and peace about them. Where they are, the air becomes purer. It becomes easier to be holy and good. It is no longer difficult to forgive an old injustice; it seems of itself to fall away. Suspicion, spite, ill will, and hostile criticism disappear in their presence. People who formerly have kept aloof from the Word of God, may even have opposed it, begin wonderingly to ask whether perhaps, after all, Christianity is a power. Before long, you hear that one after another has been won for the kingdom of God. Yea, verily: From within those that believe on Him shall flow rivers of living water. "Passing through the valley of Weeping, they make it a place of springs; yea, the early rain covereth it with blessings" (Ps. 84:6).

The life of the Spirit-filled person is his most powerful sermon. His good works prove to all the world that his Christianity is genuine. A holy life is the only testimony that can convince a world seeking for realities. "They see your good works, and glorify your Father who is in heaven" (Matt. 5:16).

In the Merchant of Venice, Portia says: "That light we see is burning in my hall. / How far that little candle throws his beams! / So shines a good deed in a naughty world."

There is a definite atmosphere around every person. It is strongest around him who has the strongest personality, but there is some of it around everyone. It is this atmosphere that delivers its silent speech to everyone, without words, even without acts. "What you are speaks so loud that I cannot hear what you say."

The Christian's life will draw a line either through his Christianity to cancel it, or under his Christianity to emphasize it. Good deeds are like an exclamation point after the sermon of a holy life. For that reason, the Christian life of the Spirit-filled person is effective also without words. The atmosphere which surrounds and speaks for him is the Holy Spirit. Therefore his life will always be a bubbling fountain of blessing in the midst of a barren and joyless world.

No one tastes the fellowship of the sufferings of Christ as fully as he who is filled with the Spirit. No one sees the world's suffering and feels it as his own in the degree that he does. The Spirit-filled person knows what responsibility is. He feels the world's need laid upon his own shoulders; his eyes are open to see the possibilities, his love urges him on so that he never lets an opportunity pass, and his strength is such that no hindrance can stop him.

The people of Israel once became a burden that overwhelmed Moses. The burden became too heavy for him to bear alone. Despondency was settling down on the strong servant of the Lord, and he reasoned with God in these words: "Why layest thou the burden of all this people upon me? Have I conceived all this people? Have I brought them forth? ... I am not able to bear all this people alone, because it is too heavy for me.—Kill me, I pray thee, out of hand—and let me not see my wretchedness."

God heard that prayer. He selected seventy men of the elders of Israel and commanded Moses to place them at the door of the tent of meeting that He might fill them with His Spirit, so they could bear the burden of the people with Moses. "I will take of the Spirit which is upon thee, and will put it upon them; and they shall bear the burden of the people with thee, that thou bear it not thyself alone" (Num. 11:17).

That land is fortunate indeed that has Spirit-filled men willing to bear the need of the people together with those whom God has appointed to be Christian leaders among the people. The truly Spirit-filled person does not isolate himself and does not hide within his own shell in order quietly to enjoy his fullness of the Spirit. He places himself shoulder to shoulder with his brothers and bears responsibilities, burdens, sorrows, and joys together with them. The Spirit-filled person is called to suffering, but his suffering must become a source of blessing.

The following legend is told of Benedict of Nursia: On one of his travels, he was overwhelmed with sorrow because of the reigning sin and unbelief. In his burning desire to become useful in the Lord's service, he threw himself on his knees on a large stone by the wayside. When he arose from his prayer, his knees had made marks in the hard stone.

Thus, every Christian who is filled with God leaves marks wherever he travels and wherever he kneels. Hearts and communities that are as hard as stone must bear marks from the prayers of a Spirit-filled Christian.

The Crimean War broke out in 1858, and with the war was an accompaniment of dreadful suffering for thousands of wounded and sick soldiers. The hospital service was in disorder, and there were no nurses. Then the English minister of war wrote a letter to Florence Nightingale and asked her to take charge of the situation and gave her absolute authority to organize the hospital service in the field. In a short time, she started out, accompanied by thirty-eight nurses. Wherever these women went, they relieved suffering, bound up wounds, and spread love and light around. The air became purer where they entered. Florence herself worked at Scutari hospital. At night she would walk among the beds, carrying her little lamp in her hand, and the soldiers would try to stay awake till she came in order to get a glimpse of the lady with the lamp. It was said of Florence Nightingale: "She belongs to a sect that, alas, is very small, namely that of the Good Samaritan." (From Welle's *Church History*.)

The self-sacrificing nurse with the lighted lamp walking at night among the beds of the sick and wounded soldiers is a striking example of what the life of every Christian should be. Toward the world's evening, it is easy to go to sleep. The only thing that can keep men awake is their expectation of the Good Samaritan walking among the world's sickbeds, where the many who have been wounded in life's hard fight lie waiting and longing for a lighted lamp and a loving hand.

The holy life of the Christian is the lighted lamp that the world is looking for toward the evening of time (Matt. 5:16). According to the Word of God, the righteous acts of the saints are the fine linen of the church of God in which she shall array herself for the marriage supper of the Lamb (Rev. 19:8-9).

Night is coming on in the world today. Thousands of wounded soldiers lie waiting. Today we who belong to the Lord must go with lighted lamps to help the sufferers with love and mercy.

Why are the lives of so many Christians of so little blessing? Because something is lacking in their surrender to God, their sanctification is hindered, they are no longer being filled by the Spirit of God.

When a Christian compromises with the world, it is inevitable that his spiritual power grows less. "What communion hath light with darkness?" (2 Cor. 6:14). A Christian who leads a life as much like the world as possible, but apparently without denying his Christian faith, will never become a blessing to those about him. "Be not fashioned according to this world: but be ye transformed by the renewing of your mind" (Rom. 12:2). The greatest hindrance to the growth of the kingdom of God today is worldly-minded Christians. A mind bent on earthly things, worldly interests and amusements are poison plants that destroy the harvest in the kingdom of God.

Our time also needs to hear these old words from Johan Arndt:

> If you wish to keep the precious treasure of the Spirit in your heart, you will be on your guard against everything that can tear God and His kingdom away from you. You are afraid of worldly company, pastimes, and hilarity. And if you must move about in worldly surroundings, you pray for self-control, turn your heart to God, and thus retain the Holy Spirit with

peace and joy in the depth of your soul."

The chief reason that the life of many Christians is poverty-stricken and void of blessing is to be found in their relation to the world. Do not expect to be filled with the Spirit of God before you are willing to be emptied of the Spirit of the world.

It is precisely the life that is separated from the world and dedicated to God that can bring most of the divine life back to the world. If you desire to be of blessing to the world, say goodbye to it, and then let the world meet you again in a new form. Only then will the world get its eye on you. And when it has seen you, it will soon behold Him whose image you bear—your Savior.

Self-centeredness, disobedience, and other sins all corrode and waste the Christian's strength. He who desires to live the abundant life must be willing to give up every sin; even his self-life must be yielded to death. The spiritual power of many a servant of the Lord is limited by an only partial surrender to the Lord. Everything has not been placed at the disposal of God. Fire from the Lord does not descend before everything is laid on the altar of the Lord. The ego appears in everything that some Christians do. They desire more for themselves than for God. That which seems to be zeal for the house of the Lord is, in reality, only a disguise for morbid ambition for personal honor. Or, their lack of boldness has its deepest cause in a towering ambition which they dare not openly display. Their lack of joy in their work is caused by envy and hard feelings toward other servants of the Lord. What appears as the tears of Jesus over Jerusalem are really only sorrow because their own advancement is so slight.

In these matters, every upright servant of the Lord must carry on a fight all his life. He will continually be reminded that the old ego is again showing his head. But he must not tolerate this without a fight if he wishes to have the power of the Spirit in his work. A right dedication of a servant of the Lord for his work consists of dedicating his ambitious self to death. And he must be in earnest about that dedication. Every time that the crucified ego announces that it still lives, he must in the power of the Spirit anew and without mercy strike the nails that are to hold the ego fast to the death. The servant of the Lord who tolerates, excuses, or overlooks the least of all this is doomed to an impotent service without blessing. He who desires to be "a vessel unto honor" must be "sanctified, meet for the master's use, prepared unto every good work" (2 Tim. 2:21).

"Whosoever shall seek to gain his life shall lose it: But whosoever shall lose his life shall preserve it" (Luke 17: 33). "No man, having put his hand to the plow, and looking back, is fit for the kingdom of God" (Luke 9:62).

God has power enough for the greatest task and the most glorious service. He does not want his servants to wear themselves out for lack of spiritual power. Samson was compelled to grind in the prison-house, the great giant doing the work of a bond-woman, and even that tired him out. That is what happens to the person who on account of disobedience has lost the power of the Lord's Spirit. By the Spirit of the Lord, the weak person becomes strong; the morbidly ambitious person begins to burn with true zeal for the house of God, the coward becomes courageous, the despondent bold, the doubter a champion of the faith.

Native endowment is not sufficient equipment for the servant of the Lord. Many a talented person, eloquent and intelligent, has passed through this world, leaving no trace, while God has made use of that which was insignificant and of small reputation in the eyes of men. To this fact, the history of the church bears abundant testimony.

It is the power of the Spirit of God that is the deciding factor. Every natural gift is a gift from God, but first God wishes to have it in His power to sanctify it. The best surgical instruments must be kept free from rust if they are to be of use. The sword of the Christian must be cleansed with the ointment of the Spirit if it is to be used in the wars of the Lord. Everything must be put at His disposal. He who desires to live so that his life shall be a blessing to others must reckon with God and not with himself.

"But we have this treasure in earthen vessels, that the exceeding greatness of the power may be of God, and not from ourselves" (2 Cor. 4:7). "But ye shall receive power, when the Holy Spirit is come upon you: and ye shall be my witnesses" (Acts 1:8). "Not that we are sufficient of ourselves, to account anything as from ourselves; but our sufficiency is from God; who also made us sufficient as ministers of a new covenant" (2 Cor. 3:5-6). "I thank him that enabled me, even Christ Jesus our Lord, for that he counted me faithful, appointing me to his service" (1 Tim. 1:12)....

So the ancient Latin saying proves true, as understood also in this connection: *Deus maximo in minimo*: "God is greatest in him who is least."

CHAPTER 9

A Living Sacrifice

James Montgomery Boice

James Montgomery Boice (1938-2000) was pastor of Tenth Presbyterian Church in Philadelphia for 32 years. From 1969-2000 he was the teacher on The Bible Study Hour radio broadcast over 238 stations and was president of the program's parent organization, the Alliance of Confessing Evangelicals. Dr. Boice held degrees from Harvard University (A.B.), Princeton Theological Seminary (B.D.), the University of Basel, Switzerland (D. Theol.), and the Theological Seminary of the Reformed Episcopal Church (D.D.). In addition to authoring numerous journal articles, he was a consulting editor for the *Expositor's Bible Commentary*. His books and commentaries include *Foundations of God's City* and the five-volume work *The Gospel of John*. The following article is taken from *Mind Renewal in a Mindless Age*, copyright ©1993 James Montgomery Boice.

> *I beseech you therefore, brethren, by the mercies of God, that ye present your bodies a living sacrifice, holy, acceptable unto God, which is your reasonable service* (Rom. 12:1).

THE FIRST POINT is the obvious one: This is to be a living sacrifice rather than a dead one. That was quite a novel idea in Paul's day, of course, though we have lost this by becoming overly familiar with it.

In Paul's day, sacrifices were always killed. In Jewish religious practices, particularly, the animal was brought to the priest; the sins of the person bringing the sacrifice were confessed over the animal, thereby transferring them to it symbolically. Then the animal was put to death. It was a vivid way of reminding everyone that "the wages of sin is death" (Rom. 6:23) and that the salvation of sinners is by substitution. In those sacrifices, the animal died in place of the worshiper. It died so that the worshiper might not have to die. But now, with a burst of divinely inspired creativity, Paul reveals that the sacrifices we are to offer are to be living, not dead. We are to offer our lives to God so that, as a result, we might "no longer live for [ourselves] but for him who died for [us] and was raised again" (2 Cor. 5:15).

Living sacrifices, yes. But with what life? Certainly not our old sinful lives in which, when we lived in them, we were already dead. Rather, we offer the new spiritual lives that have been given to us by Christ.

Robert Smith Candlish was a Scottish pastor who lived over a hundred years ago (1806-1873) and who left us some marvelous studies of the Bible. One set of these studies is of Romans 12, and in it, there is a paragraph in which he reflects on the nature of the life we are to offer God. "What life?" Candlish asks. "Not merely animal life, the life that is common to all sentient and moving creatures; not merely, in addition to that, intelligent life, the life that characterizes all beings capable of thought and voluntary choice; but spiritual life: life in the highest sense; the very life which those on whose behalf the sacrifice of atonement is presented lost when they fell into that state which makes a sacrifice of atonement necessary."[1]

What this means, among other things, is that we must be believers if we are to give ourselves to God as he requires. Other people may give God their money or time or even take up a religious vocation, but only a Christian can give back to God that new spiritual life in Christ that he or she has first been given. Indeed, it is only because we have been made alive in Christ that we are able to do this or even want to.

Offering Our Bodies

The second thing we need to see about the nature of the sacrifice that God requires is that it involves the giving to God of our bodies. Some of the older commentators stress that offering our bodies really means to offer our total selves, all that we are. Calvin wrote, "By bodies, he means not only our skin and bones but the totality of which we are composed."[2] Although it is true that we are to offer God all that we are, most commentators today rightly refuse to pass over the word bodies quite this easily, because they recognize how much the Bible stresses the importance of our bodies.

For example, Leon Morris says,

> Paul surely expected Christians to offer to God not only their bodies but their whole selves.... But we should bear in mind that the body is very important in the Christian understanding of things. Our bodies may be "implements of righteousness" (6:13) and "members of Christ" (1 Cor. 6:15). The body is a temple of the Holy Spirit (1 Cor. 6:19); Paul can

speak of being "holy both in body and in spirit" (1 Cor. 7:34). He knows that there are possibilities of evil in the body but that in the believer "the body of sin" has been brought to nothing (6:6).[3]

In a similar manner, Robert Haldane says, "It is of the body that the apostle here speaks, and it is not proper to extract out of his language more than it contains.... This shows the importance of serving God with the body as well as with the soul."[4]

Paul does not elaborate in Romans 12 upon what he means by presenting our bodies to God "as living sacrifices," but we are not left in the dark about his meaning since this is not a new idea, not even in Romans. It has already appeared in chapter 6. In that chapter, Paul said,

> *Therefore do not let sin reign in your mortal body so that you obey its evil desires. Do not offer the parts of your body to sin, as instruments of wickedness, but rather offer yourselves to God, as those who have been brought from death to life; and offer the parts of your body to him as instruments of righteousness. For sin shall not be your master, because you are not under law, but under grace* (vv. 12-14).

This is the point at which Paul first began to talk about sanctification, and the point he was making there is the same one he is making here, namely, that we are to serve God by offering him our bodies. Sin can control us through our bodies, but this need not happen. So, rather than offering our bodies as instruments of sin, we are to offer God our bodies as instruments for doing his will. To be practical, we need to think about this as involving specific parts of our bodies.

1. *Our minds.*

I begin with the mind because, although we think of ourselves largely as our minds and thus separate our minds from our bodies, our minds actually are parts of our bodies, and the victory we need to achieve begins here. In this study, I will not say a great deal about presenting our minds to God because I will be treating this more fully later when I talk about mind renewal. But I remind you that this is the point at which Paul himself begins in verse 2: "Do not conform any longer to the pattern of this world, but be transformed by the renewing of your mind" (emphasis mine).

Have you ever considered that what you do with your mind will determine a great deal of what you will become as a Christian? If you fill your mind only with the products of our secular culture, you will remain secular and sinful. If you fill your head with trashy "pop" novels, you will begin to live like the trashy characters you read about. If you do little else but watch television, you will begin to act like the scoundrels on the screen. On the other hand, if you feed your mind on the Bible and Christian books, train it by godly conversation, and discipline it to critique what you see and hear by applying biblical truths to the world's ideas, you will grow in godliness and become increasingly useful to God....

2. *Our eyes and ears.*

The mind is not the only part of our body by which we receive and filter impressions and which must, therefore, be offered to God as an instrument of righteousness. We also receive impressions through our eyes and ears, and these, too, must be surrendered to God.

Sociologists tell us that by the age of twenty-one, the average young person has been bombarded by 300,000 commercial messages, all arguing from the assumption that personal gratification is the dominant goal in life.[5] Our modern means of communication put the acquisition of "things" before godliness. In fact, they never mention godliness at all. How are you going to grow in godliness if you are constantly watching television or reading printed ads or listening to secular radio?

I am not advocating an evangelical monasticism in which we retreat from the culture, though it is far better to retreat from it than perish in it. But somehow, the secular input must be counterbalanced by the spiritual. Another simple goal might be for you to spend as many hours studying your Bible, praying, and going to church as watching television.

3. *Our tongues.*

The tongue is also part of our body, and what we do with it is important either for good or evil. James, the Lord's brother, wrote, "The tongue also is a fire, a world of evil among the parts of the body. It corrupts the whole person, sets the whole course of his life on fire, and is itself set on fire by hell" (James 3:6). If your tongue is not given to God as an instrument of righteousness in his hands, this will be true of you. You do not need to be a Hitler and plunge the world into armed conflict to do evil with your tongue. A little bit of gossip or slander will suffice.

What you need to do is use your tongue to praise and serve God. For one thing, you should learn how to recite Scripture with it. You probably know the words of many popular songs. Can you not also use your tongue to speak God's words? And how about worship? You should use your tongue to praise

God by means of hymns and other Christian songs. Above all, you should use your tongue to witness to others about the person and work of Jesus Christ.

Here is another goal for you if you want to grow in godliness: Use your tongue as much to tell others about Jesus as for idle conversation.

4. *Our hands and feet.*

There are several important biblical passages about our hands and feet. In 1 Thessalonians 4:11-12, Paul tells us to work with our hands so that we will be self-supporting and not have to rely on others: "Make it your ambition to lead a quiet life, to mind your own business and to work with your hands, just as we told you, so that your daily life may win the respect of outsiders and so that you will not be dependent on anybody." In Ephesians 4:28, he tells us also to work so that we will have something to give to others who are in need: "He who has been stealing must steal no longer, but must work, doing something useful with his own hands, that he might have something to share with those in need."

As far as our feet are concerned, Paul wrote in Romans 10 of the need that others have for the gospel, saying, "How can they hear without someone preaching to them? And how can they preach unless they are sent? As it is written, 'How beautiful are the feet of those who bring good news!'" (10:14-15).

What do you do with your hands? Where do your feet take you? Do you allow them to take you to where Christ is denied or blasphemed? To where sin is openly practiced? Are you spending most of your free time loitering in the "hot" singles clubs or in other unsavory places? You will not grow in godliness there. On the contrary, you will fall from righteous conduct. Instead, let your feet carry you into the company of those who love and serve God. Or, as you go into the world, let it be to serve the world and witness to it in Christ's name. Use your feet and hands for him....

Holiness, without Which ...

The third word Paul uses to indicate the nature of the sacrifices we are to offer God is "holy." Any sacrifice we make must be holy. That is, it must be without spot or blemish and be consecrated entirely to God. Anything less is an insult to the great and holy God all people are to serve. But how much more must we be holy—we who have been purchased "not with perishable things such as silver or gold ... but with the precious blood of Christ, a lamb without blemish or defect" (1 Pet. 1:18-19). Peter explained, "But just as he who called you is holy, so be holy in all you do; for it is written: 'Be holy, because I am holy'" (vv. 15-16). The author of Hebrews said, "Without holiness no one will see the Lord" (Heb. 12:14).

This is the very heart of what we are talking about when we speak of living sacrifices, of course. Or, to put it in other language, holiness is the end of the matter. Or, to put it in still other language, it is the point to which the entire epistle of Romans has been heading. Romans is about salvation. But, as someone has wisely noted, salvation does not mean that Jesus died to save us in our sins but to save us from them.

Handley C. G. Moule expressed this well.

> As we actually approach the rules of holiness now before us, let us once more recollect what we have seen all along in the Epistle, that holiness is the aim and issue of the entire Gospel. It is indeed an "evidence of life," infinitely weighty in the inquiry whether a man knows God indeed and is on the way to his heaven. But it is much more; it is the expression of life; it is the form and action in which life is intended to come out.... We who believe are "chosen" and "ordained" to "bring forth fruit" (John 15:16), fruit much and lasting.[6]

Is there any subject that is more generally neglected among evangelicals in America in our day than holiness? I do not think so. Yet there was a time when holiness was a serious pursuit of anyone who called himself a Christian, and when how one lived and what one was inside was vitally important.

England's J. I. Packer has written a book called *Rediscovering Holiness* in which he calls attention to this matter.

> The Puritans insisted that all life and relationships must become "holiness to the Lord." John Wesley told the world that God had raised up Methodism "to spread scriptural holiness throughout the land." Phoebe Palmer, Handley Moule, Andrew Murray, Jessie Penn-Lewis, F. B. Meyer, Oswald Chambers, Horatius Bonar, Amy Carmichael, and L. E. Maxwell are only a few of the leading figures in the "holiness revival" that touched all evangelical Christendom between the mid-nineteenth and mid-twentieth centuries.[7]

But today? In our time, holiness is largely forgotten as an important quality for Christians. So we do not try to be holy. We hardly know what holiness means. And we do not look for holiness in others. The great parish minister and revival preacher Robert Murray McCheyne once said, "My people's greatest need is my personal holiness." But what pulpit committees look for holiness in a new pastor today? Hardly any. They look for winsome personality, good communication skills, administrative ability, and other secular things.

As for ourselves, we do not seek out books or tapes on holiness or attend seminars designed to draw us closer to God. We want information on "How to Be Happy," "How to Raise Children," "How to Have a Good Sex Life," "How to Succeed in Business," and so on.

Fortunately, this lack has begun to be noticed by some evangelical leaders who are disturbed by it and have begun to address the subject. I commend Packer's book, as well as a book written a few years ago by Jerry Bridges called The Pursuit of Holiness. There is also the older classic by the English Bishop John Charles Ryle on the same topic.[8]

"Pleasing to God"

The final words that Paul uses to describe the nature of our living sacrifices are "pleasing to God." But this is also a conclusion for what I have been saying so far in this study, since the point is that if we do what Paul has urged us to do—namely, to offer our "bodies as living sacrifices, holy ... to God"—we will also find that what we have done is pleasing to him, or acceptable.

It is amazing to me that God could find anything we might be able to do to be pleasing. But it is so! Notice that the word "pleasing" occurs twice in this short paragraph. The first time, which is what we are looking at here, indicates that our offering of ourselves to God pleases him. The second time, which occurs at the end of verse 2, it indicates that when we do this, we will find God's will for our lives to be pleasing as well as good and perfect. I understand that God's will for me should be pleasing—pleasing to me, that is. How could it be otherwise if God is an all-wise and all-good God? He must will what is good for me....

The Bible tells me that, at my best, I am to think of myself as an "unworthy" servant (Luke 17:10). But it also says that if I live for Jesus, offering back to him what he has first given to me, then one day, I will hear him say, "Well done, good and faithful servant! ... Come and share your master's happiness!" (Matt. 25:21, 23).

---

1. Robert S. Candlish, *Studies in Romans 12: The Christian's Sacrifice and Service of Praise*, pp. 33-34.
2. John Calvin, *The Epistles of Paul the Apostle to the Romans and to the Thessalonians*, p. 264.
3. Leon Morris, *The Epistle to the Romans*, pp. 433-434.
4. Robert Haldane, *An Exposition of the Epistle to the Romans*, p. 554.
5. See Mike Bellah, *Baby Boom Believers: Why We Think We Need It All and How to*

THE SPIRIT OF HOLINESS & POWER

Survive When We Don't Get It, p. 27.
6. Handley C. G. Moule, *The Epistle of St. Paul to the Romans*, pp. 324-325.
7. J. I. Packer, *Rediscovering Holiness*, pp. 12-13.
8. J. C. Ryle, *Holiness: Its Nature, Hindrances, Difficulties and Roots* and Jerry Bridges, *The Pursuit of Holiness*.

All for Jesus

All for Jesus! All for Jesus!
   All my being's ransomed pow'rs,
   all my thoughts and words and doings,
   all my days and all my hours.

Let my hands perform his bidding,
   let my feet run in his ways;
   let my eyes see Jesus only,
   let my lips speak forth his praise.

Worldlings prize their gems of beauty,
   cling to gilded toys of dust,
   boast of wealth and fame and pleasure;
   only Jesus will I trust.

Since my eyes were fixed on Jesus,
   I've lost sight of all beside;
   so enchained my spirit's vision,
   looking at the Crucified.

O what wonder! How amazing!
   Jesus, glorious King of kings,
   deigns to call me his beloved,
   lets me rest beneath his wings.

                        - Mary D. James

CHAPTER 10

Have You Given Him the Reins?

Ted S. Rendall

Ted S. Rendall served for 43 years on the staff of Prairie Bible Institute, Three Hills, Alberta, Canada, as a faculty member, administrator, and editor of the Institute's monthly periodicals, *Prairie Overcomer* and *Young Pilot*. He served as pastor of Bethel Fellowship Church from 1955 until 1975. From 1986 until 1992, he served as Institute's president. For 23 years of his time at Prairie, he also served as senior pastor of the campus church, the Prairie Tabernacle Congregation. Dr. Rendall now serves as lecturer at the Olford Center and as curator of the T. S. Rendall Collection in Memphis, Tennessee. The following article is reprinted from the *Prairie Overcomer*, September 1985.

HAVE YOU EVER GIVEN ANY THOUGHT to the paradoxes of the Bible? A paradox contains a statement that appears to be contradictory but which is in fact, true. If that is not clear, then think of a paradox as truth "standing on its head to attract attention."

There are many such paradoxes in the Bible. The Lord Jesus said, for example, "Whosoever will save his life shall lose it; but whosoever will lose his life for My sake, the same shall save it" (Luke 9:24). We have Paul's testimony in 2 Corinthians 12:10—"When I am weak, then am I strong." There are many more in the New Testament. We get through giving. We enter into rest through labor. We ascend by descending.

In Romans 6:15-18, the Apostle Paul sets forth another of these puzzling but profitable paradoxes. There is, he claims, a bondage that is true freedom. Charles Kingsley, the English preacher and author put the truth this way: "There are two kingdoms: the false, when one is free to do what he likes, and the true when one is free to do as he ought." That is but another way of expressing the truth being affirmed by the apostle in this section of his dynamic teaching:

What then? shall we sin, because we are not under the law, but under grace? God forbid. Know ye not, that to whom ye yield yourselves servants to obey, his servants ye are to whom ye obey; whether of sin unto death, or of obedience unto righteousness? But God be thanked, that ye were the servants of sin, but ye have obeyed from the heart that form of doctrine which was delivered you. Being then made free from sin, ye became the servants of righteousness.

There is a blessed bondage to Christ that results in true freedom for the believer.

How, then, does Paul introduce and expound this paradox? He does so in three ways. We need to look at all three in order to grasp the paradox that there is a bondage that is true freedom.

A Startling Proposal

First, Paul repeats a startling proposal made by his anonymous questioner. He has just announced the Christian's Magna Charta—"Sin shall not have dominion over you: for ye are not under the law, but under grace." Then immediately and insistently comes the startling proposal: "What then? shall we sin, because we are not under the law, but under grace?"

Paul's unknown interrogator imagines that he has grasped Paul's teaching and has come to a proper conclusion. "If you are right, Paul, that we are no longer under law but under grace, then why cannot we go on committing acts of sin? Will there not be abundant grace to cover all our sin?"

Paul's immediate and emphatic response to that proposal is to reject it—to renounce it, to refuse it. He says, "God forbid!" or, "May it never be!" The very verbalization of the idea is abhorrent to Paul, and he vehemently and vigorously opposes it.

If you glance back at the beginning of the chapter, you will notice that Paul's inquisitor begins with a similar question: "What shall we say then? Shall we continue in sin"—that is, in the state of sin, in the realm of sin—"that grace may abound?"

If there is any distinction between the two formulations, it must be something like this: In verse 1, Paul's questioner is proposing that the Christians act as if there were no such thing as conversion. In verse 15, he is proposing that the Christian should act as if there were no such thing as consecration. The power of the Gospel, however, deals with both the guilt and the grip of sin. Thus we sing with Charles Wesley:

He breaks the power of cancelled sin;

He sets the prisoner free;
His Blood can make the foulest clean,
His Blood avails for me.

We, too, should resolutely adopt Paul's position. We cannot seriously claim to be in union with Christ and, at the same time, deliberately choose to sin against God's commandments. Paul teaches us in Galatians 5:13 that we must not use our liberty in Christ as an occasion to the flesh.

Why is this startling proposal to be summarily rejected? Why must we consistently and continually oppose any idea that grace provides us with a license to sin? Well, this proposal must be seen in at least three ways.

It Advocates Continued Sinning. We must reject this proposal because it advocates continued sinning. While we deeply disagree with the proposition, we can say this about it: It is clear! There is no beating about the bush. "Shall we sin"—the concept is not correct, but it is clear—"because we are not under the law, but under grace?" Those who advocate this proposal in principle are not always that direct. Often they twist Scriptures in order to camouflage their intent.

All through the centuries of the Church, there have been those teachers who have put forward this abominable teaching. In fact, there is a technical name for this fundamental error—we call it antinomianism. That simply means the teaching is opposed to accepting any moral restraint or rule. Such teachers want to accept God's grace but not His government. They accept Christ's atonement but not His authority.

Evidently, there were such false teachers in the early Church. Here is Peter's vivid description of them: "When they speak great swelling words of vanity, they allure through the lusts of the flesh, through much wantonness, those that were clean escaped from them who live in error. While they promise them liberty, they themselves are the servants of corruption: for of whom a man is overcome, of the same is he brought into bondage" (2 Pet. 2:18-19). Let me issue a warning, then. If some teacher, or book, or friend advocates to you that you should violate some moral principle because you are not as a Christian under law but under grace, strenuously resist and reject the proposal. Such teaching may come in the form of a dozen disguises, but if, in essence, it is proposing continued sinning, you must resolutely reject it as being unscriptural, ungodly, and unwholesome.

It Confuses Law and Grace. But that is not all we can say about this startling proposal. It not only advocates continued sinning; it confuses law and grace.

Paul's questioner had heard Paul affirm: "We are not under the law, but under grace," and had immediately jumped to an erroneous conclusion. (Someone has observed that jumping to conclusions is easier than digging for facts!) This person concluded from Paul's statement that the Christian is not under law *in any sense,* that we have been delivered from moral law absolutely, setting us free (falsely it would be) to continue sinning against God.

But that was not Paul's intention or his instruction. Paul meant that we are not under the law with regard to its demands and its decrees. The law demands perfection before it grants its blessings and passes judgment on all who fail to meet its heaven-high standards. Through grace, we have been delivered from the penalty of the law which we have broken repeatedly, and therefore from the law as a power to judge and condemn us. Now we serve God motivated by love and by a sense of appreciation for His abundant grace.

But that does not mean grace is opposed to the righteousness of the law. Indeed, grace reinforces the moral requirements of the law, for in Titus 2:11-12 Paul announces that grace disciplines us so that, "denying ungodliness and worldly lusts, we should live soberly, righteously, and godly, in this present world." And in Romans 8:4, Paul declares that the righteousness of the law is being presently fulfilled in us "who walk not after the flesh but after the Spirit." In this sense, we are under the law to Christ (see 1 Cor. 9:21). For the Christian, freedom from the law is not lawlessness.

It Misrepresents the Gospel. There is still one thing that we must say about this startling proposal that we continue to sin because we are not under the law. This proposal tragically misrepresents the saving Gospel of Christ. Jesus came to save His people from their sins. To argue that we can commit adultery, steal, and lie under the umbrella of grace is a perversion of the true Gospel. We must say emphatically that the New Testament provides no basis for using grace as a cloak under which to engage in all kinds of immoralities and impurities. Such a religion clearly earns the condemnation of the Lord Jesus when He denounced the Pharisees: "You are like unto whited sepulchers, which indeed appear beautiful outward, but are within full of dead men's bones, and of all uncleanness" (Matt. 23:27). The world of unsaved people doesn't take long to ridicule—and reject—such a faith as the hoax and hypocrisy it is.

The Basic Principle

We have examined the startling proposal. We must now look at the basic principle set forth by Paul in answer to the question put to him. We have this in verse 16: "Know ye not, that to whom ye yield yourselves servants to obey, his servants ye are to whom ye obey; whether of sin unto death, or of obedience unto righteousness?" At first glance, it is not readily apparent how this statement answers the startling proposal, but once we have thought it through, we see how appropriate and adequate is Paul's response.

The Essence of Christian Conversion. First, Paul's response represents the essence of Christian conversion. Paul's answer involves the use of a simple illustration. He compares people to servants or slaves. An individual, he claims, is either the slave of sin or the slave of obedience. If he is a slave of sin, the end result of that kind of bondage is death. If he is a slave of obedience to God, the end result is righteousness. The basic principle involved, however, is that the individual chooses which kind of bondage he desires.

Paul thus teaches that we choose to be the slaves of sin. Indeed, the Bible teaches that everyone born into the world ultimately chooses to be the slave of sin. We create the chains that bind us by choosing to serve the tyrant called sin.

There is a story that has come down to us from the Middle Ages concerning a very capable blacksmith who was taken to prison and thrust into a dungeon. There he began to examine the chain that bound him with a view to discovering some flaw that might make it easier for him to break the chain and escape. But to his chagrin, he found, from the marks upon it, that it was of his own workmanship, and it had been his proud boast that no one could ever break a chain that he had forged. So, it is with the slave of sin. His own hands forge the chains that bind him, chains that no human power can break.

Now just as we choose to be the slaves of sin, so we choose to be the slaves of obedience, the slaves of Christ. We rarely hear this emphasis in Gospel messages, but the strangeness of the truth is not because the New Testament is silent about it. The reason for our ignorance of it lies elsewhere—in our selective presentation of the Gospel, choosing only the most attractive aspects of it and soft-pedaling others.

Paul is saying here that implicit in the sinner's decision to believe on Christ is the choice to become the slave of obedience. Paul is not the only New Testament writer who stresses this. In 1 Peter 1:2, Peter states that we are elect "according to the foreknowledge of God the Father, through sanctification of the Spirit, unto (or with a view to) obedience and the sprinkling of the Blood of Jesus Christ." At the moment of your conversion, you become the slave of Jesus Christ. It is not a second experience to be entered into subsequent to salvation and as a supplement to it, but it is an obligation.

Christ's Teaching. Paul's teaching here is but a reflection and reiteration of

Christ's teaching. In John 8:34, the Lord Jesus states: "Verily, verily, I say unto you, whosoever committeth sin is the servant [or the slave] of sin." Jesus did not say here, "Whosoever commits sin becomes the slave of sin," but rather that sinning is the evidence of who is our master. Put that together with Matthew 6:24—"No man can serve two masters: for either he will hate the one, and love the other, or else he will hold to the one, and despise the other." In terms of Romans 6 you cannot be the slave of sin and the slave of obedience at one and the same time. Legally and positionally, you are one or the other.

In the days of the horse-and-buggy mode of transportation, a man was driving with his wife along a dangerous road. At a very narrow place, the wife became frightened and seized the rein nearest her. Quietly her husband passed the other rein to her and let go of it. Then she was more frightened than ever and said, "Oh, don't you let go, please!"

But her husband answered: "Two people cannot drive one horse; either I must drive or you must." She gave him back the reins, and he drove safely past the danger. Some of us imagine that we can give the reins of our lives into the hands of God and sin, but that is not possible. Either God has the reins or the Devil.

The Proposal Refuted. Seen in this light, then, Paul's basic principle refutes the startling proposal. Let me remind you of what was being put forward. Paul had announced: "You are not under the law, but under grace." Paul's questioner had replied: "Then we can continue to sin because we are not under the law with its righteous and rigorous standards but under grace."

No, says Paul, you have it all wrong. When you choose to be the slave of obedience to God, you are henceforth committed to a life of righteousness. You become the slave of obedience with a view to living a righteous life. "Not under the law" provides no escape hatch for people who refuse to face the moral demands of the law. Our union with Christ requires that we bring forth the fruit of righteousness.

Halford Luccock summarized Paul's teaching well when he wrote: "All men are prisoners of something. We merely choose our prison." When you choose Christ, you choose the best bondage in the world!

The Personal Profile

But Paul doesn't leave it there. In verses 17 and 18, he makes a personal application of the basic principle. Here we have a personal profile, a brief biography of the Christians at Rome, and by extension of all Christians throughout the world and throughout all the centuries. Did you know that the Christian's life story can be written in three chapters?

The Shameful Fact. Chapter 1 of our biography is entitled "the shameful fact." States Paul: "You were the slaves of sin" (6:17).

Is there any fact about us as Christians that is designed to humble us in the presence of God more than this: Once we were rebels against God and actually took sides against Him? I understand that one of the kings of Scotland when he was a boy, took up arms against his father. Later all through his life, he regretted that he had ever chosen to oppose his father. As a constant reminder to himself of the evil of that act, he wore an iron belt under his robes, and every year he made the belt heavier so that his repentance might be deeper each year.

As we sit at the banquet table in the palace of the King, let us not forget that once we were enemies of God and have been pardoned by His royal grace.

The Glorious Liberation. Chapter 2 of our biography is to be found in the phrase in 6:18—"You were made free from sin." Here Paul points us to our glorious liberation by the Prince of glory.

Charles H. Spurgeon tells us that a great English prince went to visit an equally famous king of Spain. The British prince was taken down to the galleys to see the men who were chained to the oars and doomed to be slaves for life.

The King of Spain promised in honor of the prince's visit to liberate any one of these men that the prince might choose.

The prince accordingly went up to one man and said, "My poor fellow, I am sorry to see you in this plight. How did you come to be here?"

"Oh, sir," said the poor wretch, "false witnesses gave evidence against me. I am suffering wrongfully."

"Indeed," said the prince, and moved on to the next man.

"My poor fellow, I am sorry to see you here. How did it happen?"

"Sir, I certainly did wrong, but not to any great extent. I ought not to be here."

"Indeed," said the prince, and he went on to others who told him similar stories.

At last, he came to one prisoner, who said: "Sir, I am often thankful that I am here, for I am sorry to own that if I had received my due, I should have been executed. I am certainly guilty of all that was laid to my charge. My severest punishment is just."

With a sense of humor, the prince replied: "It is a pity that such a wretch as you are should be chained among these innocent men, and therefore I will set you free."

Read in that parable the story of your own release from sin's chains. It was not until you were ready to confess your guiltiness that you became a candidate for freedom. As long as we hold on to our innocence or plead that our case is not really that serious, we never experience the liberation that Christ gives.

Let us recall often to our minds that had we not been set free by Christ in due time, we would face the penalty of our sins. Not that the Devil ever wants his poor dupes to see the end of their ways. He seeks to convince every sinner that his self-chosen way leads to liberty.

In the Castle of Chilion on the Lake of Geneva, there is a dungeon containing a well, at the bottom of which the tourist can discern the waters of the lake. That shaft is ironically called the Way of Liberty. Tradition claims that in centuries past, the cruel jailers would whisper to their prisoners in the darkness of the dungeon: "Three steps and liberty." The poor prisoners, deceived, would step forward in haste and plunge down the shaft, which was thickly lined with knives and spikes. Each mutilated corpse would drop into the darkness of the lake below.

That is a picture of the liberty that sin offers. "There is a way that seemeth right unto a man, but the end thereof are the ways of death." Praise God; we have been delivered from that awful end! We will never take a leap into eternal darkness, pierced through with many sorrows and regrets.

We have been set free from sin!

The New Master. The third in our spiritual biography is found in 6:18—"Ye became the slaves of righteousness." J. D. Jones, the English preacher, put the truth this way: "The art of life consists not in repudiating all masteries—nobody can do that—but in finding the right one." And in Christ, the believer has found the right mastery....

Professor Henry Drummond used to spend his summer holidays with some friends in Scotland. On one such occasion, just as he was leaving, his hostess said to him: "Would you do something for us? We're very troubled about John, our coachman. He's drinking heavily. We've warned him again and again, and he's on his last chance with us. Could you speak to him and try to help him?"

When the coachman brought around the carriage to take Drummond to the railway station, the famous professor got up beside him. He began to talk to the man about his horses, and just as they came around a dangerous bend in the road, he said, "John, what would happen if you lost control of these two horses, and they ran away with us here?"

"It would be a bad job for both of us!" said the driver.

"But if, when you found that they were out of your control," said Drummond, "you knew that I could control any horse—what would you do?"

"That's easy, sir," said John, "I'd give you the reins."

"John," said Drummond, "do you ever feel as though there was something in you like a pair of wild horses that threatens to run away with you again and again?"

John hung his head with shame, for he knew only too well what a defeated man he was. Then the professor said: "I know of One who can control all those wild passions if you will only let Him into your life to do it for you." As he parted from him at the station, he tenderly said, "John, will you give Him the reins?"

A year later, the professor met the coachman again, and as Drummond came along the platform of the station, he saw John, who immediately said to him, "I've given Him the reins, sir."

What about you? Have you given Him the reins?

Christ Reigns Within

The kingdom of God has come to reign,
  having conquered my lowly domain.
No more do I want to control my life;
  gone is fleshly resistance and strife.
Christ is King of my heart and my soul;
  to him I've given total control.
    Christ reigns within!

Once with great fear my mind debated;
  the King's demands I contemplated:
Self-surrender without condition,
  full allegiance of my volition,
To sacrifice my idol dearest,
  pledge my passions to all that's purest.
    Christ reigns within!

The kingdom of God has come inside;
  my heart, the King, has come to reside.
The standard he's raised is holiness;
  his Name will settle for nothing less.
With merciful grace he shapes my will,
  breathing his power in me to fill.
    Christ reigns within!

- Ralph I. Tilley

CHAPTER 11

The Pivot Point

Phillip Keller

Perhaps best known for his bestseller, *A Shepherd Looks at Psalm 23*, Phillip Keller (1920-1997) spent his life traveling the globe, marveling at God's creation, and writing on Christian subjects. Whether he was working as a wildlife photographer, tending livestock on his ranch, writing books, raking leaves, or washing dishes, his life seemed to radiate the joy of the Lord.

Keller was born in East Africa to missionary parents and spent many years as a shepherd. He trained as an agrologist at the University of Toronto and spent many years in agricultural research, land management, and ranch development in British Columbia. He authored more than 40 books, which have sold in the millions. The following article is taken from his autobiography, *Wonder O' the Wind*, published by Kregel Publications.

Editor's Note: Phillip Keller's spiritual pilgrimage resembles that of many in the Body of Christ. As he recounts his struggles to live a life to the glory of Christ, the reader may be able to identify with his or her own pursuit of godliness. I never read his story without being refreshed in my soul.

DURING TIMES OF QUIET REFLECTION, alone in the mountains, or ensconced in my remote cabin, I came to see clearly that I was a man of divided loyalties, divided interests, divided ambitions. It is difficult to portray on paper the peculiar pain of one "split" by counteracting tugs and pulls in life. But I must try, for it is the rock-bottom dilemma facing thousands of Christians trapped in a tormenting "wilderness experience" in their walk with God—a lifestyle in which they are going nowhere with God, simply moving in circles of selfish self-centeredness.

The Spirit at Arm's Length

On the one hand, it seemed so obvious I was "riding high" in terms of adventure and achievement. The beautiful books bearing my name were bringing wide recognition. With the royalties, I could undertake more and more extensive mountain expeditions. My wildlife studies and big-game photography provided heart-pounding excitement in the grandeur of remote wilderness areas. I was producing some remarkable films on the life habits of big game. The ranch was flourishing. My family was reveling in their new surroundings at Three Hills [Alberta].

On the surface, all seemed to be so successful, so well assured, so stimulating.

But on the other hand, I sensed a bleak barrenness within my spirit—as bare as a bleached, cast-off buckhorn lying dry and dead on a shale slope in the sun. The Spirit of the living God was present with me, yet, always standing, as it were, at arm's length from me: close at hand, it is true, but somehow strangely just out of reach, out of intimate touch.

It was Phyllis, who, from time to time, in her quiet, gentle, understanding way would remark to me, "Darling, you have such terrific drive and enthusiasm for the wilds, for mountains, for the ranch, for conservation." Then she would smile softly and pause a moment. "But you really don't seem to care that much about people or their problems. God loves them, too, you know."

She was never one to berate or belittle me. She was too loyal, too faithful a friend, too wise a woman ever to try to make her man into a mouse. Instead, with her keen, intelligent understanding, her lovely charm, her sincere praise, she made me walk ten feet tall. But God's Spirit used her gentle remarks from time to time, like polished mirrors, to make me see myself as I really was.

And what I saw, I began to abhor. My tough, hard-headed, strong-willed, self-centered determination to succeed and surpass had precluded giving Christ complete control of either my career or my character. He was there, but only as an advisor or associate, one turned to in time of stress or need. He did not govern my choices. He did not decide my deliberations. He did not command my career. He did not actually initiate or energize my enterprises.

In a sentence—I lived and worked and planned for Phillip Keller. Yet in that strange dichotomy so typical of thousands of Christians, I claimed I lived for Christ. I was caught betwixt the viselike jaws of sincerity and self-deception. How could I ever break loose out of such a constricted condition?

One of my first serious attempts was to undertake a biographical book on the *Shantymen Missionaries of the West Coast*. These were the rugged, sturdy, selfless fellows who first came ashore to our seaside cottage at "Fairwinds." Their joyous enthusiasm in God's work, their total self-giving to help others in lonely places, had partially inspired me to go to the Masai in Kenya.

Perhaps by spending weeks on their boat, Messenger II, and long hours in their company, I could or would come to a clearer understanding of what it means to truly know God. It proved to be a most profitable experience. It aroused within my spirit an even more intense desire to love Christ and commune with Him as they did.

The missionary biography, *Splendor from the Sea*, which emerged from that interlude with the "Shanty Boys," was an instant success. It was my first venture into Christian writing that opened up a whole new world of endeavor.

The work was beautifully illustrated with photographs, some of which I took. Others came from professional photographers who had done a story on the mission for *Life* magazine. It also bore exquisite line drawings executed by a dear woman who had spent long, lonely years as a lighthouse keeper's wife on the rugged west coast. One of her lifelong dreams had been to use her talent to do something beautiful for God. When I invited her to prepare the sketches for *Splendor from the Sea*, she was ecstatic. Just before the book was released to the public, I went to visit her. She had been stricken with a most malignant cancer. She lay weak and dying. Yet amid her agony and pain she held my hands in hers and whispered in my ear: "Phillip, our Father is so faithful! He has spared me to see my work and talent used to His honor!" A few days later, she was gone ... to glory. But in the stillness of that sick-room, God's Spirit had spoken to me in thundering tones heard by no other human ears. The stabbing, searching, searing question had come home to my innermost will—"Is my work, my time, my talent being used to honor God—or just me?"

Deep Calls to Deep

Steadily, surely the wondrous wind of God's Spirit was pressing upon my spirit. He was bringing me to that pivot point in life where one must decide either to step out and live wholeheartedly for God in fearless faith, or turn back to tramp the tired old trails of self-gratification and selfish self-interest. But how? How could this happen in a personality as head-strong as mine? How could such a capitulation to the control of Christ come in a will tough as tungsten steel, such as I owned?

Between my exhilarating mountain trips, wildlife studies, writing books, giving conservation lectures, and development of the ranch, I tried to squeeze in time for some of the services and speakers at Prairie Bible Institute. The school was fortunate to have great men and women of God from all over the world come to the campus for conferences, conventions, and special student sessions.

So I began to be exposed to some of the finest expository preaching and teaching to be found anywhere. More than this, new friendships were formed with devout staff members on campus. Their single-minded devotion and total dedication to the Lord moved me mightily. I saw in their joyous self-sacrifice a living, practical demonstration of what it meant to lay down one's life for others ... no matter what the cost.

But it was partially this cost of following Christ, this "price to pay" in gracious self-giving and self-sacrifice for the sake of others, that daunted me. I really was not yet ready totally to subject my will to the government of God. I was not fully prepared to capitulate yet to the claims of Christ for control of my affairs. I was not at all sure I could submit myself to the supreme sovereignty of the Spirit of the living God.

I was too tough a man. I had driven myself to the ultimate in order to succeed. I had hardened my will until like a shaft of steel nothing could bend or break or bind it. It was mine to do with as I wished—or so I assumed (wrongly). No one would lord it over me. No one would dictate to me. No one would lead me about or push me around. I was my own freewill spirit determined to fulfill my own desires.

So, in essence, it became a deadly stand-off between God and me. Looking back in retrospect to those months, twenty years ago, I marvel at the patience of God with one so petulant and perverse. Mentally, my conscious desire was to be God's man. Emotionally, all my longings were to love Christ and serve Him. But volitionally, my will had not yet submitted unequivocally to God's Spirit.

Mr. L. E. Maxwell, president and founder of Prairie, having become a dear and respected friend, with his profound insight, named me "The Maverick"— the untamed, unroped colt upon which no one had ever stamped his brand of ownership. It was a true and appropriate description.

Yet the irony of the situation was that at the school, I could see the damage done in the lives of students, who, like myself, were "mavericks." I could see the folly of flaunting God's authority. I could discern those who became derelicts because they refused to come under the divine discipline of God's Word. I could understand the utter emptiness of lives barren and wasted because they flung off the yoke of obedience and respect for God's Spirit.

In His own persistent, patient forbearance, God began to give me an insatiable thirst for His Word. I found myself, for the first time in my life, spending hours and hours searching the Scriptures, poring over its pages, exposing myself to its truth.

One of the major emphases at the Institute was the principle of each person seeking for himself to find God's wishes revealed in the Word. It was constantly reiterated that the person who sought God in His Word, would indeed find illumination there by God's own Spirit. Scripture was compared with Scripture. And the Spirit of Christ became the ultimate "teacher" who would lead one into all truth, taking the things of Christ and transmitting them to man in wondrous, living reality.

Brought Low by the Spirit

A crucial, burning issue which God's Word revealed to me at this stage of my spiritual saga was the whole matter of forgiveness. Never before had I realized the titanic cost of suffering borne by Christ at Calvary, in order to extend perfect pardon and full forgiveness to me as a man. It was His impeccable life, poured out in total self-giving on my behalf and in my stead, which atoned for all my willful waywardness and wrongdoing. Such stupendous self-sacrifice to save me humbled my spirit, pulverized my pride, and made me acutely aware of the great debt of gratitude I owed my God.

This acute awareness of my Father's forgiveness then constrained me to make right the wrong, vindictive attitude I held against those who had wronged me. I had to go to those who had injured me so deeply when "Fairwinds" [his ranch] was taken as a military base. I had to write to those who had been so unfair to mother after dad's death. I had to clear up unforgiving grudges with those who had double-crossed me in business.

This was not an easy road. It called for self-humiliation. It called for utter honesty. It called for cleansing conscience. But it brought peace, inner light, and exquisite liberty of spirit.

A Mountain-cliff Experience

It had been one of those still, serene Indian summer interludes in the northern Rockies. The days were bright, sharp, stimulating to the senses, invigorating to the soul. New-fallen snow dusted the peaks in immaculate whiteness. The lower slopes were aglow with the autumn tones of burnt-orange, gold, and rust from grass tinted with frost. Through this breathless, quiet, upland region, I had stalked the great herds of Rocky Mountain elk in their majestic migrations. I had photographed the Bighorn sheep in their rock-girt realm. I had watched the wide sweep of Golden eagles soaring above the crags on their outstretched wings.

It had been a superb season! Now I was heading home for Three Hills. Somehow my entire being was charged with vigor, with achievement, with the zest of the high country. But also, strangely, I was anxious to attend the fall Keswick Convention at the Institute. A day or so before it began, I said to Phyllis, "I have made up my mind to attend every meeting, take part in every session and participate in all the prayer times. This is the teaching Dad and Mother loved so much."

Whether or not I had a clear comprehension that I was approaching the pivot point in my walk with God is not certain. What I do know is that a burning, yearning desire to truly come to love God as I loved the wondrous wilderness world He created, engulfed me. There were times in mountains when their majestic beauty, their stimulating scenery, the cool, clean air off the heights were a heady wine to me. So I sensed deep in my spirit that in the same way a man filled, swept up in and stimulated by the wondrous wind of God's Spirit would be likewise exultant, charged with a divine dynamic.

For four full days, I attended every session at the Institute. Finally, I could not stand another service. I needed to be absolutely still before God. I needed, not more sermons, songs, and seminars, but the still small voice of God's own presence speaking to me. Moses had his "burning bush" in the desert. Gideon had his "oak tree" by the winepress. Elijah had his "cave in the rock" high on a mountain. And I had my "high cliffs" overlooking a crystal stream that cascaded out of the foothills. There I went, absolutely alone, determined that I would hear from God in a way never experienced before. For hours I paced back and forth atop the cliffs, tears coursing down my cheeks, in agony of earnestness, beseeching Christ to make Himself very real to me.

It was a man hungry, thirsty, longing for the Lord who cried aloud from those cliff tops. "Oh, God," I pleaded from the depths of my spirit, "You told us, 'Blessed are they who hunger and thirst after righteousness, for they shall be filled!'" I raised my arms in anguish of supplication, "Come now, move into my spirit, fill my life, my entire being with Yourself, just as this stream from the glaciers flows into this valley before me!"

Then there came the quiet, gentle response of God's voice: "My Spirit is imparted in plenitude to the one prepared to obey me. Your love for me is demonstrated not by emotion, but by your readiness to comply with My wishes: to do My will. Are you ready to give me your will?" There was total silence. I was astonished, taken aback at the apparent simplicity of the straightforward exchange extended to me. I would give Him my will (my heart). He would give me Himself.

In utter brokenness, compounded of joy, light relief, and surging gratitude, I fell to my knees on the wild sod, and there bowed myself before my God.

"Father, from this hour, with Your presence and Your power, I undertake to do whatever You ask; to go wherever You wish; to be whoever You desire." The words spoken audibly came in clear articulation, "I am totally available to Your purposes for me upon the planet."

A New Realm in the Spirit

It was a compact of tremendous import. It was the pivot point in my walk with God. I had crossed the "great divide" into a new region of personal, intimate contact with Christ. There was no ecstatic sensation. Rather, there enveloped the whole of my being, body, mind, emotions, will, and spirit an acute awareness of God's gracious, wondrous Presence. He was with me, in me, to empower, to direct, to abide throughout the rest of life. In calm repose and supreme peace, I went home.

Phyllis, in her cheerful, happy way, met me at the door. I had been gone all day. "Darling!" she ejaculated, surprised, and taken aback, "You are utterly radiant! What has happened?"

It was weeks before I felt free to tell her even a small part of all that took place that day. For it had been a sacred interlude shared by a common man alone with God's Spirit. But from that hour, the entire tenor and direction of my life began to change dramatically.

All sorts of people who had known me before would stop me and remark: "You seem so different now. What has happened? What did you do? How did God touch you?"

As a simple, searching layperson, there was little I could say. "Just obey Him, and He will move into your life. Resist Him, and He won't!" My favorite verse during those days became: "For it is God who worketh in you, both to will and to do of his good pleasure" (Phil. 2:13).

At last, at long last, I had been converted in the realm of my will. No longer did I evade God's hands. He was free now to work out His good purposes in my affairs. To put it in rough ranch language: My Master, at last, had flung His lariat of love around me. And now I bore His brand.

Unlike so many Christian biographies where people tell about the dreadful disasters that overtook them before they capitulated to Christ, my story at this point seemed just the opposite. Where others recount the trauma of fragmented families, criminal records, financial disasters, shattered health, or perhaps addiction to drugs or alcohol that drove them to seek God, there was, in my case, a totally different perspective.

I was at the pinnacle of prowess in my various professions. By this time, I was an author of international recognition. My outdoor photography had attracted wide acclaim. I was regarded as a leading advocate in the burgeoning conservation movement. I had earned an enviable reputation as a field naturalist. My ranches had become showplaces. I enjoyed a wide circle of friends. And my children were progressing splendidly in their studies.

It was not wreckage and disaster that I was turning over to the government of God. It was not something despicable of which I was divesting myself (except my stubborn will). It was not confusion and chaos I was leaving. Rather it was "success" by the world's standards, which I was called upon to set aside now in order to fully follow my Master.

Step by step, there would be a painful path to tread in taking up the cross that cut across all my own aims and ambitions in order to do God's will. My priorities would have to be reversed. In the process, there would be struggle, suffering, and sorrow. But with it all, would come boundless new benefits and adventures with God to equal anything in the high country.

Lord of My Real Estate

Because so much of this was so private and so personal, there is no intention to elaborate on the events here. Only the highlights will be mentioned in order that the reader understands clearly how a new foundation had to be laid in my life for future service. Nor should it be construed that others will be dealt with by God as I was. His Spirit leads each of us along a special, unique path of His own preparation.

One of the first areas of my life upon which God laid His hand was my love for the land. This instinct for enjoying and living in a country setting had always been a profound part of my life. Good soil, choice livestock, long vistas, wide skies, the fierce freedom of "being boss" on one's own domain, were a powerful force in my makeup. I had come from a family where owning land and developing it for high productivity was a surging stimulus—not only because of the intrinsic beauty of a well-managed estate but also because of the security it offered. At "Bear Claw Ranch," especially, we had ample land, abundant water from the streams and springs, plenty of timber, and excellent resources to provide for our future. Now the Spirit of the Lord began to make me aware that my resources, my security, my confidence should repose in God, my Father, not in my real estate holdings.

One would assume I should have learned this lesson well in the loss of "Fairwinds." But some of us are slow indeed to grasp the great eternal principles of God. I am one!

Increasingly, the inner conviction came upon me that I should part with the ranch. Not just dispose of it, but actually, give it away freely to those more needy than myself who were actively serving God. This was a tough request to comply with heartily. At first, I was disposed to debate the issue with Christ. How would I properly provide for my family? What about the extra costs of special Christian schooling? Where would we go to live when they went on to advanced studies?

The age-old, eternal question came to me as it did to Peter by the lake. The Master asked, "Do you love Me more than these?—these acres, streams, lake, hills, and rolling range?"

Finally, one day, sitting by the lake, utterly alone before the Lord, I completely capitulated. "Father, just as You wish, I give it all, gladly!!"

Almost overnight, after this decision was made, requests began to come in to me for feature articles, a regular magazine column, and photographs from editors I never had met. My income, instead of diminishing from the disposal of the ranch, had begun to escalate. God was simply showing me in unmistakable ways that He could easily care for all our needs. But even more important, though I knew it not at the time, I was being freed up to go and serve in city centers where God had work for me to do. Burdened with the ranch responsibilities, I would not have been available to these new purposes arranged by God.

Called to Serve

The next arena of my life to be touched by God's Spirit was the wilderness world I loved so intensely. The wilds had always provided me with enormous pleasure. I am essentially a son of the wild places. I am "at home" there, at ease, relaxed, contented in the company of trees, hills, mountains, and wildlife. I am not a sophisticated offspring of our twentieth-century civilization. In fact, I look upon our superficial society with a certain sense of disdain and disgust for its corrupt culture, its brazen ballyhoo, its false facade, its deceptive duplicity ... all of which have tainted my life.

But God was calling me persistently to disengage myself from the wilderness. He was asking me to set aside the solitude, the seclusion, and quiet serenity of my beloved mountains, rivers, and plains. Instead, He was now calling me to enter fully into the mainstream of our mad, modern world of the urban environment. There I would be finding my days filled with the burdens of broken hearts, broken homes, broken hopes, broken people.

This was not an easy transition for a man who reveled in remote places, who loved the gentle tempo of the high country, who thrived on vigorous outdoor adventures. But I had made a compact with Christ on those high cliffs. If He wanted me constricted and cramped in a city setting, I was prepared to go into the "concrete jungle." It would be a crushing, bruising adjustment, but it was His way to have my life become broken bread and poured out wine for the benefit of others.

Bit by bit, in stern reality and real-life situations, I was being shown what the Master meant when He said, "That unless a seed be buried and undergo dissimulation, it could never germinate into a fruitful, reproductive plant." So He would plant me in the soil of new situations and strange people where my life would have to be literally laid down that others might live.

It is no easy, simple thing to become the Master's man! There is a cross to carry. And that cross is the powerful principle of putting aside all one's own special interests and private preferences, to go out and do whatever God demands ... asking no questions.

A Painful Parting

The third painful parting, and one which there is no intention of dramatizing here, was a willingness to give up Phyllis. We had now been married for over twenty years. She had been a remarkable life companion. Her gracious spirit, her noble character, her strong, serene faith in Christ, her sweet disposition had all been an inspiration and strength to me during our years of adventure together.

She was stricken again with the sinister scourge of the most virulent cancer known to science. Soon she would be taken from me. In fact, it would be on the very day of our twenty-third anniversary that she would be swept away through the portal of death to enter the realm of eternal rest with her Lord. This was not an easy parting. So amid all the death to self that was endured, I could understand ever more clearly the costly path of pain my parents had trod in Africa, that others might live. This is ever God's way. For out of death springs new life. Through laid-down lives emerges God's divine energy to quicken others.

In the years ahead, in His own good time, in His own special way, God would arrange for another lovely lady to share our great new adventures together. For He is not only the God of all consolation and comfort to His people, but He is also the God of wondrous compensation in our losses.

Ursula, with her vivacious personality, her strong courage, her shining spirit would become my cheerful companion. Together we would face the future with fortitude. Quietly, calmly we would rejoice in the wonder of the way in which God's Spirit would lead us gently into ever-widening fields of service.

Reflecting back upon those crucial years following my cliff-top encounter with Christ, I marvel at His mercy, generosity, and faithfulness to me. It was as though He took me strongly by the hand to lead step by step into ever-broadening areas of service. He set before me, by His Spirit, ever wider horizons of adventure with Himself. There was a stimulating awareness of His presence to face the most formidable challenges.

Holy Ghost, with Light Divine

Holy Ghost, with light divine
Shine upon this heart of mine;
Chase the shades of night away,
Turn the darkness into day.

Let me see my Savior's face,
Let me all His beauties trace;
Show those glorious truths to me
Which are only known to Thee.

Holy Ghost, with power divine
Cleanse this guilty heart of mine;
In Thy mercy pity me,
From sin's bondage set me free.

Holy Ghost, with joy divine
Cheer this saddened heart of mine;
Yield a sacred, settled peace,
Let it grow and still increase.

Holy Spirit, all divine,
Dwell within this heart of mine;
Cast down every idol-throne,
Reign supreme, and reign alone.

See, to Thee I yield my heart,
Shed Thy life through every part;
A pure temple I would be,
Wholly dedicate to Thee.

- Andrew Reed

CHAPTER 12

My Conversion and Empowerment

Duncan Campbell

Duncan Campbell (1898-1972) was a Presbyterian minister who was mightily used of God in two significant revival periods in the first half of the 20th century in the Hebrides Islands. Entire villages were convicted by the power of God, and bars were nailed shut with signs reading, "Closed Forever." After military service during World War I, Campbell trained with the Faith Mission; he was later called to become principal of the Faith Mission's Training Home and Bible College in Edinburgh, where he served for a number of years before retiring. During his retirement, he preached at conventions in Great Britain, Ireland, South Africa, and the United States. He was also a visiting lecturer at colleges, such as Youth With A Mission's School of Evangelism at Lausanne in Switzerland, where he died while lecturing.

Editor: I was privileged to hear Duncan Campbell preach in 1969 in Grand Rapids, Michigan, a message preached in the power of the Spirit. The following account has appeared in several publications.

MY CONVERSION HAPPENED under very strange circumstances. God didn't speak to me in a church or in a mission hall, though I went to church every Sabbath. God spoke to me at a dance.

I happened to be a player and a step-dancer. I was very fond of bagpipe playing and just as fond of Scottish step-dancing. I was asked to play and dance at a concert and also to give several demonstrations of step-dancing. The concert had begun. I had already played several pieces when a minister came over to me and said, "There's a special request that you play 'The Green Hills of Tyrone'; one of our favorite Scottish tunes.

As I came to the second part of that great tune, I found my mind altogether wandering from the tune. My thoughts centered on another green hill. At family worship on the farm, we frequently sang: "There Is A Green Hill Far Away." That was the green hill before my mind as I continued to play "The Green Hills of Tyrone."

THE SPIRIT OF HOLINESS & POWER

When finished, I was so gripped by the Spirit of God and so distressed in my mind that I turned to the other players and said, "Boys, you carry on. I'm leaving the concert. One piper turned to me and said, "Are you not well? I said, "I'm very well in body, but I'm terribly disturbed in my mind."

"I saw a light in a church."

As I walked along the country road toward the farm, I saw a light in a church. I had been away on business and had just come home to play this dance. No one had told me that two workers of the Faith Mission were conducting a mission in the parish. And on that particular night, they were having an all-night affair in the church along with the minister of that parish.

I was curious to know what was happening. So I went up to the door and listened through the keyhole. Someone was praying. I listened and who did I discover praying but my own father. I am sure he was praying for his wayward son at the concert and dance. Horses could not have dragged me past that church. I was in my piper's regalia with its buckles and plates and whatnots, two swords in one hand with which I had been demonstrating sword dancing. And a set of bagpipes in the other. I laid them down in the back seat and walked up the aisle and sat beside my father.

The minister looked at me and then he looked at the two girls on the platform with him. I'm sure they thought I was either drunk or mad. Whoever heard of a piper in full regalia walking into a prayer meeting? I sat down beside my father, who turned to me and said, "I'm glad to see you here." That was all.

After that, a young woman from the island of Skye, Mary Graham, a worker in the mission, stood up and spoke for about ten minutes in Gaelic. She spoke from the text: "God speaketh once, yea twice, but man perceiveth it not."

The arrow of conviction struck home, and now I became fearfully distressed in my spirit, so much so that I was afraid I would create a scene in the church. I walked out, left the others there praying, and I made my way along the road outside of town, arriving home at about three o'clock in the morning. If I prayed one time along that country road, I'm sure I prayed ten times, crying to God to have mercy on me. I saw myself so vile and sinful.

"I found my mother on her knees ..."

Upon arriving at the farm, I found my mother on her knees by the kitchen fire. Oh, thank God for a Christian home! Thank God for Christian parents! Mother couldn't attend the prayer meeting because we had visitors on the farm that night. But she could pray at home. And there she was on her knees by the fireside. I'm sure she, too, was praying for her wayward son. I went over and told her my story, told her how distressed I was, and asked her to pray for me.

Like a wise woman, she said, "There are visitors with us this evening. Your cousins have come, and there's one occupying the bed in your room. I would suggest that you go out to the barn and tell God what you told me."

I went out to the barn and knelt in the straw prepared for the horses in the morning. I still remember the prayer I uttered. It was in Gaelic. I'm thankful that God understands Gaelic! If He didn't, I wouldn't be saved today, for I had not a word of English then. I prayed, "Oh, God, I know not how to come, and I know not what to do; but, if you will take me as I am, I'm coming now." And God, in less time than I take to tell it, swept into my life. It was miraculous! It was supernatural! Never for one minute, since that hour, have I had any occasion to doubt the work that God did that night.

"God, come into my life!"

I knew nothing about the doctrine of simply believing, or about this matter of making a decision. My cry was, "God, come into my life!" I was that night supernaturally altered, and so supernaturally altered that godliness characterized every part of my being, body, soul, and spirit.

On the following Wednesday, I walked seven miles over the hill to attend a prayer meeting. I had aspirations and longings of the soul that found expression in being at a prayer meeting.

Shortly after my conversion, I found myself along with many others, on the battlefields of Flanders, a soldier in the king's army. It wasn't long before I discovered powers resident within me that were fighting against my desire for godliness and holiness—a power well-entrenched in my nature, a power that battled my best endeavors. And with the Apostle Paul I frequently, cried, "Oh wretched man that I am, who shall deliver me from this body of death? The good that I would, I cannot do, the evil that I hate, that I do." Yet, in the midst of it all, I knew that I had entered into a saving and covenant relationship with God and that He had entered into a saving and covenant relationship with me. I knew that. And yet!—oh, the law of the spirit of life was fighting the law of the spirit of death!

However, the day came when that was changed, and changed under very strange circumstances. I found myself severely wounded in a cavalry charge outside of Amiens—The last cavalry charge of the British army, April 12, 1918. It is a terrible thing to be in a cavalry charge when machine guns are leveled at you, firing five and six hundred rounds-a-minute. That was what we had to face on that fearful morning.

I lay wounded on the battlefield; the blood was flowing freely; I believed I was dying. I was very conscious of my unfitness to appear before the judge of all the earth. Two things troubled me: I felt so impure, and I knew that I hadn't helped any soul to find the Savior. We had often sung on the farm:

Must I empty-handed go?
Must I meet my Savior so?
Not one soul with which to greet Him?
Must I empty-handed go?

Could I but recall them now,
Oh, the years of sin I've wasted!
I would give them to my Savior
To His will I'd gladly bow.

But I was dying, I thought. And then, a miraculous thing happened. The Canadian horses were called out to a second charge. They charged over that bloody battlefield toward the enemy in a body. Men were dying; men were lying wounded; the whole field was littered with men and horses in distress. As it happened, a horse's hoof struck me in the spine. The mark is still there, and I must have groaned. In the providence of God,, that groan registered in the mind of a Canadian trooper. He might have said to himself, "There's a cowardly man of the Scotch Grays. He's still alive."

After the charge, again in the providence of God, that trooper came right to the place where I lay and saw that I was bleeding profusely. He lifted me as gently as he could and placed me on the horse's back, dug the stirrup right into the horse's side, and that steed galloped with fury toward the casualty clearing station. Would I be alive to reach the casualty clearing station? Would my soul be in eternity before my body was lifted from the horse? These were the thoughts that coursed through my mind.

"Make me as holy as a saved sinner can be."

As I lay on that horse's back, I remembered a prayer Father frequently offered at family worship. The prayer came from my heart, "Oh, God, I'm dying. Will you make me as holy as a saved man can be?" It was M'Cheyne's prayer, frequently uttered by Father, "Make me as holy as a saved sinner can be."

God, the Holy Ghost, fell upon me on that horse's back. You needn't say there isn't such a thing as a definite experience of the Holy Ghost subsequent to conversion. My confession was real, my regeneration was wonderful, but they paled before the revelation of Jesus that came to me on that horse's back.

Then the horse stood at the casualty clearing station. Loving hands lifted me and laid me down on a stretcher. The place was crowded with wounded and dying, mostly Canadians. I couldn't speak English. But I tried to sing in Gaelic, and what I sang was a psalm:

Oh, thou my soul, bless God the Lord;
And all that in me is, be stirred up.
His holy name, I will magnify and bless."

Oh, I was weak. My voice wasn't strong. But God swept in. Mark you, there wasn't a man there who could understand me. To them, it was a strange language. But within that hour, seven Canadians were saved. Revival, a miniature revival, swept into the casualty clearing station! One young lad said, "Trooper, can you not speak to us in English? We are seeking Jesus." Men with little thought of God, here they were, moved by the Spirit of God, the Personality of Jesus, making His impact upon sinners.

That's why I constantly say, that, to me, the baptism of the Holy Ghost in its final analysis is the revelation of Jesus. It's not gifts. Gifts may come if God wills to give them. But I know nothing about gifts. I do know this, that when that baptism of the Holy Ghost came upon me on that horse's back, the supreme reality was Jesus. 'Twas Jesus. I loved Him "because He first loved me, and purchased my pardon on Calvary's tree."

Oh, how wonderful it was! There in the casualty clearing station, wave after wave of divine realization swept through; sinners cried to God for mercy, and sinners found the Savior.

CHAPTER 13

"Unless the Spirit . . ."

Vance Havner

Vance Havner (1901-1986) grew up in the hills of North Carolina. He began to preach at the early age of twelve and was ordained when he was fifteen. After a country pastorate, he went to Charleston, South Carolina, where he was pastor of First Baptist Church, the oldest Baptist church in the South. In 1940, he began a full-time traveling ministry, conducting local church revivals and Bible conferences.

In describing his ministry, Havner claimed that he was not a preacher, nor an evangelist, nor a teacher, nor an orator, nor a prophet. He claimed that he was simply an "exhorter." This probably is an apt description of Vance Havner, whose sharp, incisive wit and unyielding proclamation of God's message to all men, became familiar trademarks to countless congregations of people throughout the country. His ministry was effectively used and blessed by God. He was a man who remained resolutely faithful to the highest standard of his Christian calling.

Havner's message was primarily to the church and was marked by practical admonition; he penned eighteen books of sermons and devotional meditations and contributed articles for many evangelical publications. This article is taken from *Hearts Afire* by Vance Havner.

"Not by might, nor by power, but by my Spirit, saith the Lord of hosts" (Zech. 4:6)

BACK IN THE RUSTIC RURAL COMMUNITY of my boyhood days, we used to sing an old-fashioned song characteristic of the period before the Age of Amen gave way to the Era of So What? It ran like this:

Brethren, we have met to worship
And adore the Lord our God;
Won't you pray with all your power
While we try to preach the Word?

*All is vain unless the Spirit
Of the Holy One come down;
Brethren, pray and holy manna
Will be showered all around.*

I like especially that line, "All is vain unless the Spirit ..."

The plight of many churches is summed up in the words spoken to Jesus by the father who brought his demonized boy to the disciples at the foot of the Mount of Transfiguration: "I besought thy disciples to cast him out; and they could not." We are powerless before a demonized world. And it is not because we do not have knowledge, equipment, programs, activity, money. Never has the church had more—and less!

Missionaries tell us that sometimes chimpanzees imitate them by gathering wood and arranging it for a fire—but they do not know how to produce the fire. The church has her wood in excellent order today. The system is perfect, but—we have no fire.

The Old Testament tells us how Elisha sent Gehazi, his servant, to raise the Shunammite's son. He carried the prophet's staff and observed the prophet's orders, "but there was neither voice nor hearing!" Today Gehazi goes about at Elisha's orders, carrying Elisha's staff, but although he goes through the prescribed motions, the dead do not come to life. Although we say all the words, the demons do not depart.

Never has the church had more wire stretched with less power in it. "All is vain unless the Spirit of the Holy One come down." Sad to say, we seem not even to know that we have not the Spirit in power. If He ceased His work, many church members would never know the difference. Like Samson, we wist not that He has departed, but we keep "shaking ourselves" in the prescribed calisthenics.

Such was the sad plight of the churches in Asia to which our Lord spoke in Revelation. Ephesus was loveless and didn't know it. Sardis was lifeless and didn't know it. Laodicea was lukewarm and didn't know it. "Thou sayest ... and knowest not" is descriptive of altogether too many churches today. In any case, "all IS vain unless the Spirit ..."

We go to extremes, we either freeze or fry. Some services are too formal, and we come out like ramrods, having mistaken spiritual rigor mortis for dignity. We ought to be dogmatic plus, but sometimes we are dogmatic—period. So are there other fellowships coldly orthodox, having the facts but no fire. Again, we sometimes go to the other extreme, where we sit through a frenzy of evangelistic epilepsy and come out nervous, feeling more as if we had been to a circus than to a church. In either case, "all is vain unless the Spirit ..."

We do not have to choose between freezing or frying. Certainly, most of the saints do need defrosting. One thing can stop Niagara—it can freeze! The same trouble stops many a church. Deep-freeze lockers are nothing new: we have had them on street corners with steeples on top for years.

We could stand a little emotion nowadays. The World Series baseball games almost stop business in many a section of our land, so intense is the interest. If a revival so interfered with our normal processes, you would hear the complaint that we were going crazy. Indeed, that was a complaint made during the Welsh Revival. A spell of that kind of insanity would be welcome, "think" some of us who have grown weary of the present insanity misnamed progress.

We have already referred to Samson, who wist not when the Spirit of the Lord departed from him. There was a time when the Spirit was with him. It is stated in a most interesting fashion: "And the Spirit of the Lord came mightily upon him ... and he had nothing in his hand" (Judges 14:5,6). Nothing in his hand! We have too many things in our hands today, carnal weapons of our own choosing, and even God cannot fill what is already full. It was the invisible weapon that prevailed in Samson's case, as with Gideon and his "sword of the Lord." God wants us empty-handed when we go out, that we may be full-handed when we come in. Samson's hands were filled with honey for himself and others. When life is done, we want to go home full-handed: "Shall I go and empty-handed?" we sing, and the answer is "No." But the Spirit of God comes mightily on those who have nothing in their own hands, that He may fill their hands forevermore.

We are in serious danger of forgetting that it is "not by might or by power but by the Spirit of the Lord of hosts." We cannot meet the Goliath of this age in Saul's armor. When we try to grapple with the adversary in unsanctified strength, we throw away our only chance of success. The Bible is one long record of men and women who dared to be utterly ridiculous in order to prove God. Abraham, the priests at Jericho, Gideon, David facing Goliath, these and many more dared to make the glorious venture where "all is vain unless the Spirit" comes to one's aid. If it hadn't worked, they would have been laughingstocks to all subsequent generations. But it worked!

Today we are afraid to prove God. We borrow the world's program and pep and propaganda and paraphernalia and personnel. But from the world, we cannot borrow power, the power that works the works of God. Our efficiency turns out to be deficiency unless we have His sufficiency. We have a name to be alive as had Sardis, but we merely double our activities to hide our weakness. "It is not conquering energy conscious of its power but feverish energy conscious of its powerlessness." We have developed in Christian work the go-getter salesman type who "goes" more than he "gets," hunches over tables in cafeterias "making contacts" instead of getting on his knees talking to God. And all our modern St. Vitus's dance merely reveals the fact that we have not the Spirit.

There are others who sense their lack of power and set about in diverse ways to improve matters. They introduce this innovation, dispense with that, a mere reshuffling of arrangements, but the church is as powerless before the demons as ever. Rules upon rules are invented, but the sorriest hotel usually posts the most regulations, and the same holds for churches.

What to do? I suggest no "steps." There are books of them already in circulation. Until we are really convicted of our need, humble enough to acknowledge it, and desperate enough to lay hold upon God, we shall continue like Gehazi to go through all the motions in vain. And when we are so convicted and humble and desperate, we will get through to God. The best way to learn how to pray is to pray, and the man who really hungers and thirsts for God will need no "steps" to satisfy his soul.

"All is vain unless the Spirit ..." Let us pray as we ought, and "holy manna will be showered all around."

CHAPTER 14

"Look not to your own interests"

Dennis F. Kinlaw

Dennis F. Kinlaw (1922-2017) was an ordained minister in the United Methodist Church and served as a pastor, scholar, educator, and evangelist. He was a graduate of Brandeis University (Ph.D.), and served for eighteen years as president of Asbury College (now University) and was the founder of The Francis Asbury Society. For many years he served on the boards of Christianity Today, Wesley Biblical Seminary, and One Mission Society. Among the books he authored are *Preaching in the Spirit*, *This Day With the Master*, and *Let's Start With Jesus*. The following article is taken from Dr. Kinlaw's *The Mind of Christ*, copyright © 1998 by The Francis Asbury Society.

Editor: I was honored to fellowship with Dr. Kinlaw for three hours in his bedroom, two years before he went to be with Christ. I will always cherish that unforgettable experience, as the two of us discussed the things of God.

PHILIPPIANS 2:5-11 is the best-known passage of Scripture concerning the mind of Christ. Some modern translations render it in such a way that the word mind is not used; but Paul employs the same Greek verb that occurs in Mark 8, where Jesus tells Peter he does not think as God thinks. The Greek word (*phroneite*) literally means "to be minded"—in this case, to be minded as God is minded: "Let each of you look not to your own interests, but to the interests of others. Let the same mind be in you that was in Christ Jesus, who, though he was in the form of God, did not regard equality with God as something to be exploited, but emptied himself, taking the form of a slave, being born in human likeness" (vv. 5-7).

Most scholars deal with verses 5-11 as if they were a unit, an ancient Christian hymn to the Christ. Perhaps they were. But I believe Paul used these words to illustrate the message he wished to convey to the Philippians.

A state of conflict existed within the Philippian church, and Paul wrote out of his desire to see that conflict resolved. Any time people work together, tensions will develop. But unresolved tension brings reproach on the cause of Christ.

Paul knew that this conflict could be resolved only if the Philippians had a change of heart—and a change of mind.

In chapter 1, Paul observes that some people preach Christ out of right motives, while others preach Christ out of contentiousness: "Some proclaim Christ from envy and rivalry, but others from goodwill. These proclaim Christ out of love, knowing that I have been put here for the defense of the gospel; the others proclaim Christ out of selfish ambition ..." (1:15-17a). Here Paul uses the Greek word *eritheia*, which literally means "to strive." Paul condemns the tendency to contend for one's own way, which is at the heart of carnal thinking.

He introduces the second chapter with these words: "If then there is any encouragement in Christ, any consolation from love, any sharing in the Spirit, any compassion and sympathy, make my joy complete: be of the same mind, having the same love, being in full accord and of one mind" (2:1-2). The basic problem at Philippi was that the Christians had different "minds"; each one thought his own way. So if Paul was to heal their division, he had to deal with the mind. He describes the sort of mind they must have: "Do nothing from selfish ambition [Greek, *eritheia*] or conceit, but in humility regard others as better than yourselves. Let each of you look not to your own interests, but to the interest of others" (2:3-4).

The first time I read that in the Greek, I thought, Wait a minute. Where is the word "only"? The King James Version put the word only in italics, which indicates it is not in the original Greek text. Try as I might, I couldn't find it in the Greek. So I went to our classical Greek specialist at the college, who has a Ph.D. in classical languages from St. Louis University, and I said, "Help me here." He cast about for awhile and then wrote me a note that said: "It isn't there, Kinlaw."

I went to Bob Mulholland, who has a Ph.D. from Harvard in New Testament. I said, "Bob, I've got a question...." He pulled books down and looked all around his office. Finally, he said, "Kinlaw, it isn't there."

Now, why is the word only inserted in that verse, in most modern translations of the Bible? Why do most versions read, "Let each of you look not only to your own interests, but also to the interests of others"? Because we 20th-century Christians don't believe the Lord can deliver us from self-interest, so we insert our assumptions into Scripture.

Four Ungodly Characteristics

In verses 3 and 14, Paul lists four characteristics that should be alien to the

Christian life. He says that every Christian should act (1) without self-interest; (2) without vain conceit; (3) without grumbling; and (4) without questioning.

Self-interest (v. 3) is the supreme characteristic of a sinful person. It has been said that sinfulness is to be "curved inward upon oneself." Conversely, the purpose of the redemption offered by Christ is to undo our distorted orientation—to turn us outward, so that we are not interested in ourselves but in the well-being of others. When we understand sin in these terms, we begin to break down the traditional dichotomy between evangelism and Christian social action. After all, the Christian life is not an "either/or" proposition: "Either I enrich my own relationship with Christ, or I go out and show others who Christ is, through my selfless service." Outwardness is all there is to the gospel. The essence of Christian living is making oneself a servant as Christ is a servant.

It is no accident that John Wesley became a paragon of Christian social action. He engaged in prison reform, slave emancipation, hospital work, and other activities that modern evangelicals sometimes disparage as the concerns of "the social gospel" (as if it were different from the gospel of Christ). These activities were a normal consequence of Wesley's message about the necessity of entering into the Christ-life.

Self-interest is well demonstrated by the question, "What's in it for me?" Jesus never strived to get something for himself. The Gospels relate no instance in which Jesus' self-interest was his first consideration!

Imagine the scene when Jairus asked Jesus to heal his daughter. Suppose Jesus had said, "Yes, I could do that. I could go home with you and lay my hands on your daughter, and she would get well. But what's in it for me?" My mentioning such an idea must offend you, because that attitude is utterly antithetical to what Jesus represented. He came to lay down his life for his sheep (John 10:15). He did not come to protect himself; rather, he came to spend himself.

The Old Testament lifestyle may have been expressed by the statement, "Love your neighbor as yourself" (Lev. 19:18). But Jesus expressed the New Testament lifestyle like this: "Love one another as I have loved you. No one has greater love than this, to lay down one's life for one's friends" (John 15:12-13). Jesus changed the pattern of personal priorities when he became the Shepherd, who sacrificed himself for his sheep.

Conceit (v. 3) is the common English translation of the New Testament Greek term *kenodoxia*, which comes from the word *kenos*, meaning "empty." In other words, a Christian should be unconcerned about elevating his own status or doing things for the sake of appearance.

How often we fall short of doing God's will because we are overly concerned about appearance! I have noticed that at an annual conference of ministers, when someone asks, "What can you tell me about your church?" a fellow will quail or strut, depending on the position of his congregation in the "pecking order." I don't think I have ever heard a minister say, "I have the appointment of my life. There are dozens of people in that community who don't know Christ, and I have an opportunity to reach them." We think instead of our status and position.

Jesus exemplified a life unconcerned with appearance. He talked with a Samaritan woman; he touched lepers; he cared nothing about his appearances before his disciples or the public.

Murmuring (v. 14) is the self-pitying attitude that says, "I deserve better than this." Self-pity is another mark of our fallenness.

When Helen Roseveare graduated from Cambridge in the early 1960s, she went to an area of Zaire where two-hundred thousand people lived without a doctor. She made that her mission field. As her medical work progressed, she decided to build a hospital. She wrote her mother, asking for a book about how to build a hospital; her mother was unable to find such a book, but sent her a book about how to make bricks. So Helen Roseveare found herself teaching the African natives how to make kiln-fired bricks.

As they were taking the first load from the kiln, and she began pulling the spines off of the new bricks, she realized that her fingers were wet. They were dripping blood, where she had broken her fingernails. She thought, Lord, I didn't come to Africa to make bricks; I came here to be a surgeon. Surely there's someone in England who could come to do this.

While she stood there feeling sorry for herself, a runner came from the hospital and said, "We have an emergency. Come! You must perform surgery immediately!"

She went to the infirmary and began to prepare for surgery. She gritted her teeth as she scrubbed her hands with a brush; then, she let her assistant pour alcohol over them, and her protest became a scream.

A few weeks later, one of the African workers at the kiln said, "Doctor, when you are in the surgery, you are like a god. You terrify us. But when you're at the brick kiln and your fingers drip blood like ours, you're our sister. We love you!" At that moment, she realized God had not sent her to Africa to be a surgeon; he had sent her there to show the love of Christ. What did she deserve? Merely an opportunity to show the love of Christ. And she could not do that if she got what she thought she deserved!

Arguing (v. 14) is the mentality that tries to bargain with God. It is the attitude that says, "Yes, Lord, but...." Or, "Isn't there a better way to do this, Lord?" It professes a willingness to obey, but it hedges.

Arguing is the attitude of a Christian girl who marries a fellow that she knows is not really God's choice. It is the attitude of a young man who is called to serve God overseas, but allows himself to get trapped by career or family obligations at home. Arguing rears its head in a thousand ways, as we compromise the will of God in our lives by placing conditions upon it....

How We Can Have the Mind of Christ

Becoming like Christ is a work of grace. It occurs only as Christ lives within us, not as we strive to be like him. Is this possible? Of course, it is! Christian history is brimming with examples of men and women who have responded to life as Christ responded. They did it because Christ lived within them.

During Samuel Brengle's senior year at Boston University, he was offered the pastorate of a wealthy congregation in South Bend, Indiana. He had an opportunity to begin his ministry at the top of the social roster. But he felt that God was calling him to join the Salvation Army, so he crossed the Atlantic and presented himself to General William Booth.

"We don't want you. You're dangerous," Booth said.

"Dangerous? What do you mean?" Brengle asked.

"You would not take orders."

"But you haven't given me a trial," Brengle pleaded.

"You have too much education. You would not be willing to subordinate yourself to one of the officers here. Converted drunks and prostitutes are the staff leaders."

"Please give me a chance," Brengle said. So General Booth sent him to one of his sons, Ballington Booth, who put him through a similar interrogation. When Brengle still insisted on trying the Army, Booth's son made him bootblack for the Central Salvation Army Corps in London. In an unfinished basement, on a dirt floor half-submerged in water, Brengle began cleaning mud off of the boots of converted street bums who were now soldiers in the Army. One day he seemed to hear a voice that said, "You're a fool!"

I am not! he thought.

"You're a sinner, too."

What do you mean?

"Remember the man who buried his talent in the earth?" the inner voice said. "What are you doing here? Think of all the training you've gotten. You're just throwing it away."

Brengle sank into a depression. After awhile he prayed, "Lord, have I failed you? Did I miss your leading?"

And the Lord replied, "Remember, Sam, I washed their feet!"

That muddy cellar became an anteroom to heaven, as Brengle sensed the reassuring presence of his Lord. From that day forward, Brengle knew that he was called, not to invest himself, but to spend himself for others. He realized that Christ is a servant who looks for others to serve with him.

The Holy Spirit makes this sacrificial thinking possible. Jesus' ministry began when the Holy Spirit descended upon him. His disciples' ministry began when the Holy Spirit came upon them on the day of Pentecost, empowering them to "turn the world upside down." Likewise, the Spirit of Christ must control us if we are to be conformed to the character of Christ and be filled with his power.

Christ must be free to spend us. As long as we attempt to save our own lives, we shall lose them; but if we surrender our lives to be controlled by his Spirit, we shall live and bear fruit for him. The Bible says very little about self-enrichment; but it says a great deal about giving our lives for the enrichment of others.

Letting Go of the Strings

I recently got acquainted with Josef Tson, the pastor of a large Baptist church in western Romania. Until a few years ago, the Romanian Communist Party was one of the most brutal in the world. As a Christian pastor, Josef spoke out on some issues and angered the government. So they decided to destroy him. They came in and stripped his library of all his books. Two books were quite worn and had no jackets on them, so the soldiers left them behind. One was Martin Niemoller's account of his suffering under Adolf Hitler. The other was *Abundant Living*, a devotional book by E. Stanley Jones.

This Romanian pastor put Martin Niemoller's book on his nightstand to give him strength through the night. He put E. Stanley Jones' book on the shelf in his study.

The government then sent the police to interrogate Josef five days a week, and up to seven hours a day. The intent was to destroy him. Oftentimes they would interrogate him with a loaded pistol on the table in front of the interrogator. One day, after a very grueling period of questioning, Josef went into the study, locked the door, and fell to the floor, sobbing. He said, "God, I can't take any more."

He thought he heard a voice. The voice said, "Josef, get up. Read the book on the shelf."

Josef said there was no problem knowing which book to read; there was only one left! So he pulled down E. Stanley Jones' book and opened it. The devotional for that day was on "How to Live Above Your Circumstances." It was about Jesus' facing the cross. Stanley Jones said Jesus did not resist the cross. Jones said that Jesus embraced the cross instead of resisting it.

Josef said, "God, you surely don't mean I'm supposed to embrace my interrogators!"

"Yes," the Lord said, "that's exactly what I mean."

"Well, God, if you want me to do that, you must do something in my heart that you have never done before."

Josef said that's exactly what the Lord did. He walked back into the interrogation room, ready to embrace his trial. He said the change in the atmosphere was almost comical. Before that time, the pastor had been in trauma; but now the chief interrogator was in trauma because he had lost control of his subject! The chief interrogator was beside himself. He finally spun in anger on the pastor and said, "You are stupid. I guess we'll just have to go ahead and kill you."

Josef found himself saying, "I understand, sir. That's your ultimate weapon. When everything else has failed, you can always kill. But you know, I have an ultimate weapon too. And when you use your ultimate weapon, I get to use mine."

"And what's your ultimate weapon?" the Communist angrily demanded.

"Your ultimate weapon is to kill," Josef said. "Mine is to die. When I die, I will be much better off. But your troubles will just be beginning. You see, every tape of every sermon that I have ever preached will be sprinkled with my blood. So you'll have much more trouble with me dead than you have with me alive!"

The Communist shouted, "Take him out!"

A few weeks later, the pastor heard through the grapevine that the Communists were saying Josef Tson was crazy because he wanted to be a martyr. "But we're no fools!" the Communists said. So they stopped interrogating him. Josef said he could not even argue them into killing him then.

"When I was pulling every string to try to save my life, I was at wit's end," Josef told me. "But when I turned the strings loose and let Christ control my life completely, I was free."

CHAPTER 15

Transfiguration of Character

J. Sidlow Baxter

J. Sidlow Baxter (1903-1999) was born in Sidney, Australia, and grew up in Lancashire, England. He trained for the ministry at Spurgeon's College, London, where the foundations were laid for a life of fruitful ministry; he was a pastor in Scotland and England. He later moved to the United States, where he eventually retired and died. His ecclesiastical roots were in the Calvinistic Methodist Church.

Dr. Baxter was not only a preacher of outstanding ability, but first and foremost, he was an excellent Bible teacher. He was in great demand as a speaker at conferences and conventions. Among Baxter's best-known books are *Awake My Heart, Divine Healing of the Body, The Strategic Grasp of the Bible*, and *Rethinking Our Priorities*. His most popular work is *Explore the Book*, a 1760 page tome that analyzes and summarizes each book of the Bible. He also authored a trilogy on the doctrine of sanctification: *A New Call to Holiness, His Deeper Work in Us*, and *Our High Calling*, which were later published in one volume. The following article is taken from *A New Call to Holiness*, published by Kregel Publications.

WHATEVER OTHER ISSUES may be involved in this subject of scriptural holiness, never for one moment must we forget that the supreme purpose of the Holy Spirit's deeper work in the believer is the *transfiguration of character*. However often we may fight it down, there is a reassertive tendency in most of us to think that the infilling of the Holy Spirit is mainly an emotional experience. Perhaps this misunderstanding is the more persistent because of our knowing that sudden envelopments by the Holy Spirit have not infrequently been *accompanied* by an eruption of ecstatic emotion. It is important that we distinguish between the purposive and the merely associative.

The human mind is usually conceived of as having three main areas or centers of activity: (1) intellect, or reason, (2) volition, or free will, (3) emotion, or feeling. Which is the true order of precedence? The intellect is meant to be king, with the will as prime minister, or executive of the crown, and the emotions as obedient subjects. When that order is violated, and especially when the emotions run amok, we are soon in trouble, either physically or psychopathically, or both. We live in an age of suspense and nervous tension. Emotional behaviour patterns and disturbances are receiving more attention than ever. We dare not understate the importance of the emotions. Yet when we have said the most and the last about them, it still remains true that they are comparatively the *least* important. They are the most volatile, the most variable, the most unpredictable, the most *superficial* part of us.

Is it thinkable, then, that the Holy Spirit comes to do His deepest work in the least substantial part of us? No, whatever emotional accidence there may or may not be, that major invasion by the Holy Spirit ... designs a renovation in the deepest depths of the human personality. It is meant to effect such a purification and refinement within the moral nature that there shall be a transfiguration of *character*.

I have made a distinction between "nature" and "character." Nature is the raw material, so to speak. Character is what we make out of it. In the final consummation, we shall all be presented "faultless" in our nature; but does that mean we shall all be equal in *character?* No, for as "one star differeth from another star in glory" (1 Cor. 15:41), so will there be greater and lesser resplendencies of character developed by our voluntary reactions while living on earth in the mortal body. (Oh, how important is this present span on earth!). In that gracious suffusion by the Holy Spirit, which effects inwrought holiness, the divine purpose is not only even the correcting of wrong bias, and the cleansing of impure impulse and the refining of desire; it is that *nature*, being thus renewed, may be developed into holy *character*.

In other words, inwrought holiness is not only negative; it is both negative and positive. Wonderful as are the aspects of it which we have already mentioned, those more negative features (i.e., cleansing, correcting, renewing, refining) are the clearing away of obstructions, so that all those traits and qualities which are most natively human, "after the image of God," may be unimpededly developed, even sublimated, in the transfiguration of character. Holiness is not only a reclamation of the garden of weeds, but a filling of it with fragrant flowers. It is not only (negatively) a clearing away of obnoxious undergrowths from the orchard, but (positively) a producing of gracious fruit, even "the fruit of the Spirit ... love, joy, peace, longsuffering, kindness, goodness, faithfulness, meekness, godly self-control" (Gal. 5: 22-23), and all manner of "good works which God afore prepared that we should walk in them" (Eph. 2:10).

The kind of character-beauty which true holiness begets is not that of elegant marble statuary, charming in profile, graceful in silhouette, yet cold and hard to the touch, voiceless, uncommunicative, and locked up in itself. Any kind of holiness which turns the inner life into a mental monastery, and the outer life into a walled-off enclosure, is not holiness according to Christ. One of the loveliest traits of character engendered by true holiness is a self-forgetting otherism. Instead of a continually in-looking self-culture, there is an out-looking diffusion of goodness to others.

Genesis 1:11 tells how God caused the earth to bring forth herb and fruit tree "whose seed is in itself." The miracle of herb and fruit self-propagation has been going on for all the thousands of years since, and it always happens at the point of full development or ripeness. Similarly, holiness in full development or ripeness expresses itself in an outreaching graciousness of character, which propagates goodness and moral beauty everywhere. Except where there is Satanic resistance or Pharisaic hypocrisy, it gently "provokes to love and good works" (Heb. 10:24) in other hearts and lives. It is never self-advertising, yet neither can it conceal itself. It continually reaches out in soul-winning activity and atmospheres evangelism in the very love of God. It is full of effort, yet somehow it is effort with ease. Its hands are full of "good works." It produces character which visibly incarnates those words of the Apostolic benediction, "the grace of the Lord Jesus Christ, and the love of God, and the fellowship of the Holy Spirit."

Inward Metamorphosis

Now, of course, there are many New Testament verses which bear on this matter of Christian character; but I here call special attention to two, because of their using a certain Greek verb, i.e., *metamorphŏō*, which, incidentally, seems to have found new vogue today in our rather modern word, "metamorphosis." Both in the Greek and in the English, the meaning is to transform. That Paul should speak about a *character-metamorphosis* through inward renewal is, to say the least, arresting. In Romans 12:1-2, he writes,

> *I beseech you, therefore, brethren, by the mercies of God, to present your bodies a living sacrifice, holy, acceptable to God, which is your reasonable service. And be not fashioned according to this world; but be ye transformed [metamorphosed] by the renewing of your mind, that ye may prove what is the good and acceptable and perfect will of God.*

It is interesting to see how different translators try to bring out the full force of the meaning in these two verses. From a dozen or so, I pick out the rendering given by Weymouth's *New Testament in Modern Speech*.

> *I plead with you, therefore, brethren, by the compassion of God, to present all your faculties to Him as a living and holy sacrifice to Him—a spiritual mode of worship. And do not conform to the present age, but be* TRANSFORMED BY THE ENTIRE RENEWAL OF YOUR MINDS, *so that you may learn by experience what God's will is, namely, all that is good and acceptable to Him, and perfect.*

This metamorphosis is here connected with certain factors that immediately catch the eye. (1) *Separation* from the world: "Do not conform to the present age." Our Lord could transfigure a Stephen, but never a Demas who "loved this present age." (2) *Consecration* to God: "Present all your faculties to Him as a living and holy sacrifice." Our Lord may bless others in many ways, but it is only the completely yielded whom He transfigures. (3) *Renovation* inside the human personality: "the entire renewal of your minds." Nothing less than this can really transfigure character. (4) *Realization* of the divine will by new perception and in actual experience: "that you may learn by experience what God's will is...."

All these will merit separate consideration, but the central and vital thing to grasp is that this character-transformation is wrought by *"ENTIRE RENEWAL" OF THE MIND*. If anything could unanswerably show to us how astray both the eradication theory and the conventional counteraction theory [of the doctrine of sanctification] are, this second verse in Romans 12 does. If, as eradicationism says, the Second Blessing completely extirpates the so-called *"old* nature," leaving only the *"new* nature," then Paul's exhortation here, in Romans 12:1-2, must be to that *"new* nature," which, however, makes the exhortation a useless redundance. For if the so-called "new nature" is (according to theory) sinless, why need Paul to exhort *it* to separation from the world, and consecration to God, and inward renewal? On the other hand, if, as says the "counteraction" idea, the "old nature" must persist within us as an inerradicable evil entity to our dying day, how could Paul exhort us to *"ENTIRE RENEWAL OF THE MIND"*?

How long must some of us continue to sponsor such exegetically untenable concepts in the name of scriptural holiness? How long must unsuspicious audiences be a prey to such misguidance and its hurtful after-effects? How long are we to let well-meant theory, venerated names and tenacious shibboleths blindfold us to the true, precious teaching of our New Testament? With such clear guidance flowing to us through Apostolic pens, why are we so slow to see the real truth about regeneration and sanctification? Regeneration, other than being merely the superinducement of a (suppositionary) "new nature" which is not the human "I" or "me," is the Holy Spirit's transfusing of a new spiritual *life* into our human nature itself. And, through His *further* work in us, this new life may fill, may interpenetrate, may "renew" our whole moral and spiritual nature—not to a static ethical absoluteness but to moral and spiritual *fullness of health* in which inward purity, at last, has the upper hand over all animal appetites, over all temptations injected from without, and over every wrong response from within. *That* is the true New Testament teaching as to regeneration, inward renewal, inwrought holiness, and transfiguration of character.

Yes, that is the central, vital thing: true Christian character-transformation issues from this "entire renewal of the mind." Our Lord said of John the Baptist, "He was a burning and a shining light" (John 5:35). The burning was inward. The shining was outward. There would have been no outward shining without the inward burning. The inward burning was sanctification through the infilling Holy Spirit (Luke 1:15). The outward shining was that of transfigured character. It is *still* true that there cannot be a true outward "shining" without the same inward "burning." Many of us are needing to learn that more deeply. So, then, let us briefly analyze this character-transfiguration in its inwrought and outwrought features.

Transformation of the *Mind*

First, there is a transformation of the *mind*. The word which Paul uses in Romans 12:2 (*metamorphose*) is used of our Lord's mountain-top transfiguration: "He was transfigured before them" (Matt. 17:2, Mark 9: 2). Luke's verbal variation of it is, "the fashion of His countenance was altered" (Luke 9: 29); it was the same face, yet not the same. Correspondently, there can be such a transfiguration of the mind, by the Holy Spirit, that the very "fashion" of its thinking is changed; so that although it remains the same mind as to personal identity, it is no longer the same in its deepest impulses and responses. It means that all the thoughts, imaginations, emotions, motives, ambitions, yearnings, joys and loves of the heart and mind are made to become radiant with "the joy of the Lord." I myself have known persons who have given every convincing evidence, under widely varied testings, of this fundamental refashioning of the mind.

Transfiguration of the *Personality*

Resultantly, there is a transfiguration of the *personality*. This is the very opposite of self-decoration. It is also quite different from a prepossessing natural charm, which in its own way, of course, can be quite delightful. It is no mere exterior impressiveness of figure or feature, nor is it any kind of personal force which is self-achieved. It is an inner radiance which somehow shines through the personality, not in *any* way because of natural appearance or engaging gifts, but, as often as not, despite the *absence* of them. It is an indefinable but unmistakable glow which tinges and lusters one's way of saying and doing things. It is utterly unconscious of itself, yet it *atmospheres* the whole personality, expressing itself most often through the most ordinary activities of the most ordinary days. It shows itself distinctly to the public through the ministry of public men, but it shows itself most clearly to those who live nearest to it and observe it continually in private life.

I remember reading about a man who once went to breakfast with the saintly John Fletcher (whom John Wesley described as "the holiest man in England"). The breakfast was very plain fare, in itself, but the visitor afterward described the meal in this way: "Do you know, taking breakfast with John Fletcher was like taking the Sacrament!" This transfiguration of the personality is a lovely fulfillment of that prayer in Psalm 90:17, "Let the beauty of the Lord our God be upon us."

Transformation of the Countenance

We may go further and say, with all due cautiousness, that this "entire renewal" of the mind often gradually transfigures *the face.* This may not be one of its most solidly important effects, but it is one of its most appealing adjuncts. It must have been transfixing to the gathered members of the Jewish Sanhedrin when they saw Stephen's face become "as the face of an angel" (Acts 6:15). Of course, it still remained the same human face, but some unearthly sheen must have shown through it.

I never thought I would ever see anything on earth near enough to that to remind me of it, but I did a few years ago. My dear wife and I were traveling through what was then the Belgian Congo. On the occasion of which I now speak, I was addressing a crowd of between twelve and fifteen hundred negro men and women of varying ages, from several different tribes, many of whom had come, in larger or smaller contingents, two or even three days' trek through the jungles in order to be present at our Conference. I had asked beforehand for guidance as to my type of message and had been told, "They will go as deep in the Word as you can take them"—which proved to be true. I believe that many of those beaming-faced African brothers and sisters in the Lord knew more about implicit trust in the Word, and about deeply experienced sanctification than I did myself. My subject was: "Out of Egypt and into Canaan"—and oh, how they listened, even though it had to be through two interpreters, because of different tribal languages.

Because of needing to preach through *two* interpreters, I practiced, as closely as possible, one complete thought to each complete sentence. Next to me, on my left, a lady missionary interpreted, and next further left was a negro interpreter. In that way, the main two groups of languages were covered. I could not help noticing how the people looked at that negro interpreter. Maybe *they* could not help noticing how *I* kept looking at him. I became so absorbed in watching his face that sometimes, when it was time for me to add my next bit, I had momentarily forgotten the thread of my discourse!

Oh, that face! I have seen many beautiful faces in my time, but never one quite like that. I have seen eyes shine, and features beam, but never elsewhere quite like that. Using the word in its finest, uttermost sense, that negro's face was *radiant*. If ever I saw the "spiritual glow," I saw it there. As evidently as anything could be, it was the outshining of an inward purity. In Scriptural phraseology, it was "the *beauty* of holiness." I learned afterward that the beauty of his character matched the radiance of his face.

That was not the only thing that we learned afterward. On our way back from the meeting to the missionary's dwelling, we passed a group of naked natives—six or seven men, squatting at the base of a great tree. Never before in our travels had we seen human beings so facially ugly, or with such prominent suggestion of the ape. I suddenly realized how easy it would be, if we had no authentic guidance from the written Word of God, to believe in human evolution from the anthropoid apes. One of those men was so strange-looking, so gorilla-like, it was disturbing to look at him, yet we could scarcely turn away our gaze. As soon as we were past them, our missionary friend said, "I know what you were thinking. We missionaries have thought the same at one time or another. You were shocked at the appearance of that big one, with the coarse hair and ugly gorilla face. Well, he is the brother of the man who interpreted your sermon just now; and your radiant-faced interpreter was even *uglier than that* before his conversion to Christ"! For the moment, we were dumbstruck. The contrast between the two was so great that such a transformation seemed incredible, but the missionary assured us that similar transfigurations had occurred in tens of hundreds of lives. When, despite their crudeness, those dark-minded people are brought to the point of simple yet vital faith in the Saviour, and become truly regenerated by the Holy Spirit, there is such a sheer contrast between their new life in Christ and what they were before, in their pre-conversion mental darkness and animalism, that the gracious shock of it causes wonderful *facial* transfigurations.

In a gentler, less vivid, yet equally real way, I have seen transfigured character and transfigured faces in England and America. Pure-hearted Christian saints, I think of them now, and my memory of the gentle light shining through some of those dear faces tempts me to fill pages here, telling about them and the gracious witness for Christ which they diffused. But I must forbear. I would only say that those faces, some masculine, some feminine, some younger though perhaps the more of them rather older, some naturally well-featured, others rather peculiar or else of the plain Jane type, have all had a radiance, a light, an expressive something which transfigured whatever kind of natural cast or feature they had. There was that Shekinah light within which tinges with beauty *whatever* it shines through.

Transfiguration of Disposition and Behaviour

Then again, going with this inward renewal and transfiguration of character, there is always transfiguration of disposition and behaviour. "Entire renewal of the mind" inevitably registers itself in refined and tempered attitudes. Hasty verdicts and drastic reactions drop away. The way of looking at things and dealing with things is modified. There is a new interest in others, a new tolerance of others, a new warmth of kindliness toward others. In matters of faith and conviction, there is a new firmness which is the more Christlike because it is firmness without fierceness. The very manner of doing things is changed, even in the commonplace duties, chores, and contacts of everyday living; the way of answering questions, the way of conversing, the exhibiting of charitableness to those who differ—oh, in so many ways, transfigured character communicates itself through transformed disposition and behaviour.

Have we not seen such transformation of character, of personality, of countenance, of disposition and behaviour? It sheds abroad the most winsome of all influence for Christ. It is the most magnetic of all apologetics for the Christian faith. It generally shines out with its most victorious splendour amid life's darkest experiences. With heaven-reflecting eyes, it smiles upon us even through sickness, and somehow gives the thin, wan face of the wearied invalid a soft, gentle light and beauty which transfigure even the mystery of permitted pain. It is indeed the transfiguration which comes from the Holy Spirit's deeper work in the entirely sanctified believer. It is the inner glory-light of inwrought holiness, gleaming through the outer windows of the consecrated personality.

Or, in those words of Romans 12:2, it is "entire renewal of the mind," expressing itself through a metamorphosis *of* character.

Progressive Christlikeness

This brings us to a point where we ought to glance at the other place where Paul uses the verb *"metamorphose"* in connection with transfiguration of character. It is Second Corinthians 3:17-18, "But we all, with unveiled face, beholding [or, possibly, 'reflecting'] as in a mirror the glory of the Lord, are transformed [*metamorphosed*] into the same image, from glory to glory, even as from the Lord, the Spirit."

There is some doubt as to whether Paul here means (1) that *we* are the reflecting mirror, or (2) that our Lord Jesus is the mirror, reflecting "the glory of the LORD," i.e., of Yahweh, or (3) that the Gospel, as the "new covenant" (see verses 6-11) is the mirror, reflecting the glory of Christ. Perhaps number three best fits the context, but, yes or no, the central idea remains the same, namely, that *we,* by beholding with "unveiled face," our glorious Lord, are "transformed into the same image."

It is a striking figure and flashes with meaning for us. Like Romans 12:2, it certainly teaches a transfiguration (metamorphosis) of character. The phrase, here, "with unveiled face," means with unveiled eyes of the *mind.* With our outer, physical eyes, we cannot see our Lord at all, for the present; but, with unveiled *inward* vision, we may see Him as being luminously ever-present to the mind. Let us be quick to notice the four aspects of this character-transfiguration, which are here indicated and blended.

1. *It is transfiguration through communion.* The participle clause, "beholding-as-in-a-mirror" is all one word in the Greek (*katoptrizomenoi*), meaning a beholding or mirroring which is contemporaneous and *going on.* One of the things which we never dare forget, especially in teaching inwrought holiness through consecration and faith, is, that no matter what crisis we may experience or what spiritual elevation may come to us, *no* blessing of the Christian life ever continues with us unless there is continuous communion with Christ. Moreover, this "beholding" or "reflecting" is that kind of communion which we call *contemplation*—of which, in this age of inane rush, there is so little that we are spiritually poverty-stricken.

2. *This transfiguration is progressive.* The verb is in the present tense: *"being* transfigured." In these chapters, we have emphasized that in no sense is inwrought holiness our reaching a fixed point of static sanctity. No, this deeper

renewal within us marks a crisis-point of new departure into a *progressive* transfiguration of character. Heart-holiness is never a reservoir, but, in Frances Ridley Havergal's words, a "river glorious."

3. *This transfiguration is inwrought by the Holy Spirit.* It is "from the Lord the Spirit," that is, it is a result of His activity in the mind. The noteworthy thing is that He affects His transfiguring work through the believer's adoring contemplation of "the glory of the Lord." In Romans 12:2, the transfiguration begins with the "entire renewal of the mind." Here, in 2 Corinthians 3:18, it is developed through communion; through an adoring contemplation, which absorbs into itself the very impress of that beloved heavenly Lord.

4. *This transfiguration is approximating likeness to Christ*—"transformed into the same image." Yes, that is the supreme goal of true, Christian sanctification: to become ever-increasingly conformed in character to the sublime character of Christ, "the Altogether Lovely." Let it be reiterated yet again: entire sanctification, or restoration to holiness, is *not,* according to the New Testament, either a man-achieved or God-inwrought ethical top-level, an accomplished *goal* of moral perfectness; it is restoration from moral and spiritual disease to fullness of health, making possible there from an ever-developing likeness to the character and beauty of the Lord Jesus, who is the ineffable moral loveliness of God Himself in visible embodiment.

Inwrought holiness through "entire renewal of the mind" certainly *is* both restoration to moral fullness of health and an elevation to a new high plane impossible of attainment by merely human struggling; but instead of its being a high level from which we look *down,* conscious of an exalted superiority, it humbles us with a prostration deeper than any ever caused by the heartbreaking repentance of a prodigal returning from his wallowing in the mire. Why? Because, on that higher level of holiness through "entire renewal of the mind," we see as never before, "with unveiled face," the "heavenly vision" of the ineffable, all-holiness and all-loveliness of Jesus; the very "glory of God in the face of Jesus Christ" (2 Cor. 4:6); the one, ultimate attraction of all holy heart-longing; the solitary, absolute all-perfection in the universe; the one-and-only, all-eclipsing, ever-alluring *GOAL* that ever fills the gaze of all the truly sanctified. When once, through inwrought holiness, we have seen *that* exquisite Goal, we never again talk about our own holiness, much less of "perfection"!—for the *nearer* we get to that beatific Goal, so the more do we realize how *far* we are from it. The more truly we approximate to *that* perfection, the less conscious of it we are, and the more humblingly conscious are we of our own *im*perfection. That which lifts us highest brings us lowest.

Is not that the reason why, in this matter of "Christian perfection," John Wesley is far safer as an example than as teacher? However insistently he may have preached and urged "Christian perfection," he never once claimed it. Nay, he *disclaimed* it. In a letter to Dr. William Dodd, he writes, "I tell you flat, I have not attained the character I draw." As time went on, the Wesley teaching of Christian "perfection" became so pared and trimmed that, in reality, it was no more than a self-contradictory concept of *im*perfect perfection.

So, then, to summarize. The supreme purpose of the Holy Spirit's deeper work in us is transfiguration of character. That inward transfiguration begins through "entire renewal of the mind," or inwrought holiness, and is revealed outwardly through transfigured personality, facial expression, disposition, attitude, and behaviour. It develops especially through communion with God. It is not suppositionary ethical immaculateness of the religious perfectionist, but a growing *likeness to Christ.*

Oh, for a deeper knowledge of such character-transfiguration through "entire sanctification"! Is not this inwrought holiness the "perfect love," which "casteth out fear"? (1 John 4:18)—and is not this character-transfiguration that which John means when he says, *"AS HE IS,* even so, are we in this world"? (v. 17)—and is not the most thrilling prospect of the coming Rapture just this: "When He shall appear, we shall be *LIKE HIM"*?

Now, O my King above,
  Now, even more,
Thee for Thyself I love,
  Thee I adore;
For 'tis the glorious loveliness
  Thou art
Which captures and subdues my
  wondering heart.
Now, all my prayer is this:
  More, more of Thee.
Thou art the perfect bliss;
  Live, live through me.
Let me Thy life absorb, diffuse,
  express,
Till heaven itself unveils Thy
  loveliness.

CHAPTER 16

I Met a Man with a Shining Face

Harry E. Jessop

Dr. Harry E. Jessop (1884-1974) was a faithful exponent of the doctrine of holiness and the Spirit-filled life. He was the second president of Chicago Evangelistic Institute (later renamed Vennard College), pastored Northwest Gospel Tabernacle (Chicago), served as editor of the *Heart and Life* periodical, and authored over 20 books. The following article is taken from *I Met a Man with a Shining Face* by Harry E. Jessop.

Editor: An esteemed sister in Christ and a former parishioner of mine, who also possessed a shining face and is now with the Lord, gave me a copy of this book many years ago.

I MET A MAN with a shining face—and I mean really shining. It was a face having upon it the glow of heaven and the glory of God.

Let there be no mistake about it. My language is not mystical; I am not thinking about the face of Moses as described in the Scriptures, neither am I speaking of the face of the Lord Jesus beheld by the eye of faith in contemplative meditation, true though it be that "God, who commanded the light to shine out of darkness, hath shined in our hearts, to give the light of the knowledge of the glory of God in the face of Jesus Christ" (2 Cor. 4:6).

The face was the face of a man, a man of my own generation, a young man, probably not more than ten years my senior. Only a few years before this incident he had entered the Christian ministry, and because of his unswerving loyalty to a newly-discovered spiritual experience to which he declared he must testify, he had met the full force of an unexpected blast of ecclesiastical opposition issuing from a church board composed of men ready to fight for things they considered fundamental, yet without any notion concerning the deep things of God.

They were determined that their church should not be disturbed by this young upstart who was daring to preach such radical notions among them.

To the amazement of all concerned, the opposition did not silence him, and to their further amazement, their persecution did not sour him. When he was denounced, he did not fight back, and when evicted, he quietly withdrew. On being told that in view of his heresy the church could no longer support him, neither would the pulpit be open further for his ministry, he launched out into a life of faith, preaching, like John Wesley, wherever an opening could be found and trusting God to meet his needs. This God did in a marvelous way.

The opposition drove him deeper and still deeper into God, until on his countenance as naturally as his own complexion, there shone the radiance which I have described.

My First Meeting

My first meeting with this man was in the month of May 1906, and, little as I dreamed it then, that meeting was destined to prove the crossroad, which was to lead to the settling of one of the greatest issues of my life.

Certainly, I needed to meet somebody, for spiritually, I had a deep-rooted need. I had known the Lord Jesus in saving power for more than five years. My conversion had been intensely real. It was so very definite that I knew the date. It had produced an incontrovertible testimony which I found it a delight to give. I knew I had been born again. It happened on the last Sunday of January 1901, about four o'clock in the afternoon. That day I had come into personal contact with Jesus Christ and had received my pardon at His hand. I passed from death unto life; the Spirit's witness came into my heart.

So real and definite was all this that all who knew me became aware of the marked change that had taken place. From that moment to the time at which I now write, the fact of my salvation has never once been in doubt.

Yet I was puzzled—sadly puzzled. Somehow, within my experience, Scripture and the practical outworkings did not agree. Certainly, I could find isolated verses, which taken from their context and separated from their historical setting, would for the moment silence my heart cry and condone my defeat, but my trouble was that my heart cry would not remain silenced, and when I honestly faced my defeats in my Lord's presence in the place of prayer, I was utterly ashamed.

My Search

I had only a little knowledge at that time concerning the laws of Bible exegesis, yet I felt within my soul that those verses—often only parts of verses—so often emphasized by my religious teachers in support of their "must sin every day in thought, word and deed" theory, did not represent full-orbed Bible truth, and that such a theory was not worthy of the price my Lord had paid for my redemption. There were other Scriptures which, to say the least, did not emphasize that phase, and although at the time the thought seemed so strangely contradictory, I became increasingly conscious that somewhere there must be a key which as yet I had not found.

Among the numerous Scripture passages which troubled me was Paul's magnificent declaration. "Nay, in all these things, we are more than conquerors through him that loved us" (Rom. 8:37). When I honestly faced such a declaration, I knew that my experience did not match it. Not that I ever hoped to match it in the things which this mighty warrior of the Cross actually endured, but I felt very definitely that God expected me to be as gloriously triumphant in my circumstances as Paul had been in his.

When at length, I ventured to voice such a thought among my religious associates, they insisted that I was taking the Bible far too literally. It did not mean, they declared, that we could be conquerors in everything but in things in general. To make the Bible apply to every detail was going too far. "And yet," they went on to say, "in reality, you are more than a conqueror, because Christ is the conqueror and you are in Him. You, of course, are always failing, but all the time, His victory is put to your account. He conquered on Calvary, and even though every day you may fall and be defeated, you are credited with what He has done, not with what you are doing, therefore in the sight of God, defeated as you are, you are more than a conqueror."

Frankly, I did not know what to make of it. It seemed to me that if this was the best God had to offer, Christ and Calvary were set to condone rather than to conquer. It did not seem to make sense, and certainly, it did not bring glory to God. The more I thought and prayed about it, the more puzzled I became.

It was during this time of spiritual perplexity that I met my friend with the shining face, and by that period, God had graciously prepared me for the meeting. I shall always believe that just as definitely as Philip was sent to meet the eunuch by the way of Gaza and Paul was directed to the disciples at Ephesus, that man was divinely placed in my path that day. How that face did shine! If my own experience perplexed me, that face perplexed me more. It betokened an evident satisfaction, for it radiated a rare spiritual glow. Young and inexperienced as I was in the things of God, I could detect the difference between this spiritual glow and a natural grin. But how had that glow of spiritual satisfaction come there? What deep divine secret had he found?

The Disturbing Question

Then came my second surprise; it was in the form of a question. It became evident that the interest was not all on one side; that while I had been studying him, he, too, had been studying me, and had rightly appraised my inward need. It seemed as though he had been looking down into the deep places of my spiritual nature, had seen my emptiness, and recognized my hunger.

"Brother," said he, "have you been baptized with the Holy Ghost and fire?" To say the question surprised me would be, to put it mildly indeed. I was startled, almost stunned. A later contemplation of that hour has seemed to bring a comparison with the incident of Paul and the Ephesian disciples as recorded in Acts 19:1-7. Acknowledging their present experience, yet recognizing their apparent lack, he inquired, "Have ye received the Holy Ghost since ye believed?" So puzzled were these men that in their perplexity, they stammered out, "We have not so much as heard whether there be any Holy Ghost." It could hardly be that they were entirely unaware of the existence of the third Person of the Trinity; surely Apollos, their pastor, had at least taught them that. What they seem to be saying is exactly what I said to my questioner nearly nineteen centuries later, when hardly knowing how to frame my reply, 1 said, "I don't know what you mean by being baptized with the Holy Ghost and fire, but if that is it that shines on your face, I want it."

The Story

He then began to tell me his story, the substance of which was as follows:

"There was a time when I was as hungry-hearted as you are today, but I did not know what it was I was hungry for. Following my ordination, I had gone to my first church, a keen young minister with lots in my head but with a heart that was becoming lean and dry. My sermons were intellectual and were, I fear, designed to please rather than to convict. After some weeks of my ministry, I was met at the foot of the pulpit stairs one Sunday morning by a strange little woman—at least that was my estimate of her at the time—who shook my hand cordially, smiled at me sweetly, and then amazed me by saying, 'Young man, that was a very clever sermon you preached this morning, but do you know you are as blind as a bat? I am praying for you,' and before I had time to recover from my astonishment, she had disappeared.

"Now whether that old lady showed the best judgment in the way she approached me, might, of course, provide a subject for discussion. Certainly, I was not flattered by her remark, and I did not fail to show it. It is not to my credit when I say I began to make pointed remarks in my sermons, especially for her benefit, and for these, later, I found it necessary to make an open apology. The thing that puzzled me, however, was that she never argued with me. The more cutting my remarks became, the more she beamed, and each time she met me, she greeted me with a warm 'God bless you! I am praying for you,' and much as I hated to acknowledge it, I knew deep down in my heart that the strange old lady, as I had chosen to call her, possessed something to which I was a total stranger.

"At last I could bear it no longer, and going to her with my hungry heart, I asked her to forgive me, pray for me, and tell me the secret of her radiant experience. She told me that since the first day I entered the church, she had prayed and intended to continue as long as I remained. Then looking me straight in the eyes, she asked, 'Did you ever hear about the Second Blessing?' 'No!' I replied, 'I have never heard of it. What is it?' 'Well,' said she, 'it is what John Wesley preached [Wesley refrained from using this term], what the Bible teaches, and what I've got. Everybody ought to have it, and God wants you to have it.' I asked the old lady to pray that God would give me that experience. She did; I began to pray for it myself; I placed all I had on the altar of consecration, and God met my need. Thank God I have the blessing today."

As I stood in that humble Yorkshire home, the earnestness of spirit in my new-found friend, and the evident satisfaction he enjoyed only made me hunger the more. For the first time in my life, I felt I was looking into the face of a man who really knew God and found complete satisfaction in Him. He did not seek to press me into any undue acceptance of doctrine, but with an earnestness that was deep and meaningful, he said, "And brother, God can do the same thing for you." He invited me to attend a holiness convention to be held in the city two days later and then said goodbye.

The following Thursday found me attending my first holiness convention. The afternoon service only tended to increase my hunger and my determination to have that hunger satisfied.

I remained between meetings for tea and fellowship. I was not at ease, for I did not know what to talk about. These men seemed to live in a realm to which I was a stranger; they talked about things which bewildered me. To them, God seemed to be so intensely real. The Bible was a book which they seemed to think had been written especially for their benefit. They talked about the promises God had given them, about things they had been led to do, and so on.

That night David Thomas, a London dry goods dealer, preached. Preached, did I say? Measured by canons of homiletics, it was a poor sermon indeed. Evidently, he was not a trained preacher, but as I learned afterward, a businessman who delighted to give both time and money to the proclamation of full salvation truth. Yet, whatever may be said of his sermon, there was no doubt about his message. It would have been a very dull member of that congregation who missed what he was trying to say. He preached with an unction that betokened a divine indwelling. There was something about both message and messenger, which only the fact of an indwelling God could explain.

The message was based on Acts 1:8, "But ye shall receive power, after that the Holy Ghost is come upon you; and ye shall be witnesses unto me." The Holy Ghost! It thrilled my soul to hear this man use the term. The Holy Ghost! He was to come upon me! To possess me! To use me! It seemed too good to be true, and yet God's Word said it; therefore, it must be true.

That night found me kneeling as a seeker at the altar of prayer.... From that night onward, I was never the same man again.

Jesus, Rose of Sharon

Jesus, Rose of Sharon, bloom within my heart;
Beauties of Thy truth and holiness impart,
That where'er I go my life may shed abroad
Fragrance of the knowledge of the love of God.

Jesus, Rose of Sharon, sweeter far to me
Than the fairest flow'rs of earth could ever be,
Fill my life completely, adding more each day
Of Thy grace divine and purity, I pray.

Jesus, Rose of Sharon, balm for ev'ry ill,
May Thy tender mercy's healing power distill
For afflicted souls of weary, burdened men,
Giving needy mortals health and hope again.

Jesus, Rose of Sharon, bloom forevermore;
Be Thy glory seen on earth from shore to shore,
Till the nations own Thy Sov'reignty complete,
Lay their honors down and worship at Thy feet.

- Ida A. Guirey

CHAPTER 17

The Story Behind *Streams in the Desert*

Lettie Cowman & Ed Erny

Listed among the twenty most widely read books of all time, *Streams in the Desert* was born out of the suffering that Lettie Cowman (1870-1960) endured during her husband Charles' six-year battle with heart disease. Lettie was the wife of Charles Cowman (1868-1924), founder of the Oriental Missionary Society (now One Mission Society).

Streams in the Desert is a daily devotional compiled by Lettie Cowman from various sermons, writings, and poetry she had read over the years. The immense popularity of this book has allowed multiple editions to be printed. This article is taken from *The Story Behind Streams in the Desert*, copyright © 1994 OMS International.

MY MOTHER, for many years a close friend of Lettie Cowman, once asked Mrs. Cowman, "How do you account for the fact that *Streams* is so much more popular than your other books?" After a moment's silence, Lettie looked at mother with the dramatic solemnity that marked her public speaking. "Esther," she said quietly, *"Streams* was born. The other books were written."

In reading Lettie Cowman's 1924 diary, the reader is ushered into the inner sanctum of two lives subjected to excruciating torment, a fiery crucible from which *Streams in the Desert* sprang. To appreciate this diary, it is important that the reader know something of the events leading to the drama of 1924, climaxing in the death of Charles Cowman, Lettie's husband.

Conversions

As a young man, Charles Cowman was a prominent executive in the Western Union office in Chicago. Though he had a pious upbringing, he was convinced that one could simply not live a committed Christian life and succeed in the hurly-burly Chicago business world. His wife, Lettie, came from a distinguished banking family. Charles and Lettie had been childhood sweethearts, back in Iowa. Lettie, whose refinement was immediately apparent to all who met her, loved music, particularly opera. It was this that drew her to Grace Methodist Church one evening in 1892 to hear a converted opera singer. At the invitation, Lettie went to the altar, kneeling among a cluster of children to receive Christ as her Savior.

Lettie could be persuasive, and thus despite his reservations, Charles a short time later found himself at a revival service at the same Grace Methodist Church. In giving the invitation, the evangelist departed from the traditional form. He asked that Christians come to the front to pray while the unconverted remained in their seats.

Lettie rose from her seat and walked slowly down the long aisle, leaving Charles behind. As her husband watched, it seemed a great gulf was widening between him and his beloved. After the service, Charles was in torment. When they arrived home, without even turning on the light, he fell on his knees, and with tears of repentance, asked Christ into his heart.

Charles, never one to do things halfheartedly, was a living embodiment of the "all or nothing" principle. The following day he led his colleague, Ernest Kilbourne, to Christ, and in the months that followed, they proceeded to bring seventy-five of their fellow telegraphers to the Savior. Eventually, these men formed The Telegraphers' Band, an organization that sought to network with telegraphmen throughout the continent in an evangelistic outreach. At the same time, Cowman opened a small mission for derelicts in a Chicago slum known as "Little Hell."

God's Call to Serve

In God's providence, two events now impacted the lives of Charles and Lettie Cowman. These resulted in their giving up their lucrative and comfortable lives in Chicago for Japan and a lifetime commitment to foreign missions.

The first of these was a missionary meeting led by A. B. Simpson, the famed founder of the Christian and Missionary Alliance. At the appeal for contributions, Charles pulled out a wad of bills, his entire week's salary, and dropped it into the offering plate. Lettie did the same with her diamond wedding ring. When an invitation for volunteers followed, the Cowmans walked forward to offer themselves for missionary service.

A short time later, Cowman and Kilbourne met a Japanese minister at Grace Methodist Church. Juji Nakada had come to Moody Bible Institute to, as he said, "get filled with the Holy Spirit." A unique bond was forged between the three men with the result that in 1901 Cowman and Nakada opened the Central Gospel Mission in the heart of Tokyo. Ernest Kilbourne joined them a year later.

Thus, The Oriental Missionary Society and the Japan Holiness Church were born. In time, the work spread throughout Asia and later into South America and Europe. In 1907, Korean students came to Tokyo to be trained in the OMS Bible School. This was the beginning of what one day would be the largest church ever planted by a faith mission in Asia.

Observing the effectiveness of his colleague, Nakada, Cowman concluded, "If Japan is to be won, it will be won, not by Western missionaries, but by trained, Spirit-filled nationals. Hence the most important thing a missionary can do is to devote himself to the training of nationals." This dictated the strategy of OMS work in every country. Cowman called it, "the pattern shown us on the mount."

A new dimension to Cowman's work and vision was 1911. Discovering that missionary effort was, for the most part, concentrated in the large cities to the neglect of the interior villages, he resolved to, as literally as possible, fulfill the great commission by reaching every home in Japan with the Gospel. Cowman and Kilbourne organized, later joined by young volunteers from the United States, to walk across Japan placing scriptures in every home. The campaign completed in 1918 had put scripture portions in Japan's 10,400,000 homes.

This effort, called the Great Village Campaign, later known as the Every Creature Crusade, was duplicated in Korea, China, and other OMS fields.

Cowman gave himself unsparingly to the task of missions. He had a relentless passion. One colleague recalled that "whenever the evangelization of the Orient was mentioned, his soul took fire and you felt he would die a martyr through his own fervor. He belonged to the class of martyrs whose love for souls made an early holocaust of the physical man."

Said another friend, "He was on fire for souls. I do not know that he ever took a vacation from the time he went to the field until his fatal breakdown."

Oswald Chambers, who visited the OMS work in Japan, said, "The thing that strikes you about Charles Cowman is his absolute abandonment to Jesus Christ."

The *Desert* Begins

On August 15, 1917, as the Every Creature Crusade was nearing completion, Cowman wrote in his diary, "Experienced a strange pain in my heart in the night, but prayed and it left me. I can see no place to stop in the work."

Within a year, however, it was clear that he could not continue. "Worn out" was the doctor's diagnosis. Only an immediate change of climate and prolonged rest would save his life, the physician warned.

Early one morning that fall, Charles Cowman, with his wife Lettie, boarded the steamer that was to take them forever from his beloved island home. A group of workers and students were there, and Mrs. Cowman recalled they felt a "strange presentiment that their next meeting would be in the presence of the King. But Charles bade them farewell with the same old cheery smile and assured them that he would soon be well and back at his post again."

On the boat, he turned to his wife. "I love them so dearly," he wept. "How utterly vain to express the emotion of my soul. No, never can any finite being know. Never."

In California, Charles recovered a measure of health, and with strength came the restless urge to communicate the burden of the Orient to Christians in America. He set out, and for six months, he mounted platforms from California to Michigan, telling the miracle story of the Village Campaign.

Everywhere he went, he carried a large map of Japan and Korea. Standing beside it, he would point to the areas marked in red, indicating the provinces covered by the crusade teams. Often he would break down and weep as he recalled the struggles and the triumphs.

But the candle of his life was burning low. That summer, while on the train nearing Owosso, Michigan, he was stricken with a severe heart attack and was unable to proceed. "You must stop your public work at once," the doctor insisted. "Return to California and rest. Frankly," he said, "your work is at an end."

Healing Withheld

To fully appreciate the drama of these years of invalidism leading to Charles' death in September 1924, we must understand the influence of A. B. Simpson on the Cowmans. If Charles and Lettie had a hero, it was A. B. Simpson. They had answered God's call to the mission field under his ministry and had patterned their little work in many ways after the Christian and Missionary Alliance.

The mission statement of faith reflected Simpson's strong position on the subject of healing. As a young minister, Simpson had been struck down, debilitated, his life work apparently finished. As he sought God in prayer, he gained insight on the subject of faith healing and the doctrine of "healing in the atonement," derived from scriptures like Isaiah 53:5, "and by his stripes we are healed." As a result, the young minister was totally and completely healed, gifted with a heretofore unknown vitality. He moved to New York, pastored a huge downtown church, and founded the Christian and Missionary Alliance. He also pioneered a score of other enterprises. His evangelistic campaigns were marked now by a strong, unapologetic emphasis on healing. So much so, that he was characterized in the secular press as a "fanatical faith healer."

The Cowmans and Kilbournes, deeply influenced by Simpson, espoused the same views, and in their work, likewise placed great stress on healing. They frequently held healing services, laid hands on the sick, and saw many in this way restored to health. Like Simpson, they believed "healing, like the forgiveness of sins, is provided for through the blood of Jesus Christ; and it is the Christian's privilege and right to exercise faith and thus appropriate healing power for all human disease." Failure to obtain healing, they believed indicated some deficiency of faith. Echoes of these sentiments appeared throughout Charles' and Lettie's diaries.

Hence, when the pronouncement of doom came from the lips of physicians, the Cowman's response was simple and automatic. Though Charles was suffering and there was doubtless divine purpose in that, in time, God would glorify Himself in Charles' body through miraculous healing and full restoration of the warrior to the field of battle.

In Lettie's biography of Charles Cowman entitled *Missionary Warrior,* she writes,

> His faith in God's power to heal never wavered throughout the six years, a perseverance so characteristic of the man. He fought day and night with what was considered unbelief that prevented the healing touch and felt that something must be lacking in his prayers. Days and weeks were spent in searching the Word, and he kept on praying. Indeed his every breath was a cry for life for his broken body. When the best physicians told him plainly he could never hope to recover, he only smiled and replied, "But they do not know that God can heal when the case is impossible. Most of the people whom Jesus healed during the earthly ministry were impossibles." Nothing staggered his faith. Often he attempted to act out his faith and taking a few feeble steps, he would walk slowly for a block or so until the heart weakness would seize him. Then he would sit on a curbstone for an hour or more, waiting for strength to return home. After such attempts, there would be added weakness for days and even weeks.
>
> Thousands of people were praying for him, and nothing was a greater stimulus to his faith than the letters received during those years. Several times when life seemed to be ebbing away, and he was being tested to the

uttermost concerning his recovery, a message would be received that would give a momentary lift. Hope would revive, and a fresh grip be taken upon the promises for healing. A letter was received from a beloved missionary in South Africa. It read, "Last Sabbath I asked my congregation of Zulus to join with me in prayer for your healing and one after another prayed. One big black chief, who has been recently converted, prayed with tears rolling over his cheeks, and it almost overwhelmed me."

B. H. Pearson, Lettie Cowman's biographer, in his book, *The Vision Lives*, writes,

> Charles desires to go to a public healing service, and she takes him. Hundreds of sick are waiting to be prayed for. The man lays his hands on Charles and prays. Charles feels strengthened. After a luncheon, they ride with the minister until four o'clock, and the weakness does not reappear. A great hope is dawning. The Christian doctor lays hands on Charles and prays for him. An outstanding Christian leader comes. He says, "Charles, I have come to anoint you and pray for your healing." How to explain the fearful attack that night?
>
> She must confess that the more they pray, apparently the less the answer. Seemingly there is no response from God. So pressed are they over this that they scarcely know where they are or what they believe. But she must cling to the Word. It is His will to heal. The Word says so. Charles believes in divine healing. With all of his heart, he has always believed it. "Healing is the children's bread," he would say. "A crumb picked up under the table was sufficient for healing the Syrophenician daughter." Why then should he not be healed? He weeps when friends discuss it. He is so hungry for healing.

Streams in the Desert

It is out of this context that *Streams in the Desert* is born. The ever-darkening valley through which the Cowmans pass lasts a long, an incredibly long, torturous six years. And from the standpoint of physical healing, it is marked by slowly diminishing hope. Gale winds of unanswered questions are battering them.

In a desperate effort to fortify her trembling faith and find comfort for her breaking heart, Lettie lives in the Word. Beyond this, she begins to seek out the great writings that have sustained the saints in years gone by. She develops a ravenous appetite for this precious food for comfort. When she has exhausted their personal library and that of their friends, she begins to haunt the Los Angeles' second-hand bookstores. Again and again in her writing crop up words such as, "enjoyed the bookstores today ... Was in second-hand bookstores ... Charles and I went to bookstores."

From this treasure trove of collected writings, she begins to prepare devotionals which she sends to *God's Revivalist,* published by their friends at God's Bible School in Cincinnati. These writings appear in each issue under the title, "Thoughts for the Quiet Hour."

There seems something almost uncanny about the way she day by day discovers devotional readings and words of encouragement that perfectly suit their situation. Throughout her life, in fact, she felt that God, in some sweet providential way brought to her the materials that would one day find their way into her books, and become a source of blessing to millions. "I do not find material," she once said. "Materials come to me, fly to me, from all over the world—in an unlikely tract, an old faded booklet, crumpled church bulletin, a tattered songbook."

These collected writings published first in *God's Revivalist* became the famed daily devotional, *Streams in the Desert*—the title deriving from Isaiah 35:6.

Lessons Learned in God's School of Suffering

January 1924 begins the sixth year of the Cowman's ordeal. Though a fierce resolve to appropriate by faith the long-delayed healing is in no way relinquished (and is reflected on nearly every page of her journal throughout the early months of the year), entries begin to reflect a thought process which might be summarized as follows:

1. God is delaying Charles' healing for some mysterious purpose, one which we cannot begin to comprehend. More than this, through the fires of testing, He is accomplishing in me a very necessary death in order to more perfectly endue me with His life.

On January 28 she wrote,

When we got up after a restless night, the thought came to me, "Why things are just the very same and no visible change whatever." Instantly, the words came from the Lord, Isaiah 56:9, "Shall I bring to the birth and not cause to bring forth." It was wonderful to my soul. I scarcely know just what the Lord is doing, but He is doing something which we shall see with our eyes. I am sure we have come to the birth of something in our experience, which shall be wonderful.

On Sunday, February 17, she writes, "I read Psalm 66 and Job, and God witnessed to it. I see it as never before. God is breaking down our own humanity, and that is the meaning of this prolonged trial. God was dealing with Job humanly, and he had to pass under the crucible."

The most oft-read passage of scripture during these months is Exodus 14, which chronicles Israel's crisis at the Red Sea, with the great body of water hemming them in on one side and Pharaoh's approaching armies of doom on the other. This for Lettie symbolizes their position, one which from the human standpoint is utterly hopeless. Yet like Moses, she feels that God is saying to them, "Fear not, stand still and ye shall see the salvation of the Lord" (Ex. 14:13). This chapter was read, again, and again, the pages marked, annotated, and wept over.

2. As Charles' condition worsens, a new thought begins to express itself in Lettie's writings: Perhaps, after all, it is not God's will to heal Charles. In fact, He may very well not heal him, but God is accomplishing here in this mysterious furnace, something even greater than healing.

Her entry for June 28 reads:

A memorable day when God said, "There is more than healing." There came to me today a thought that I believe was given me of God that there is something greater than healing for us. God may have a far deeper purpose than just healing. We shall yet see it. Now I feel that instead of confining myself to pray for Charles' healing, God will lead me out in the direction He would have me walk in. God is using this affliction to teach us of Himself, and when it is complete, we shall find we have much more than healing.

Part of her entry for August 2 reads,

I have been much impressed that God was wanting me to restfully wait for Him. For what? He has not told me, but He will show me His glory as He has promised, and it will be so exceeding abundantly above all I could ask or think that it will make up a thousand-fold for the delay and strangeness of it all. God does things on a grand scale, and He knows just what He is doing in this case.

While I was ironing about 3 p.m., He gently whispered, "In some happy, bright tomorrow" and the thought came He was speaking of a tomorrow in heaven, but when I took the hymnal, it impressed me differently. It is the hymn, "Trust and Rest." He said, "Be content to accept things you cannot understand, wait patiently, presently I will reveal to you the treasures of darkness, the riches of the glory of the mystery." Mystery is only the veil of God's face. Do not be afraid to enter into the cloud that is settling down on your life. God is in it. The other side is radiant with His glory. "Think it not strange concerning the fiery trial which is to try you as though some strange thing happened unto you, but rejoice inasmuch as you are partakers of Christ's suffering." God is nigh. He is in the dark cloud. Plunge into the blackness of its darkness without flinching. Under the shrouding curtain of His pavilion, you will find God awaiting you.

The final months of Charles' life are ones of excruciating pain. He finds it impossible to sleep for more than a few minutes at a time, and to find relief, he must be kept in a sitting position. The doctor begins administering morphine. At one point, Lettie tries to give him chloroform. The strain is telling on Lettie, and she begins to suffer from weakness and heart problems of her own.

In August, Lydia Bemmels, a devout woman and gentle nurse offers her services. She is a God-send and is destined to be Lettie's companion throughout most of the remainder of her life. Others volunteer to come in evenings and sit up with Charles. At one point, Lettie goes seven days without a night's rest.

3. The month of September, there comes to Lettie the final disclosure of God's purpose in the long ordeal. Charles is clearly on the threshold of death. She has relinquished him to the Lord. Healing, it seems, is not a part of His plan for her husband. A friend accompanies her to the Hollywood cemetery to choose a burial plot.

Nevertheless, God's plan and purposes are not to be aborted by Charles' death. His vision and his mission will be, in fact, extended for many years through her own ministry. She is convinced that far from this being the end, she is about to enter upon a whole new life for which all that she has experienced hitherto has been but a preparation.

On September 21, Lettie wrote, "I shall see the glory as God promised in the days ahead. I yield to Him absolute control of my life, my all. 'I will make the darkness light before them.'"

The next day, in her September 22 entry, she wrote, "God had a plan to bless the world through Mary and Martha, but their brother died. I have thy promise, O Lord, and if thou dost take my loved one, I shall see thy glory somewhere. Only God can interpret this strange dealing. I leave it wholly to thee, O my Father."

And then on the 24th, the day before Charles' passing, she writes,

"In quietness and confidence shall be your strength." Shall we let the Lord make us a new creation in Christ Jesus, old things passing away and all things becoming new? Shall we let Christ be our head and henceforth our thinking and planning and managing, and we be ready as a body to take our place and follow all His commands, walking in obedience and having Him glorified in our lives, as well as our work? Expect God to do the work, count Him faithful who has promised to work in you. To will is to do. We do the reckoning; He does the slaying.

The pages of Lettie's diary for 1924 are, in effect, the distillation of experiences and thoughts that had been in process since Charles' first attack in 1917. The trials of faith, dark agony, physical, spiritual and emotional torment—the whole matrix from which *Streams in the Desert* was born—is best seen in these pages, which epitomize Charles and Lettie Cowman's experience. So the 1924 diary events give dramatic expression to all that had been going on in a lesser degree through the preceding five years.

Take My Life, and Let It Be

Take my life, and let it be
Consecrated, Lord, to Thee;
Take my moments and my days,
Let them flow in ceaseless praise.

Take my hands, and let them move
At the impulse of Thy love;
Take my feet and let them be
Swift and beautiful for Thee.

Take my voice, and let me sing
Always, only, for my King;
Take my lips, and let them be
Filled with messages from Thee.

Take my silver and my gold;
Not a mite would I withhold;
Take my intellect, and use
Every power as Thou shalt choose.

Take my will, and make it Thine;
It shall be no longer mine.
Take my heart; it is Thine own;
It shall be Thy royal throne.

- Frances Havergal

CHAPTER 18

Power from on High

Leslie D. Wilcox

Leslie D. Wilcox (1907-1991) was converted at the age of 16 in a Wesleyan Methodist Church revival service in Silver Creek, New York, at which time his parents and siblings were also converted. He was a graduate of God's Bible School & College (Th.B.), University of Cincinnati (M.A.), and received an honorary degree from God's Bible School & College (D.D). During his ministerial career, Dr. Wilcox served his Lord as a pastor, church administrator, author, and preeminently as a college professor. As a college teacher, he taught New Testament Greek, Bible, and theology. Dr. Wilcox loved language; he was proficient in Spanish, Hebrew, German, Greek, Italian, and developed a working knowledge of ten others. The following article is taken from *Power from on High* by Leslie D. Wilcox.

Editor: Dr. Wilcox was my first New Testament Studies and New Testament Greek professor; he was also my first church administrator. I will be forever indebted to him for his Christlike example and teaching expertise.

And, behold, I send the promise of my Father upon you: but tarry ye in the city of Jerusalem, until ye be endued with power from on high.
Luke 24:49 KJV

NOTE THE THREE FEATURES stressed by the promise that the disciples were to be endued with "power from on high."

A Positive Experience

Sometimes we have so strongly stressed the cleansing aspect of the work of entire sanctification that we may have tended to give the impression that it is merely a subtraction. The stress is usually placed on purging or purifying, eradication or removal of carnal traits, or on release from the inner power of sin. All of these are true and deserve their place in any exposition of the second work of grace. But we must not forget that there is a positive side. A new power is added. An inner fortification is accomplished. This is the true meaning of all the language that talks about a baptism with the Spirit. Jesus' promises in John 14-16, especially stress what the Spirit will do for us when He comes. And this is the thrust of this promise. There is to be an enduement. This is an addition. There is a cleansing but an empowerment as well.

An Experience Affecting Character

One of the expressions used in our text is the word enduement. I suspect that this and the accompanying word power have tended to make many persons think only of the miraculous, the supernatural, the unusual manifestation. When we put all the stress on this, or even a major stress, we depart from the basic meaning of Pentecost. The whole charismatic movement is based on a misunderstanding of the basic meaning of what the baptism with the Spirit is supposed to do for men. *Miracle* is one of their favorite bywords. They are more concerned with doing something that is eye-catching and attention-getting than they are in finding holiness of heart, of character, and of life. An examination of the word "endue" will help us at this point.

"Endue" is almost an exact repetition of the Greek word it comes from. But it has taken on overtones in English that lead us away from its basic meaning. The word means basically "to clothe." It is used literally of wearing clothes in many passages. The following analysis will show its use in the New Testament.

The word is found 28 times, of which 13 refer to the literal wearing of garments, including such times as John the Baptist's camel hair garments, Christ's purple robe, and the angels and saints in Revelation wearing fine linen. Then it is used five times, mostly in 1 Corinthians 15, of the putting on of the new resurrection body. This is literal also, although in a slightly changed application. This leaves ten times when it is used of a figurative "putting on" of some spiritual quality, equipment, or characteristic; four of these times it refers to putting on the armor of God. Twice it urges us to put on Christ, and twice it is a command to put on the new man. This leaves two other passages, the text, and a very significant passage in Colossians 3:12, which reads as follows, "Put on, therefore, as the elect of God, holy and beloved, bowels of mercies, kindness, humbleness of mind, meekness, longsuffering." Let us tabulate these so we can see how the whole thrust of this word points to a transformed character. According to these passages, we are to be "endued" as follows:

- endued with the armor of God

- endued with the new man
- endued with the Lord Jesus Christ
- endued with mercy, kindness, humbleness, meekness, and longsuffering
- Endued with power from on high

Does not this list give a splendid example of what that enduement means? Whether or not it is exactly the same things as those given in the list above, this certainly indicates a new quality of life, a new protection from the attacks of evil, a new power to withstand such attacks, and a new and deeper manifestation of the Christ-spirit, when the believer is endued with power from on high.

An Experience Producing Strength

The word for "power" that is used in this passage has also been interpreted in ways that have had misleading effects. It is frequently noted that the English word dynamite comes from this Greek word. This leaves the impression this power is of an explosive nature, or at least that it produces a big bang. This impression of something very conspicuous or arresting is very unfortunate. Why do we not note that the English words dynamo and dynamic also come from the same Greek word? These words would suggest an idea much more to the point and much nearer the meaning of the original word.

To examine the Greek word which is here translated power would involve a more detailed study than we can give in this booklet. The word covers a wide range of circumstances and applications, but its basic meaning is *ability*, since it comes from the Greek word that means to be able. Certainly, a man needs a new inner ability if he is to live a life of holiness both inwardly and outwardly. But since this word power has been misused by certain considerations in connection with it, these basic considerations will be indicated by the next three section headings.

Meaning of "Power" in this Context

The Greek word, which is translated "power," occurs 120 times in the New Testament. Of these 120 times, the King James Version uses the translation power only 77 times. Since the word is used so frequently, to examine in detail all the ways in which it is used would be impossible. So we will limit our study to places where the word is used in connection with the word "Spirit" and so would relate to the context of our study.

Two times in Romans 15, we find these two words associated. In verse 13, the power of the Holy Ghost is described as producing "joy, peace and hope." In verse 19, Paul tells of the Spirit's work in his own ministry, producing mighty "signs and wonders" so that he was enabled to preach fully the gospel of Christ. In comparing these two passages, we observe that for an apostle, there was power to make the message effective, while for the common believers, the same power produced inward spiritual results.

Another passage that links the word power with the Spirit is 2 Timothy 1:17, which reads, "God hath not given us the spirit of fear; but of power and of love, and of a sound mind." Here the power associated with the Spirit is not something miraculous or spectacular, but an inner fortitude and transformation which enables one not to be ashamed of the testimony of our Lord as the following verse points out. These passages are enough to show us that the Power of the promised Spirit is always inner, spiritual strengthening, and may, on occasions when needed, be an enabling force for the spread of the Gospel. The power that we need to look for is not a power of a Samson or a Hercules, but the power of a Barnabas, who was a man full of the Holy Ghost. There is no record that he ever performed a miracle or preached a mighty stirring sermon, but he was a man who stood in the gap, a man with a spiritual vision to see possibilities and then step in and do whatever was needed. Yet he was a man who was not merely filled with the Holy Ghost on some mighty occasion, but one whose settled steady character is described as "full of the Holy Ghost" (Acts 11:24).

To conclude our consideration of the meaning of "power" in this context, we go back to our list of scriptures which described what happened at Pentecost, and to Peter's identifications of the meaning of those passages. We remember that one identification which Peter made was that the baptism of the Holy Ghost produced a purifying of their hearts. So here is the real heart of power. It is the power of purity, cleansing the heart, providing an inward strength and stamina, which were impossible as long as there were remains of sin in the heart. But now the source of weakness has been purged away, and with it a new enabling of the Holy Ghost has come. This is the real heart of power without which all other kinds of power or claims to power, turn out to be but a mere sham in the eyes of God.

Miracle Power

One of the doctrinal emphasis that one finds today is to the effect that the baptism of the Spirit is proved or authenticated by power to work miracles. Much emphasis is placed upon miracle-working power, and this is supposed to be a return to New Testament Christianity. But let us examine these claims a bit in the light of the Word.

It is claimed that miracles are to be expected today because "Jesus Christ is the same yesterday, today and forever." The implication is that whatever Christ did when on earth, His disciples can do today. There are two difficulties with taking this scripture in this way. In the first place, the passage (Heb. 13:8) does not say what this usage infers. It says that Christ is unchanging. That is to say, that He is the same in nature, in power, in essential being. But it does not say that He does the same things today as He did then. Manifestly, He does not. He is not now on the earth in His human bodily form as He once was in Galilee. He is not now doing the many things that He once did during His earthly ministry. So the text cannot possibly prove that He now does whatever He once did. He once created worlds, but He is not now employed in creation. An unchanging Christ, whose power is unchanging and unchangeable may not necessarily always manifest that power in the same way. So the text does not prove what it is claimed to teach.

Furthermore, the very persons who appeal to this text to prove the present possibility of miracle-working power, are not consistent in their application. Jesus wrought miracles which they do not. They seem to specialize in certain areas. Healing, speaking in tongues, material riches, and handling snakes seem to be the special areas which this general group prefers, although they do not all emphasize or practice all of them. But if Jesus' power in working miracles is now to be duplicated by those who have this special power, where are the multiplied loaves and fishes, where is the water changed to wine, where are the corpses called out of a cemetery? If Jesus is "the same," these should be duplicated as well as others, should they not?

But the basic assumption back of this claim to work miracles is the belief that miracles authenticate the Gospel, or at least they authenticate the fact that a person has received the baptism with the Holy Ghost. We feel this claim is false and unscriptural.

We fully believe that God answers prayer in healing sick bodies, in supplying material needs and in many other ways of blessing for the good of His children. But these answers to prayer are not an authentication of any spiritual possession or experience. Miracles were used as an authentication for the ministry of Christ and His apostles in the beginning of the Gospel. This is plainly declared in Hebrews 2:4, where we read that God bore these early Gospel preachers witness with "signs, wonders and divers miracles and gifts of the Holy Ghost." This plainly appeals to these mighty works as proof that this message, which began to be spoken by the Lord, was from heaven. Jesus Himself appealed to the works that He did as a proof of His commission from heaven. In John 14:11, He says, "Believe me for the very works' sake." In other passages, such as John 10:37-38, He uses essentially the same appeal. But while Jesus and His apostles could appeal to miracles for authentication, we cannot do that today.

For our day, a very different situation is found. Jesus looked ahead, and He told of those who would claim the right to eternal life because they had done many wonderful works (Matt. 7:21-23). But Jesus called them "workers of iniquity" and His treatment of this subject is found in the passage where He describes false prophets. The danger of appeal to miracles as proof of God's approbation in our day is further shown when we are told of the miracle-working power which the Antichrist will be able to exercise. Certainly, his miracles would not prove that he was from God!

All of this has been said to expose the fallacy of supposing that the power given by the baptism with the Holy Ghost is miracle-working power. It is *primarily moral and spiritual power*, manifested in the ability, the stamina, the strength, needed to be a holy person through and through.

Power for Service

While there are those who stress miracles as proof of the power of the Holy Spirit, there are others who place an almost exclusive emphasis on the power for service. They draw this emphasis from Acts 1:8, where the promise of receiving power is coupled with being witnesses. Those who make this their strong emphasis also deny that the baptism with the Holy Ghost delivers from sin. For this reason, holiness people have usually tended to avoid this interpretation in their effort to keep the emphasis on the power of pure hearts.

But while we insist on the primacy of heart purity as the real power of Pentecost, we must not ignore the clear association in this text with the task of witnessing for Christ. The power of the Spirit is to give enablement for witnessing, too. Let us see what a witness needs, and in so doing, we can see what the Holy Spirit gives to make his witness effective.

A witness must be capable. He must be able to speak forth the truth he has found and exalt the Savior whom he has come to know. It may not be eloquent oratory. It may be in simple, homespun fashion. But certainly, a divinely given ability is implied in this text in Acts.

A witness must be credible. No amount of talking will do any good, unless his life is such that it renders his testimony credible. Unless there has been something happen to make the man over, the crowd is not going to listen to what he has to say.

A witness must be convincing. This is not the power of a high-pressure salesmanship, but a conviction borne in upon the hearer that this witness knows what he is talking about and that there is something more than mere human opinion in what he has to say. This is not to say that all, or even large numbers, will yield to his witness. Sin has too great a hold on the multitudes, but again and again, they will have to take knowledge of these witnesses that they have been with Jesus, even though they refuse to personally acknowledge His claims.

Summary

Perhaps all we have been trying to say about the subject of power can be best seen by a good look at a statement describing the early church right after Pentecost. In Acts 4:33, we read, "With great power gave the apostles witness of the resurrection of the Lord Jesus; and great grace was upon them all." Here we find power for witnessing for those whose duty called them to the public place, but for all the others, the rank and file, there was "great grace." The basic thing that God gives is a new inner fortitude and an enabling to be and do whatever God has for one to do. It may be "great power" in witnessing. But whether it is that or not, it will always be "great grace"!

CHAPTER 19

The Cost of Service

John E. Hunter

John E. Hunter (1909-2005) was an educator, Bible lecturer, and Christian counselor. He spoke many times at Mount Hermon Christian Conference Center, California. He was associated with evangelist and author Major Ian Thomas, *The Torchbearers*, and the work of Capernwray Hall, England. He authored more than 20 books, including *Limiting God, Going On to Maturity, Knowing God's Secrets*. Dr. Hunter's resources are available at Fresh Springs Foundation. This article is taken from *The Christ-filled Life* by John E. Hunter.

Editor: When requesting permission to reprint this article in *Life in the Spirit Journal* in 2005, a staff person at the Fresh Springs Foundation informed me, "Your request comes at a sad time since Dr. John Hunter passed away at his home in England this past Thursday evening, October 6. He was 96 years young and lived his message until the end. He finished well." What a beautiful testimony!

MANY CHRISTIANS TODAY are busily engaged in serving the Lord under the wrong terms of service. In some cases, they regard the service itself as the object of their Christian life; the act is made the end and not the means to an end. As long as they are engaged in a busy round of church activities, they are satisfied with their service. As long as they can point to membership of this society and that society, on the committee of this group and that group, their consciences are at rest—they are busy serving the Lord.

This [article] is an attempt to analyze Christian service in its simplest terms, and then to see how we fit into God's plan.

What Service is Not

First, let us see what service is not.
America today, more than ever before, is a land of big business. Millions of

dollars are invested in the training of staff, in research in the preparation of the product, analysis of market, advertising of goods, etc.

Yet big business is not a philanthropic society; all these dollars are invested and spent with the ultimate object of acquiring a return. As long as returns are greater than expenditures, then the company can make a profit and survive. But if the returns drop for too long, the company will have to fold up.

If we looked at Christian service as a big business, what tremendous activity we would find! There is expenditure of millions of dollars, training of staff, advertising of goods—but there the comparison ends. The visible results in many fields of Christian service are pitiful compared with the expenditure. From a business point of view, much Christian service in many churches is practically useless—unless the ultimate aim is to keep the members on the move.

But what fruit is there for Christ? Much of this misguided service comes from imitation of the world. Jesus said: "They are not of the world, even as I am not of the world" (John 17:14).

The Lord's methods were so different from the accepted standard of His day. He was revolutionary in His ways, His works, and His teachings. Today we tend to copy the best ways of the world in our techniques, but He broke away from accepted techniques and tradition.

Philippians 2

The whole secret of the Lord's life of service is hidden in Philippians 2:7.

See, first, these words: "But made himself." All things were made by Him, and the last thing He made was "Himself of no reputation." He was rich; He was Deity, and yet He emptied Himself of power, and He stripped Himself of His glory. He took the first step—"He made himself."

Secondly, the verse goes on to say, "He was made." We must be careful not to miss the absolute simplicity of this. Many of God's great lessons are very simple; in fact, so simple we overlook them. This verse is an excellent example.

The words, "He made himself," are in the active voice in the English grammar. This means that He was the one who did the actual making. He initiated the process.

Conversely, the words, "he was made," are in the passive voice in the English grammar. This means that other people did the making. His hands were off His own life. He was the one who was made....

Notice how limited He was. He was born a helpless baby, dependent on his parents. He was made a refugee as an infant and was made to flee to Egypt. They made Him carry His cross at the end. All through His blessed life, He was subject. He had taken His hands off His own life, and He was going to take the consequences.

But how wonderful is Philippians 2:9. The ultimate end to His subjection was exaltation—above every name—with every knee bowed and every tongue confessing. Our hearts cry, "Hallelujah!"

Why was this passage in Philippians written? As an encouragement or a "happy ending"? Verse 5 contains a command: "Let this mind be in you." This is no trivial request but a divine command from Almighty God. The example has been shown, the pattern has been proved. God has been satisfied, and now the word comes to you and me: "Let this mind be in you." We, too, have to take these steps that the Lord took.

First, there must be a moment in our lives when we realize God's perfect plan of service when we are willing to humble ourselves and to "make ourselves." We must deliberately take our hands off our own lives and, regardless of the consequences, accept the second step of the perfect plan of God—become willing to "be made."

This comes as a costly challenge to every man or woman because all the glamour and the glory are gone, and we are left with the chill of obedience.

In the story of the Prodigal Son in Luke 15:11-24, we can see how the two stages in the boy's life are revealed in verse 12: "Give me," and verse 19: "Make me." At first, it was all "give me"—all for self. Later on, as God worked in his heart, he speaks those precious words—"make me."

Many of us are like the son before he came to God in our service. We are "give me" Christians, always doing and going and getting. But Philippians 2:7 is very clear; there are just two simple steps: make ourselves nothing; then be made.

As Christians, we so often seek to gain a reputation as a good organizer, a good singer, a regular attendee, a cheerful giver. The trouble with gaining a reputation is that we want to keep the reputation that we have gained. So, in the end, our Christian service is concerned with doing things so that I will live up to my reputation! Christ made Himself of no reputation—dare we!

Paul followed Christ. He said in 1 Corinthians 9:19, 22: "For though I be free from all men, yet have I made myself servant unto all, that I might gain the more.... To the weak became I as weak, that I might gain the weak: I am made all things to all men, that I might by all mean save some."

Here is the secret of Paul's service—"I made myself" (verse 19) and "I am made" (verse 22).

Just as the service of Christ ended in the exaltation, so, too, will ours. "His lord said to him, 'Well done, good and faithful servant; you were faithful over a few things, I will make you ruler over many things. Enter into the joy of your lord.' " (Matt. 25:21).

To the one who, like the son in Luke 15, has said, "Make me ..." will come the words of the Master, "Well done, thou good and faithful servant."

God's Plan is Different from the World's

We must realize continually how completely different is God's plan from the world's plan. The world's way is doing; God's way is being made. To obey God, we must take our hands off our own life and then ask God to do with us just what He wants.

Why are so few of us prepared to do this? The answer is simple—it hurts, it costs, it humbles, it denies self—it is not "natural." If we want to bear, however, we should be ready to step aside and let the Lord Jesus, who lives in us by the power of His Holy Spirit, take over the doing and the making and the being.

It costs to be a committed Christian. If I honestly take my hands off my life and say, "Lord, make me what You will," I am opening the door to possible disturbance and difficulty.

If you are a parent, God may want your child for the mission field. If you are younger, your ambitions may have to go.

God took everything when Nate Saint and his companions prayed this prayer. They had committed all to Him, and there were no strings left for them to pull. But God had a magnificent plan whereby He shocked the Christian world out of its lethargy. Certainly, there will be a great Auca harvest, and more certain there will be a divine, "Well done, thou good and faithful servant!"

Which would you rather do—grow old, fat and prosperous as a "give me" Christian with no real fruit to show, or live a glorious adventure in the uncertainty of being made by God, losing things, and realizing no reputation—being a "fool for Christ's sake."

Emotionally, every one of us would say: "Me for Christ." Many will say it, but few will take the first step of "nothingness" for Christ's sake, to follow Christ's example, and to obey the command: "Let this mind be in you."

When I was staying at the Firs Conference Center in Bellingham, Washington, I was intrigued by the sunlight each morning. Through the window, I saw shadows cast on the road as the sun shone through the tangled mass of fir tree branches. As I studied these patches of sunlight scattered on the road, I suddenly saw something I had learned at school. Among all the varied shapes were a few perfect circles. If the sun is allowed to shine through a hole, whatever shape the hole may be, as long as it is a "nothing" with a complete circumference, the image cast by the sun is always a perfect replica of the shape of the sun—that is, a perfect circle.

As I looked, I remembered the words of our text: "He made himself nothing ... Let this mind be in you." If I am prepared to make myself nothing, to empty myself, then He, shining through me, can reproduce Himself in this dark world below.

The question is, "Dare you so hand over your life to Christ that, as you make yourself nothing, He may move into your entire being to make you according to His own plan and desire?"

The main difficulty in this study is the simplicity of the thought. In our busy world today, we are apt to dismiss a thing as trivial if there is a very simple explanation to it.

We are impressed by the achievements of the rocket scientists and the others who put things in orbit, while we take for granted many of the simpler precious achievements of other men.

Philippians 2:7 is divine simplicity, but too many of us are like Naaman, the military leper who at first refused to make himself of nothing by bathing in the poor waters of Jordan. We still cry—"Are not Abana and Pharpar, rivers of Damascus, better than all the waters of Israel?" (2 Kings 5:12).

We fail to remember that it was only when Naaman made himself of no reputation, that God made him clean!

The world's idea of success is not God's idea. At the end of three years' perfect ministry, the Lord Jesus had but twelve apostles, one of whom betrayed Him, one who denied Him, and all forsook Him. From the world's point of view, He was a failure, but He could say: "I always do those things that please him" (John 8:29).

He had made the great stoop, had made Himself nothing so that God could take and make Him. His perfect obedience was the answer to it all.

It may come as a shock to some of us that Philippians 2:5 is not a request; it is God's command: "Let this mind be in you, which was also in Christ Jesus."

In other words, if we don't do this, then we are disobeying God. The surrounding materialism is such a burden and a barrier. It is so easy to follow the pattern of other much-admired Christians and go their way, letting their mind be in us instead of following the mind of Christ. We use this so often as an excuse for not making ourselves of nothing, avoiding thereby the cost, and the shame, and the ridicule.

We should call to mind the names of many missionaries and servants of God who "made" themselves of no reputation so that God could move into their lives and use them as He willed. Like Paul, they so often went down in the world's estimation, yet they had a greater joy in their nothingness than others had with their possessions.

But God is still no man's debtor. The more you have given, the more God is sure to bless you, even if only to maintain His glorious promises.

All to Jesus I Surrender

All to Jesus I surrender,
All to Him I freely give;
I will ever love and trust Him,
In His presence daily live.

All to Jesus I surrender,
Humbly at His feet I bow;
Worldly pleasures all forsaken,
Take me, Jesus, take me now.

All to Jesus I surrender,
Make me, Savior, wholly Thine;
Let me feel the Holy Spirit,
Truly know that Thou art mine.

All to Jesus I surrender,
Lord, I give myself to Thee;
Fill me with Thy love and power,
Let Thy blessing fall on me.

All to Jesus I surrender,
Now I feel the sacred flame;
Oh, the joy of full salvation!
Glory, glory, to His Name!

- Judson W. Van DeVenter

CHAPTER 20

The Minister with a Laughing Face

Warren W. Wiersbe

The author of this biographical sketch, Warren W. Wiersbe (1929-2019), was a well-known international Bible conference teacher and writer with a heart for missions and former pastor of Moody Church in Chicago. He served for ten years as General Director and Bible Teacher for Back to the Bible. Dr. Wiersbe authored more than 80 books, including the best-selling "BE" series. He was known as a "pastors' pastor," and his speaking, writing, and radio ministries have delighted the hearts of thousands of God's people around the world. This article is taken from *Victorious Christians You Should Know* by Warren Wiersbe, copyright © 1984 Baker Books.

ONE OF THE RICHEST EXPERIENCES you can have is reading the diaries and journals of great men and women in Christian history. Among many that I enjoy, perhaps my favorite is *The Diary and Life of Andrew Bonar,* edited by his daughter, Marjory Bonar, and published by Banner of Truth Trust.

Most people know Andrew Bonar as the brother of hymnwriter Horatius Bonar, and the close friend of Robert Murray McCheyne. He was also the editor of the best edition of Samuel Rutherford's *Letters,* and the author of a devotional commentary on Leviticus and *Christ and His Church in the Book of Psalms,* which has been reprinted by Kregel Publications.

But when you read his journal, you will meet and learn to love a truly great man of God. He lived and labored at a critical time in the church in Scotland, and God used him in wonderful ways to uphold his truth and build his people.

Andrew Alexander Bonar was born on May 29, 1810, in Edinburgh, Scotland, the seventh son of James and Marjory Bonar. He was surrounded by spiritual influences, but not until he was twenty years old and in college did he have assurance of his salvation.

Later, he became a divinity student, and during that time cultivated his friendship with McCheyne. He served as an assistant pastor and city missionary in Jedburgh and at St. George's in Edinburgh, and was licensed in 1824. In 1836, he candidated at St. Peter's Church, Dundee, but the congregation called McCheyne instead.

In 1838 Bonar accepted a call to the Presbyterian Church in Collace, where he was ordained and remained for eighteen fruitful years. When he arrived, there were probably only half a dozen true believers in the parish; but God sent revival to the area, and many turned to Christ. While Bonar and McCheyne were on a special missionary deputation to the Holy Land in 1839, God used William Burns to bring a fresh wind of the Spirit to McCheyne's church in Dundee, and the blessing spread to other churches.

The year 1843 was difficult for ministers and churches in Scotland, for in that year, more than four hundred dedicated ministers left the Established Church and founded the Free Church. Those who seceded protested the modernistic tendencies of the denomination and the interference of the civil courts in church affairs. At Collace, Bonar preached in a tent until the congregation, which had forfeited its property, could build a new place of worship.

In 1856, Bonar became pastor of a new church on Finnieston Street in a needy area of Glasgow; and there he remained until his death on December 30, 1892. Before long, what had been a small work when he began had grown to a congregation of more than a thousand members, with a strong Sunday school program and an evangelistic outreach into the city. The work was difficult, but Bonar preached the Word and trusted God. When a friend asked one day how things were going, Bonar replied, "Oh, we are looking for great things!" When his friend admonished him not to expect too much, Bonar replied, "We can never hope for too much!"

A confirmed premillennialist, Bonar enjoyed preaching about the return of Jesus Christ. He had a remarkable ability to remember names and faces. One day he addressed by name a little girl on the street, and she ran home and announced, "Mother, Mother, he knows me!"

He could detect when a member was absent on Sunday and during the week would visit to see if there were a special problem or need. He also had a marvelous sense of humor. One child called him "the minister with the laughing face." One day he told an invalid he was visiting, "I have a new medicine for you: 'A merry heart doeth good like a medicine.'" When a man told Bonar he had felt an angel touch him during an illness, Bonar said, "Have you a cat in the house? Don't you think it may have been the cat?"

He believed in pastoral work, particularly visiting in people's homes. "There is a blessing resting on visiting," he wrote to a pastor friend. "What else is fitted to make us know the state of our flocks? Were it not for their good but only for our own, is not this department of work most important? It is only, thus, we can know our people's spiritual state." He usually visited every afternoon from one o'clock to five, walking great distances to bring encouragement and help to his beloved people.

I think the greatest value of the *Diary and Life* is its record of Bonar's interior life. He was able to accomplish much with men in public because he spent time with God in private. There are scores of references in these pages to prayer, meditation, and self-examination. They also record times of discouragement and defeat when Bonar felt he had failed the Lord and his people. God's choicest servants rarely evaluate their own ministries with accuracy and balance, and often Bonar was too hard on himself.

During the Kilsyth Revival of 1839-40, Bonar wrote to his brother Horace: "Pray for Collace. We have no more than a few drops as yet, and I believe I am to blame. I *work* more than I *pray.*" Later he wrote in his journal: "I was living very grossly, namely, laboring night and day in visiting with very little prayerfulness. I did not see that prayer should be the main business of every day." Again, he wrote: "I see that prayerlessness is one of my great sins of omission. I am too short, ask too little, ask with too much want of forethought. Then, *too little meditation upon Scripture.*"

He discovered that even his books and his literary ministry could create problems in his spiritual life. "Tried this morning specially to pray against idols in the shape of my books and studies. These encroach upon my direct communion with God, and need to be watched." As he was writing *Christ and His Church in the Book of Psalms,* he noted in his diary: "I distinctly see now that Satan's chief way of prevailing against me is by throwing in my way a great deal of half literary work, half biblical." When he was preparing *Rutherford's Letters,* he wrote: "A piece of extra work this year has been an edition of *Rutherford's Letters,* which I fear has been a snare to me, inasmuch as it has sometimes shortened prayer, yet it has also helped me."

Bonar tried to keep each Saturday evening as a time of prayer and special preparation of his own soul for the ministry on the Lord's Day, a practice I strongly recommend to preachers today. But he discovered that he was especially vulnerable to Satan's attacks on Saturday evenings and Monday mornings. He often sought for "Saturday assurances" from God to encourage him for his Sunday ministry. He observed that Christ, after a busy day of ministry, arose early to pray (Mark 1:35); and he tried to follow that example on Monday mornings.

In spite of his success as a pastor, preacher, and writer, Bonar often saw himself as a failure in the pulpit. On December 5, 1857, he wrote in his diary: "Got such a sight of the impotence of my preaching that I felt as if I need never attempt it more." One day he received special encouragement from Proverbs 23:16, "Yea, my reins shall rejoice, when thy lips speak right things." He wrote in his journal, "Christ listening to our sermons!"

Bonar realized that he could not go on forever, no matter how much his people loved him. There is a deeply touching entry in his diary for September 11, 1890, when he was eighty years old.

> I see distinctly that my Lord is teaching me to "glory in my infirmities" and to be willing to be set aside. My voice fails; some of my people, specially the younger part, going elsewhere; my class melts away, Some very mortifying cases of ingratitudes on the part of some; my influence with brethren manifestly declines—all this is saying, "He must increase, but I must decrease."

On October 14, a committee met with him to arrange to call a successor. "I read with them Numbers 27:15-18, and prayed with thanksgiving, and the business went on pleasantly," he wrote. "Oh, I don't think anything about growing old," Bonar once told D. L. Moody's associate, Major D. W. Whittle. But those closest to him detected a gradual failing of his strength, even though he continued in ministry as much as possible, and after only two days of illness, he went Home to Glory on Friday, December 30, 1892.

Each time I read Bonar's *Diary and Life,* I find something new to ponder, or I am reminded of something I had already read and underlined but had forgotten. His personal character has always impressed me. He was not envious at the success of others, but rejoiced at God's blessing, even if he disagreed with the methods other men used. When many Calvinists were opposing Moody and Sankey, Bonar was praying for them and laboring with them. Moody invited him to minister at this Northfield Conference, and in 1881 Bonar sailed to America and ministered in several cities. Like F. B. Meyer, Henry Drummond, and many other ministers of the Word, Bonar was greatly helped by his friendship with Moody.

I have also been impressed with Bonar's emphasis on evangelism. He kept two texts (in the original Hebrew) in his study: "He that winneth souls is wise" (Prov. 11:30) and "For yet a little while, and He that shall come will come and will not tarry" (Hab. 2:3). When the church in Finnieston Street moved to a new location in 1878, "He that winneth souls is wise" was carved in Hebrew over the front door. Bonar had a special burden for the Jews, and he hoped that the text would not only attract them but also remind his own people of the importance of witnessing.

Although Bonar was criticized by some and ignored by others, he stuck to his premillennial interpretation of the Word and greatly advanced the study of prophecy in Great Britain. He viewed the Lord's return as a practical motivation for life and ministry. His views closed doors for him, but they also opened many hearts.

Bonar noted in his diary on July 5, 1847: "I have been much impressed with the sin of choosing my text without special direction from the Lord. This is like running without being sent, no message being given me." He also tried to relate each text to the needs of his people. "I feel as if I had not got my subject from the Lord," he wrote in 1858. "This whole matter had led me to search into my feelings toward my people, and I have discovered that I do not sufficiently think of them individually and pray for them.... Lord, give me a larger heart."

In my own preaching ministry, I have quoted some of Andrew Bonar's "spiritual sayings," and I want to close with some of my favorites.

The best part of all Christian work is that part which only God sees.

Let us be as watchful after the victory as before the battle.

God likes to see His people shut up to this, that there is no hope but in prayer. Herein lies the Church's power against the world.

Love is the motive for working; joy is the strength for working.

Bonar was pleased when the University of Edinburgh granted him a Doctor of Divinity degree in 1873. But when he was made Moderator of the Free Church Assembly, he said: "Alas! How far down our Church has come when it asks such as me to take this office!"

I hope you will get acquainted with this delightful man of God—a wholesome example in ministry, and a saint who encourages us to live in the Holy of Holies with God.

CHAPTER 21

How God Revived Me

Barry Shoemake

Barry Shoemake has been the senior minister of Whitesburg Christian Church, Whitesburg, Georgia, since 2006. Before his Georgia pastorate, Barry was pastor of the First Christian Church in Borden, Indiana, for 22 years. He began pastoring the Borden church while a seminary student. The church steadily grew under Barry's ministry, as did his positive influence for Christ in the community. Barry is a graduate of Johnson Bible College (B.A.) and Southern Baptist Theological Seminary (M.Div.).

Editor: Barry and I, with two other ministerial colleagues, met weekly for prayer and fellowship for several years until the Lord led us to a change in our respective fields of service. We will long cherish those special times together when pastors gathered to meet with the Lord and one another. One church member remarked on Barry's pulpit ministry before and after his post-conversion experience: "His preaching is as different as night and day."

IN OCTOBER OF 2002, I went over to my study to work like I did almost every morning. As I sat at my desk, my mind began to wander, and I found myself thinking, "My daughter has a basketball game tonight, and tomorrow I'm playing golf." Suddenly, the still small voice of God said to my heart, "Yeah, you'd rather do those things than to spend time with me."

It was a very gentle and tender message. I think I could have ignored it and gone on as usual. But for some reason, this time I listened. And this became the biggest turning point in my ministry and perhaps in my life. I said, "Lord, I know You're right. Help me. I don't know what to do." And He began to lead me to a restored relationship with Himself.

You see, I had been a minister for seventeen years. I went right out of high school into Bible college and then to seminary. I started preaching at a small church in southern Indiana while I was in seminary, and had been there ever since. I loved the church, loved the people, loved the town, but I didn't love the

Lord. I was trying to serve the Lord and wanted to do what's right, but I didn't *love* Him. I could remember times in my late teens and in Bible college when I had felt close to God. A small group of us used to have some awesome prayer times in dorm rooms or on camping trips.

"God was just so near."

I remember one time, in particular, the students and faculty were having a forty-eight-hour prayer chain, and I had signed up for 3:00 a.m. Walking up the hill toward the prayer room in the middle of the night, God was just so near. I was in awe. Remembering that moment still brings tears to my eyes. But I had not valued those moments. I didn't realize that God wanted to have those moments with me. In my practical mind, I wasn't accomplishing anything. I wasn't teaching a class or witnessing to a lost person or writing a sermon. So the relationship with God took a back seat to the work of the ministry.

It'll be no surprise to most of you that, since I wasn't allowing God to fill my heart with His Spirit, I ended up trying to fill that void with other things—television, eating out, golf, my children's sports teams, a growing church attendance, lust, tobacco, pride, image. The list is almost endless.

The heart affects every area of life, and my ministry was not an exception. My focus was on people rather than on the Lord. There was almost no vertical dimension. Sometimes I leaned toward legalism and other times toward entertainment. I wrote the sermons, but I knew almost nothing of waiting for a word from the Lord. If the attendance was up, I was up. And if the attendance was down, so was I. I don't mean to imply that nothing good happened during those years. At least I knew enough to keep things biblical. And God was gracious enough to work in spite of my shortcomings. He is such an awesome God.

And on that wonderful morning in 2002, He stepped in. That was over six years ago [from the time this article first appeared in *Life in the Spirit Journal*], so in my description, I may get some details out of order. But let me try to describe what happened following that encounter.

I began to listen, to be open to God's leading. He had pointed out my problem, and I was inviting Him to point me to the solution. I developed a hunger to read—something I had never had before. In the bookstore, my attention was drawn to a book by David Yongi Cho, pastor of the world's largest church in Sol, Korea. The book was called *Prayer That Brings Revival*. I read the entire book, but one paragraph stood out like a light. Cho said that he prays for an hour a day because he has two options: he can operate out of his own strength and resources, or he can operate out of the strength and resources of God. And there is no way he can lead a church of 700,000 with his own resources. My first reaction to that was, "An hour! I don't have an hour! I'm busy. I've got sermons to write, and lessons to prepare, and a preschool ministry to manage, and people to ..." Then it hit me. He has 700,000 people to minister to, and he has an hour. And I've got 120 people, and I don't have an hour. Something about that doesn't make sense. After a few days of resisting, I finally said, "Okay, Lord, I'm just going to do it. I can't imagine how I'm going to get everything done, but I'm just going to trust You."

I still remember the first time I took my Bible and a lawn chair and went to the lake. I sat in the sun, but I bathed in the Presence of the Lord. He ministered to me, restoring my soul. After that, I started making my time with God my first priority. When I walked into the church, Satan would throw a dozen tasks in front of me. "These things have got to be done!" he would shout. And I would have to close my ears and eyes to those distractions. My Lord had called me to spend time with Him. Oh, bless His name!

"Oh, God, change my heart. Please, change my heart."

For the first several months, I would often spend all morning in prayer. I was on my knees and on my face. I was desperate for His presence. He pointed me toward those "rivers of living water" that He promised, and I said, "Lord, I don't have anything like that in my life. Please help me!" He reminded me of the fruit of the Spirit, and I cried for Him to produce them in me. I spent a great deal of time repenting in agony. I saw how selfish I was and how prideful. I begged Him to change me. I remember being curled up on the floor, pleading, "Oh, God, change my heart. Please, change my heart."

My sermon preparation began to change drastically. Before, I would pray for a few minutes and then say, "That's all the time I've got, Lord. I've got a sermon to write." Now my sermons began to come out of my prayer time. I wrote many sermons on my knees as thoughts and images would come to me. The most prominent image was of a church building, with people inside. I saw horizontal lines from the people to the world. God was saying, "This is what you've been doing wrong. The church has been trying to impact the world without being impacted by Me. The result is that the world has come into the church rather than the church changing the world."

Then I saw vertical arrows coming from God into the church, and *then* out to the world. God was showing me that we've got to call on Him, depend on Him, seek Him. It has to be Him working in us and through us. I knew that I was saved by grace, that it was only by the shed blood of Jesus that I could come into the Kingdom. But I thought that after that, it was pretty much up to me—my determination, my commitment, my effort.

God was showing me that, just like I was totally dependent on God to save me, I am still dependent on God to give me the ability to live for Him and to obey Him. I was talking to a fellow minister about this, and he said, "It's not determination, it's dependence, isn't it?" I said, "That's exactly what it is." God is looking for people with broken and contrite hearts, who know that they can't do anything without Him.

God began to give me regular confirmation that He was leading me in my preaching. I wanted to preach exactly what He wanted on a given Sunday. I remember one week I was feeling led to preach from Luke 17, about Jesus returning "like lightning which flashes and lights up the sky from one end to the other." I asked God to show me that He was leading. No one knew what I was preparing.

On Friday morning, I was praying with a small group. The first words out of the mouth of the first lady who prayed were these: "Oh, Lord, I see you returning like lightning flashing from the east to the west." When she said this, I just burst into laughter, as I knew God was talking to me. That season of regular confirmation only lasted for about a year or two. Now He seems to be saying, "Just trust me."

"Now look at my church. They are just like you were."

After God had dealt with me personally for several months, there came a time when He seemed to open up the blinds and say, "Now look at my church. They are just like you were. They don't love me. They love everything else. They are materialistic. They are prideful. They are self-absorbed. They are idolatrous." (God was so gentle and kind with me, that He didn't even use the word "idolatry" when He was dealing with me. But later, I realized that that is exactly what I was practicing.) One verse that was constantly before me was Matthew 15:8, "These people honor me with their lips, but their hearts are far from me."

The most powerful communication came a few years ago. I had preached two Sundays in a row on the subject, "Repent, for the Kingdom of heaven is at hand," which to me was bad news and good news. The bad news is that we have to turn from something. We have to turn from what we've been holding onto. But the good news is that we can turn to something better—the Kingdom of God. But the message was heavy on the people. I could see it.

The second Sunday, when I got home, I went for a walk. I said, "Father, You know that I want to say whatever You are telling me to say. But please let me know this is You, because these people don't want to hear what I'm saying." The next morning when I woke up, in my mind was a Scripture reference and a phrase. The Scripture reference was Ezekiel 33:11 (and one other verse that was for me), and the phrase was "God consciousness/gold consciousness." I went to my study, took my Bible, and began to open. My hands were trembling. I didn't even know if Ezekiel had 33 chapters. I found chapter 33. I read verse 11: "Say to them, 'As surely as I live, declares the Sovereign Lord, I take no pleasure in the death of the wicked, but rather that they turn from their ways and live. Turn! Turn from your evil ways! Why will you die, O house of Israel?'"

That was the morning that Hurricane Katrina hit. I said, "Lord, what about the phrase, 'God consciousness/gold consciousness.' What does that mean?" What came to me was, "During the gold rush, what were peoples' hearts set on? Gold. They had other things to do, but their hearts were always on gold. That's what I want—a people whose hearts are always on Me."

You understand that these are some highlights of several years of process. Most of the time, I'm grappling to understand what God is saying. I'm still asking God to crucify my flesh. Sometimes the process is excruciating. I can remember riding in my truck, yelling, "Don't let me quit, God! Don't let me quit!" Sometimes I'm broken, and sometimes I'm proud of how broken I've been. Sometimes I'm praying for revival, and sometimes I need it more than anybody, and often I'm frustrated that He is not pouring out what He's had me praying for. But I do see Him working. I keep meeting people from different places and different churches who are being stirred up spiritually. And I can say this: Our God is an awesome God. He's for real, and He is working. Praise His Holy Name!

CHAPTER 22

Used of God

Jonathan Goforth

Jonathan Goforth (1859-1936) was the first Canadian Presbyterian missionary to China with the Canadian Presbyterian Mission, with his wife, Rosalind. He attended University of Toronto and Knox College, where he graduated in 1887 and awarded the Doctor of Divinity in 1915. In 1900, the Goforths had to flee for many miles across China during the Boxer Rebellion. Jonathan was attacked and injured with a sword, but they both survived and escaped to safety.

Dr. Goforth remained active into the 1930s, especially in Manchuria. He died at his son's manse in Wallaceburg, Ontario, after preaching the previous evening in nearby Wyoming, Ontario. The following article is taken from *By My Spirit* by Jonathan Goforth, copyright © 1942 by Zondervan.

IF THE ALMIGHTY SPIRIT moves in sovereign power on the hearts and consciences of men, the outcome must be above the normal. In his introduction to Miss Dyer's *Revival in India*, Dr. A. T. Schofield says:

> One thing to be borne in mind is that since the days of Pentecost, there is no record of the sudden and direct work of the Spirit of God upon the souls of men that has not been accompanied by events more or less abnormal. It is, indeed, on consideration, only natural that it should be so. We cannot expect an abnormal inrush of Divine light and power, so profoundly affecting the emotions and changing the lives of men, without remarkable results. As well expect a hurricane, an earthquake, or a flood, to leave nothing abnormal in its course, as to expect a true Revival that is not accompanied by events quite out of our ordinary experience.

Movements of the Spirit

Perhaps no movement of the Spirit since Pentecost has seen so productive of results as the Moravian Revival of the eighteenth century. We read that about noon, on Sunday, August 10th, 1727, "while Pastor Rothe was holding the meeting at Herrnhut, he felt himself overwhelmed by a wonderful and irresistible power of the Lord and sank down into the dust before God, and with him sank down the whole assembled congregation, in an ecstasy of feeling. In this frame of mind, they continued till midnight, engaged in praying and singing, weeping and supplication."

The accounts that we have of "the Love Feast in Fetter Lane," London, New Year's Day, 1739, give us an insight into the beginnings of another great movement that originated in that same period. We are told that there were about sixty Moravians present at the meeting, together with seven of the Oxford Methodists, namely, John and Charles Wesley, George Whitefield, Wesley Hall, Benjamin Ingham, Charles Kinchin and Richard Hutchins, all of them ordained clergymen of the Church of England. Of that meeting, Wesley writes: "About three in the morning, as we were continuing instant in prayer, the power of God came mightily upon us, insomuch that many cried for exceeding joy, and many fell to the ground. As soon as we were recovered a little from that awe and amazement at the presence of His Majesty, we broke out with one voice—'We praise Thee, O God; we acknowledge Thee to be the Lord!'"

I was a student at Knox College when Mr. [Dwight] Moody conducted a three days' series of meetings in Toronto, during the winter of 1883. One of his noon meetings was about as melting as anything I have ever seen. I hardly think there was a dry eye in the assembly that day. No one who attempted to pray could go very far without breaking down.

Normal Christianity

But though we speak of the manifestations at Pentecost as being abnormal, yet we maintain that Pentecost was normal Christianity. The results, when the Holy Spirit assumed control in Christ's stead, were according to Divine plan. Each one was strengthened with might by His Spirit in the inner man. Christ then did dwell in their hearts by faith, and they were rooted and grounded in love. They were filled unto all the fullness of God, and God did work in and through them above all that they had asked or thought, even unto the "exceeding abundantly."

Anything short of that would have defrauded their Lord of His Calvary merits. The purpose of the Holy Spirit was to glorify the Lord Jesus Christ every day from the crowning to the coming. It is unthinkable that He should grow weary in well-doing. My conviction is that the Divine power, so manifest in the Church at Pentecost, was nothing more nor less than what should be in evidence in the Church today. Normal Christianity, as planned by our Lord, was not supposed to begin in the Spirit and continue in the flesh. In the building of His temple, it never was by might nor by power, but always by His Spirit.

The Lord Himself met and foiled Satan after first being filled with the Spirit. And no child of God has ever been victorious over the adversary unless empowered from the same source. Our Lord did not permit His chosen followers to witness a word in His name until endued with power from on high. It is true that before that day, they were the born again children of the Father and had the witness of the Spirit. But they were not the Lord's efficient co-workers and never could be until Spirit-filled. This Divine empowering is for us as for them. We, too, may do the works which our Lord did, yea, and the greater works. The Scriptures convey no other meaning to me than that the Lord Jesus planned that the Holy Spirit should continue among us in as mighty manifestation as at Pentecost. One should be able to chase a thousand and to put ten thousand to flight—as of old. Time has not changed the fact that "Jesus Christ is the same yesterday, today and forever."

A Growing Dissatisfaction

Upon returning to China in the fall of 1901, after having recuperated from the harrowing effects of the Boxer [Rebellion] ordeal, I began to experience a growing dissatisfaction with the results of my work. In the early pioneer years, I had buoyed myself with the assurance that a seed-time must always precede a harvest, and had, therefore, been content to persist in the apparently futile struggle. But now, thirteen years had passed, and the harvest seemed, if anything, farther away than ever. I felt sure that there was something larger ahead of me if I only had the vision to see what it was, and the faith to grasp it. Constantly there would come back to me the words of the Master: "Verily, verily, I say unto you, he that believeth on Me, the works that I do shall he do also; and greater works than these shall he do ..." And always there would sink deep the painful realization of how little right I had to make out that what I was doing from year to year was equivalent to the "greater works."

Restless, discontented, I was led to a more intensive study of the Scriptures. Every passage that had any bearing upon the price of, or the road to, the accession of power became life and breath to me. There were a number of books on Revival in my library. These I read over repeatedly. So much did it become an obsession with me that my wife began to fear that my mind would not stand it. Of great inspiration to me were the reports of the Welsh Revival of 1904 and

1905. Plainly, Revival was not a thing of the past. Slowly the realization began to dawn upon me that I had tapped a mine of infinite possibility.

Late in the fall of 1905, Eddy's little pamphlet, containing selections from *Finney's Autobiography* and *Revival Lectures*, was sent to me by a friend in India. It was the final something that set me on fire. On the front page of this pamphlet, there was a statement to the effect that a farmer might just as well pray for a temporal harvest without fulfilling the laws of nature, as for Christians to expect a great ingathering of souls by simply asking for it and without bothering to fulfill the laws governing the spiritual harvest. "If Finney is right," I vowed, "then I'm going to find out what those laws are and obey them, no matter what it costs." Early in 1906, while on my way to take part in the intensive evangelistic work which our mission conducted yearly at the great idolatrous fair at Hsun Hsien, a brother missionary loaned me the full *Autobiography* of Finney. It is impossible for me to estimate all that that book meant to me. We missionaries read a portion of it daily while we carried on our work at the fair.

It was at this fair that I began to see evidence of the first stirrings in the people's hearts of the greater power. One day, while I was preaching on I Timothy 2:1-7, many seemed deeply touched. An evangelist behind me was heard to exclaim in an awed whisper, "Why, these people are being moved just as they were by Peter's sermon at Pentecost." That same evening, in one of our rented halls, I spoke to an audience that completely filled the building. My text was I Peter 2:24: "He bore our sins in His own body on the tree." Conviction seemed to be written on every face. Finally, when I called for decisions, the whole audience stood up as one man, crying, "We want to follow this Jesus who died for us." I expected that one of the evangelists would be ready to take my place, but what was my surprise, when I turned around, to find the whole band, ten in number, standing there motionless, looking on in wonder. Leaving one to take charge of the meeting, the rest of us went into an inner room for prayer. For some minutes, there was complete silence. All seemed too awed to say anything. At last, one of the evangelists, his voice breaking, said: "Brethren, He for Whom we have prayed so long was here in very deed tonight. But let us be sure that if we are to retain His presence, we must walk very carefully."

Confessing My Faults

In the autumn of 1906, having felt depressed for some time by the cold and fruitless condition of my out-stations, I was preparing to set out on a tour to see what could be done to revive them. There was a matter, however, between the

Lord and myself, that had to be straightened out before He could use me. I need not go into the details. Suffice to say that there was a difference between a brother missionary and myself. I honestly felt that I was in the right. (Such, of course, is very human. In any difference, it is always safe to divide by half.) At any rate, the pressure from the Spirit was quite plain. It was that I should go and make that thing straight. I kept answering back to God that the fault was the other man's, not mine; that it was up to him to come to me, not for me to go to him.

The pressure continued. "But Lord," I expostulated, "he came to my study and in tears confessed his fault. So, isn't the thing settled ?" "You hypocrite!" I seemed to hear him say, "you know that you are not loving each other as brethren, as I commanded you to." Still, I held out. The fault was the other man's, I kept insisting; surely, therefore, I couldn't be expected to do anything about it. Then came the final word, "If you don't straighten this thing out before you go on that trip, you must expect to fail. I can't go with you." That humbled me somewhat. I did not feel at all easy about going on that long and difficult tour without His help. Well, I knew that by myself, I would be like one beating the air.

The night before I was to start out on my trip I had to lead the prayer meeting for the Chinese Christians. All the way out to the church, the pressure continued: "Go and straighten this thing out, so that I may go with you tomorrow." Still, I wouldn't yield. I started the meeting. It was all right while they were singing a hymn and during the reading of Scripture. But as soon as I opened my lips in prayer, I became confused, for all the time the Spirit kept saying: "You hypocrite! Why don't you straighten this thing out.?" I became still more troubled while delivering the short prayer address. Finally, when about halfway through my talk, the burden became utterly intolerable, and I yielded. "Lord," I promised in my heart, "as soon as this meeting is over, I'll go and make that matter right." Instantly something in the audience seemed to snap. My Chinese hearers couldn't tell what was going on in my heart, yet in a moment, the whole atmosphere was changed. Upon the meeting being thrown open for prayer, one after another rose to their feet to pray, only to break down weeping. For almost twenty years, we missionaries had been working among the Honanese and had longed in vain to see a tear of penitence roll down a Chinese cheek.

It was late that night when the meeting closed. As soon as I could get away, I hastened over to the house of my brother missionary, only to find that the lights were out and that the whole family was in bed. Not wishing to disturb them, I went back to my home. But the difficulty was settled. Next morning, before daybreak, I was on my way to the first out-station. The results of that tour far exceeded anything that I had dared hope for. At each place, the spirit of judgment was made manifest. Wrongs were righted, and crooked things were made straight. At one place, I was only able to spend a single night, but that night all present broke down. In the following year, one out-station more than doubled its numbers; to another, fifty-four members were added, and to another eighty-eight.

A Channel of Blessing

Make me, O Lord, one of your channels of blessing,
  a life poured out in service to you.
Filled with Jesus' love and compassion for others,
  may Christ be seen in all that I do.

In the presence of selfish ambition and strife,
  a bearer of holy peace make me.
Save me from all pettiness that drives men apart,
  promoting the Spirit's unity.

Where cruel pride pervades men's thoughtless agenda,
  using others to achieve their end,
Show me the footprints of him who became a slave,
  stooping low to serve—willing to bend.

In this impersonal world of sorrow and stress,
  where many callously look away,
May I bring Christ's presence to your hurting children—
  comfort and cheer, just like the sun's ray.

When an obstruction emerges in this channel,
  let me not sin attempt to excuse,
But flee directly to the cross of Christ Jesus—
  grace to receive that I you might use.

Make me, O Lord, one of your channels of blessing,
  a life poured out in service to you.
I seek no gain or rewards down here;
  I'm content to keep your smile in view.

- Ralph I. Tilley

CHAPTER 23

Amy Carmichael: The Radiant Life

V. Raymond Edman

V. Raymond Edman (1900-1967) was the son of Swedish immigrant parents; he joined the Army in 1918 and served for one year, spending much of that time in Allied-occupied Germany. After returning home, he attended college and became a missionary to the Quichua Indians in Ecuador from 1923 to 1928. Edman earned a Ph.D. from Clark University in 1933. He went to Wheaton College in 1936 as an associate professor of history and became the college's fourth president in 1940, a position he held until he became chancellor in 1965. He died on September 22, 1967, while preaching a chapel message entitled, "In the Presence of the King."

Among the several volumes Dr. Edman authored is *They Found the Secret*, a book consisting of twenty biographical accounts of Christians who experienced a profound deepening in their walk with Christ. This article is about one of those individuals, Amy Carmichael. The Introduction and article are taken from *They Found the Secret* by V. Raymond Edman © 1960, Zondervan Publishing House.

Introduction

EVERY NOW AND THEN, we come across a life that is radiant, revealing a richness, a warmth, a triumph that intrigues and challenges us.

These lives we find in biographies out of the past; and just when we begin to think that such people lived only in other days, we meet one in real life, right in the middle of the twentieth century!

The details of their experiences are usually quite different, yet as we listen to their stories and watch their lives, either in our reading or in our contact with them, we begin to see a pattern that reveals their secret. Out of discouragement and defeat, they have come into victory. Out of weakness and weariness, they have been made strong. Out of ineffectiveness and apparent uselessness, they have become efficient and enthusiastic.

The pattern seems to be: self-centeredness, self-effort, increasing inner dissatisfaction and outer discouragement, a temptation to give it all up because there is no better way; and then finding the Spirit of God to be their strength, their guide, their confidence and companion—in a word, their life.

The crisis of the deeper life is the key that unlocks the secret of their transformation. It is the beginning of the *exchanged life.*

What is the exchanged life? Really, it is not some *thing*; it is some *One*. It is the indwelling of the Lord Jesus Christ made real and rewarding by the Holy Spirit.

There is no more glorious reality in all the world. It is life with a capital L.

It is a new life for old. It is rejoicing for weariness, and radiance for dreariness. It is strength for weakness, and steadiness for uncertainty. It is triumph even through tears, and tenderness of heart instead of touchiness. It is lowliness of spirit instead of self-exaltation, and loveliness of life because of the presence of the altogether Lovely One.

Adjectives can be multiplied to describe it: abundant, overflowing, overcoming, all-pervading, satisfying, joyous, victorious; and each is but one aspect of a life that can be experienced but not fully explained.

Said the Savior: "I am come that they might have life, and that they might have it more abundantly." We find newness of life in Christ by receiving Him as our own Savior from the penalty of sin. Abundance of that life we find by surrendering self and drawing upon the unfailing resources of the Almighty. There is life; and then there is life more abundant. This is the exchanged life.

The expression, "the exchanged life," was first used, as far as I know, by J. Hudson Taylor, founder of the China Inland Mission. Out of striving and struggling, out of discouragement and defeat, he came to the realization of life more abundant in Christ. I have found no happier description than his: The Exchanged Life.

And I have found no more concise contrast between the old and the new than that stated by the late Dr. A. B. Simpson in his poem entitled *Himself.*

Once it was the blessing,
  now it is the Lord;
Once it was the feeling,
  now it is His Word;
Once His gifts I wanted,
  now the Giver own;

Once I sought for healing,
  now Himself alone.
Once 'twas painful trying,
  now 'tis perfect trust;
Once a half salvation,
  now the uttermost;
Once 'twas ceaseless holding,
  now He holds me fast;
Once 'twas constant drifting,
  now my anchor's cast.
Once 'twas busy planning,
  now 'tis trustful prayer;
Once 'twas anxious caring,
  now He has the care;
Once 'twas what I wanted,
  now what Jesus says;
Once 'twas constant asking,
  now 'tis ceaseless praise.
Once it was my working,
  His it hence shall be;
Once I tried to use Him,
  now He uses me;
Once the power I wanted,
  now the Mighty One;
Once for self I labored,
  now for Him alone....

[There are] testimonies of men and women who have found the promise of life more abundant to be true. With procedure proper to a witness they tell us what happened, rather than attempting to teach us in fine detail the doctrine of their experience.... The pattern of their experiences is much the same. They had believed on the Savior, yet they were burdened and bewildered, unfaithful and unfruitful, always yearning for a better way and never achieving by their efforts a better life. Then they came to a crisis of utter heart surrender to the Savior, a meeting with Him in the innermost depths of their spirit, and they found the Holy Spirit to be an unfailing fountain of life and refreshment. Thereafter life was never again the same because in one way or another they had learned what the Apostle Paul had testified: "I am crucified with Christ; nevertheless I live; yet not I, but Christ liveth in me: and the life which I now live in the flesh

I live by the faith of the Son of God, who loved me, and gave himself for me." New life had been exchanged for old.

Amy Carmichael

Amy Carmichael first met the living Lord on the streets of Belfast. She was just a girl then, in her teens. The meeting with the Savior was sudden and startling, wholly unexpected. In *Gold Cord,* the autobiographical account of the background and the building of the Christian home for girls and boys at Dohnavur in South India, she relates that meeting, as important in her life as was the revelation of the Lord Jesus to Saul of Tarsus on the way to Damascus.

> It was a dull Sunday morning in Belfast. My brothers and sisters and I were returning with our mother from church when we met a poor pathetic old woman who was carrying a heavy bundle. We had never seen such a thing in Presbyterian Belfast on Sunday, and, moved by sudden pity, my brothers and I turned with her, relieved her of the bundle, took her by her arms as though they had been handles, and helped her along. This meant facing all the respectable people who were, like ourselves, on their way home. It was a horrid moment. We were only two boys and a girl, and not at all exalted Christians. We hated doing it. Crimson all over (at least we felt crimson, soul and body of us) we plodded on, a wet wind blowing us about, and blowing, too, the rags of that poor old woman, till she seemed like a bundle of feathers and we unhappily mixed up with them. But just as we passed a fountain, recently built near the kerbstone, this mighty phrase was suddenly flashed as it were through the grey drizzle: "Gold, silver, precious stones, wood, hay, stubble; every man's work shall be made manifest; for the day shall declare it, because it shall be revealed by fire; and the fire shall try every man's work of what sort it is. If any man's work abide ..." (1 Cor. 3:12-14).
>
> "If any man's work abide"—I turned to see the voice that spoke with me. The fountain, the muddy street, the people with their politely surprised faces, all this I saw, but nothing else. The blinding flash had come and gone; the ordinary was all about us. We went on. I said nothing to anyone, but I knew that something had happened that had changed life's values. Nothing could ever matter again, but the things that were eternal.

That afternoon the eighteen-year-old Amy shut herself in her room, talked to God, and settled once and for all the pattern of her future life. Amy had found the Lord Jesus as her personal Savior two years before when a student at school in Harrogate, North Ireland. In the moments of quiet at the conclusion of an evangelistic message, "the Good Shepherd, she said, "answered the prayers of my father and mother and many other loving ones, and drew me, even me, into His fold."

At the age of nineteen, she attended a convention in Glasgow. There she heard the "Keswick Testimony" of the life of victory by the Holy Spirit for the first time. She recalled:

> I had been longing for months, perhaps years, to know how one could live a holy life, and a life that would help others. I came to that meeting half hoping, half fearing. Would there be anything for me? I don't remember feeling there was anything (my fault) in either of the two addresses. The fog in the hall seemed to soak into me. My soul was in a fog. Then the chairman rose for the last prayer. Perhaps the previous address had been about Peter walking on the water, and perhaps it had closed with the words of Jude 1:24, for the one who prayed began like this, *"O Lord, we know Thou art able to keep us from falling."* Those words found me. It was as if they were alight, and they shone for me."

In exaltation of mind and spirit, she left the meeting and went with her hostess to a restaurant for lunch. "The mutton chop wasn't properly cooked, and somebody said so," wrote Amy Carmichael. "I remembered wondering, *Whatever does it matter about mutton chops? O Lord, we know Thou are able to keep us from falling.*"

Assurance of salvation at Harrogate ("the one watered moment in an arid three years"), awareness of eternal values by the Holy Spirit at Belfast ("something had happened that had changed life's values"), and the actuality of the new life in Christ at Glasgow ("Thou art able to keep us from falling")—these were the spiritual milestones of Amy Carmichael's awakening and preparation for her long and fruitful service for the Lord Jesus.

Early did this Irish girl learn the sensitivity to the Holy Spirit that is indispensable in a close walk with God. Still in her teens, she was led to Christian service in a Belfast mission, "The Welcome." For some nights, there were souls saved night after night, then suddenly the meetings went dead. As she prayed and searched her own heart, she remembered "a rollicking hour when we reached home after the meeting and, as usual, it was my fault. There was nothing wrong in the fun, *but it was not the time for it.* I have never forgotten the shock of that discovery. *Grieve not the Spirit,* that was the word then. In His mercy, He forgave; and the work went on again."

There was the implicit and wholehearted response to the call for foreign service, quite unthought of even the day before it came, on January 13, 1892. Obedient to that call of *Go Ye,* she was appointed the first missionary under the Keswick convention and within a few months went to Japan. Though her service there was brief she learned many lessons that were invaluable later in the fifty-five consecutive years that she served in India.

Not long after she arrived in Japan, she learned the importance of simplicity of dress and appearance on the part of missionaries and the value of adaptability to the clothing and the standards of the people among whom one had come to witness for the Savior.

It was a hard lesson learned in a sad way. With her Christian fellow-worker, Misaki San, she had gone to visit an old lady who was ill. In response to Miss Carmichael's word, translated by Misaki San, the needy heart seemed just about to turn to the Savior when she noticed fur gloves on the missionary's hands and was distracted from the message. "I went home," said the young missionary, "took off my English clothes, put on my Japanese *kimono,* and never again, I trust, risked so very much for the sake of so very little ..."

Another valuable lesson came out of that experience. Said Miss Carmichael:

The touch of that old lady on my fur gloves set free, though I never imagined it, thousands of hours of time; for the saving of time is great when a company of people live for many years without having to spend any time in giving thought to their clothes. And it set free hundreds of pounds; for the saving of money is also great, when at a stroke all the extras of dress are cut off, and nothing need be spent on them. And all this time and money saved has meant just so much the more to give to Him Who gave us all. But more than that, as I believe, it led to the opening of doors never opened before. It would have been impossible for one in foreign dress to go to the places to which I had to go if I were ever to discover the truth about things in India. And more, far more than that, it opened doors to hearts. If any question that, I can fall back on this: it made it just a little less easy for the great enemy to distract a soul who was drawing near to its Savior.

Early in her missionary life, she also learned the strength of the Strong One. A Buddhist neighbor in the Japanese village of Matsue was possessed by the "Fox spirit," as they called it. The Japanese knew the reality of demon possession but had heard nothing of deliverance from that dreadful bondage. Miss Carmichael and Misaki San went uninvited to pray for a demon-possessed man, only to be driven away, but not before they had assured the wife that they would pray at home until her husband was delivered from the power of the Fox spirit. Within an hour, a messenger came to say that all the Foxes, six of them, were gone; and the next day, the man, perfectly well, came with a branch of pomegranate flowers to express his appreciation for their prayers. Some months later, he died of malaria, peacefully, with his New Testament clasped in his hands. Thus she learned in actual combat that "greater is he that is in you than he that is in the world."

Such was the beginning of her deep acquaintance with the Lord and her preparation for service in India. One day in India, while sitting under a wide-spreading tree with her Tamil grammar and dictionary before her, she became conscious of the "unfolding sense of a Presence, a Listener." It seemed to her He looked for someone to listen with Him, to listen to the voice of one's brother's blood crying unto Him from the ground. Time ceased for the lady under the tree, and she sat all that day in His presence. That day on the hillside influenced all the years that were to follow for Amy Carmichael and gave depth to them all.

When she was called by the Lover of little children to the rescuing of girls from the temple, and later of boys in danger, few missionaries or Indian Christians were in sympathy with her. Of this, she wrote: "Sometimes it was as if I saw the Lord Jesus Christ kneeling alone, as He knelt long ago under the olive trees. The trees were tamarind now, the tamarinds that I see as I look up from this writing. And the only thing that one who cared could do was to go softly and kneel down beside Him so that He would not be alone in His sorrow over the little children."

The sensitivity to spiritual and eternal values gave her not only insight to discern the presence of her Lord, but also outer sight to "see things as they are." The publication of a volume by that name, *Things As They Are,* in 1903, caused tremendous stir in India, and also in Britain, so much so that a committee on the field was appointed to ask her to return to England. She found, however, that the Lord of the Harvest overruled in her behalf when others misunderstood her obedience to marching orders and her understanding of the battle.

She had, by the Holy Spirit, a wonderful gift of teaching others to trust the Faithful One. When the First War brought great hardship and uncertainty to the work in Dohnavur, there were opportunities to help the children learn the simplicity and sweetness of faith in God. In her 1915 diary we read:

October 26. Had children in field weeding. Told them of need of money—a new idea to them. Explained a little to older girls about our way of working, and what it involved of careful sensitiveness towards God. Finally got them, and all, to the point of willingness to give today (Festival Day) to weeding. Girls splendid over it, children very sweet and good. Inwardly prayed for a quick assurance from our Father that He was pleased. It would be like Him to do this.

October 27. Mail in today, and 50 from a friend of Irene Streeter, the soldier brother's money left to her. Took letter up to field where children were weeding, and we all praised God standing in shadow of cactus hedge. There was other money too—more in one mail than has come for many months. All much cheered, and much awed too.

The Spirit-filled life is a practical one. Amy Carmichael found it so. In the problem of guidance, she learned to pray, to trust, to obey, and not to look back.

When decisions have to be made, don't look back and wonder what I would have done. Look up, and light will come to do what our Lord and Master would have you do.

It may be that decisions which seem to change the character of the work will have to be made. But if the root principles which have governed us from the beginning are held fast, there will be no real change. The river may flow in a new channel, but it will be the same river.

If you hold fast to the resolve that in all things Christ as Lord shall have the preeminence, if you keep His will, His glory, and His pleasure high above everything, and if you continue in His love, loving one another as He has loved you, then all will be well, eternally well.

Amy Carmichael had a singing heart. Sensitive, artistic, and radiant, her gift of song found expression in her poetry. Few writers in our generation have had the ministry of pen in poetry and also prose as has Amy Carmichael of Dohnavur. These responses of her heart to trials of faith and triumphs of God's faithfulness have been printed and reprinted in every quarter of the globe.

One poem will suffice to illustrate all the rest:

From prayer that asks that I may be
Sheltered from winds that beat on Thee,
From fearing when I should aspire,
From faltering when I should climb higher,
From silken self O Captain, free
Thy soldier who would follow Thee.

From subtle love of softening things,

From easy choices, weakenings,
Not thus are spirits fortified,
Not this way went the Crucified,
From all that dims Thy Calvary,
O Lamb of God, deliver me.

Give me the love that leads the way,
The faith that nothing can dismay,
The hope no disappointments tire,
The passion that will burn like fire,
Let me not sink to be a clod:
Make me Thy fuel, Flame of God.

The ultimate source of her overflowing life was far beyond, out of sight and reach, because it was in God. The "pool" from which her life poured forth was the meeting with the Lord Jesus on Belfast's rainy streets with its challenging words that changed all of life's values: *if any man's work abide*!

CHAPTER 24

The Irreducible Minimum

D. Martyn Lloyd-Jones

D. Martyn Lloyd-Jones (1899-1981) grew up in Welsh Calvinistic Methodism, first as a boy in Wales and then as a teenager and student in London. Pursing a future in medicine, he completed his academic education and training in London, and by the age of 26, he also became a Member of the Royal College of Physicians. With a brilliant and lucrative career in front of him, God had other plans for Lloyd-Jones to be a physician of souls rather than of bodies. Though raised in the church, it wasn't until he was a young doctor that Lloyd-Jones came to a saving knowledge of the Lord Jesus Christ. Sometime later, he was called of God to preach and took his first pastorate in Wales.

It was as the pastor of Westminster Chapel, London, (1938-1968) where "The Doctor" (as he was affectionately called), eventually reached a global audience through his published sermons and writings. His consuming desire to live and minister to the glory of God, his passionate love for Christ, and his keen sensitivity to the ministry of the Holy Spirit—pervaded his spoken and written ministries.

This article is taken from *God's Ultimate Purpose: An Exposition of Ephesians 1:1-23,* © Copyright 1979 by D. M. Lloyd Jones, published by Baker Books.

Editor: I shall be forever grateful to the Lord for the influence Martyn Lloyd-Jones has had in shaping much of my theology of the Holy Spirit over the past 50 years. I never read after him but what I am made hungrier for the God he served so faithfully.

IT IS CHARACTERISTIC of human nature that we always prefer to have things cut and dried rather than have them in the form of principles. That is why certain forms of religion are always popular.

The natural man likes to be given a definite list; then, he feels that, as long as he conforms to the things stated in the list, all will be well. But that is not possible with the gospel. That was partly the position under the Old Dispensation, and even there, it was carried too far by the Pharisees and scribes. But it is not at all like that under the New Testament dispensation. However, we still tend to like this sort of thing. It is very much easier, is it not, to think of holiness in terms of observing Lent for six weeks or so during the year, rather than to be living with a principle which demands and insists upon application day by day.

We always like to have a set of routine rules and regulations. That is why I am pressing this point. If you take the Sermon on the Mount with these six detailed statements [Mt. 5:21, 27, 31, 33, 38, 43] and say, "As long as I do not commit adultery—and so on—I am all right," you have entirely missed our Lord's point. It is not a code of ethics. He is out to delineate a certain order and quality of life, and He says in effect: "Look, I am illustrating this kind of life. It means this type of behaviour." So we must hold on to the principle without turning the particular illustration into a law.

Let me put it again in this form. Any man in the ministry has to spend a good deal of his time answering the questions of people who come and want him to make particular pronouncements upon particular questions. There are certain problems that face us all in life, and there are people who always seem to want some kind of detailed statement so that when they are confronted by any particular problem, all they have to do is to turn up their textbook, and there they find the answer. Catholic types of religion are prepared to meet such people. The casuists of the Middle Ages, ... those so-called doctors of the Church, had thought out and discussed together the various moral and ethical problems likely to confront Christian people in this world, and they codified them and drew up their rules and regulations. When you were faced with a difficulty, you immediately turned up your authority and found the appropriate answer.

There are people who are always anxious about something like that in the spiritual realm. The final answer to them in terms of this Sermon can be put in this form: the gospel of Jesus Christ does not treat us like that; it does not treat us like children. It is not another law, but something which gives us life. It lays down certain principles and asks us to apply them. Its essential teaching is that we are given a new outlook and understanding, which we must apply with respect to every detail of our lives. That is why the Christian, in a sense, is a man who is always walking on a kind of knife-edge. He has no set regulations, instead he applies this central principle to every situation that may arise.

All this must be said in order to emphasize this point. If we take these six statements made by our Lord in terms of the formula "Ye have heard" and "I say unto you," we shall find that the principle He uses is exactly the same in each case. In one, He is dealing with sex-morality, in the next with murder and in the next with divorce. But every single time, the principle is the same. Our Lord, as a great Teacher, knew the importance of illustrating a principle, so here He gives six illustrations of the one truth.

Let us now deal with this common principle, which is to be found in the six, so that when we come to work each one out we shall always be holding this central principle in our minds. Our Lord's chief desire was to show the true meaning and intent of the law, and to correct the erroneous conclusions which had been drawn from it by the Pharisees and scribes and all the false notions which they had founded upon it. These, I suggest, are the principles.

First Principle

First, it is the spirit of the law that matters primarily, not the letter only. The law was not meant to be mechanical, but living. The whole trouble with the Pharisees and the scribes was that they concentrated only on the letter, and they did so to the exclusion of the spirit. It is a great subject—this relationship between form and content. Spirit is always something that must be embodied in form, and that is where the difficulty arises.

Man will ever concentrate on the form rather than on the content, upon the letter rather than upon the spirit. You remember that the apostle Paul stresses this in 2 Corinthians, where he says: "The letter killeth, but the spirit giveth life," and his whole emphasis in that chapter is that Israel was so constantly thinking of the letter that they lost the spirit. The whole purpose of the letter is to give body to the spirit; and the spirit is the thing that really matters, not the mere letter.

Take, for example, this question of murder. As long as the Pharisees and scribes did not actually murder a man, they thought they had kept the law perfectly. But they were missing the whole point and spirit of the law, which is not merely that I should literally not commit murder, but that my attitude towards my fellow men should be a right and loving one, likewise, with all these other illustrations. The mere fact that you do not commit adultery in an actual physical sense does not mean that you have kept the law. What is your spirit? What is your desire as you look, and so on? It is the spirit, not the letter, that counts.

It is clear, then, that if we rely only upon the letter, we shall completely misunderstand the law. Let me emphasize that this applies not only to the law of Moses but still more, in a sense, to this very Sermon on the Mount. There are people today who so look at the letter of the Sermon on the Mount as to miss its spirit. When we come to details, we shall see that in practice. Take, for instance, the attitude of the Quakers with regard to taking the oath. They have taken the letter here literally, and, it seems to me, have not only denied the spirit but have even made our Lord's statement almost ridiculous.

There are people who do exactly the same with turning the other cheek and giving to those who ask gifts of us, bringing the whole teaching into ridicule because they are constantly living on the letter, whereas our Lord's whole emphasis was upon the primary importance of the spirit. That does not mean, of course, that the letter does not matter, but it does mean that we must put the spirit before it and interpret the letter according to the spirit.

Second Principle

Now take a second principle, which is really another way of putting the first. Conformity to the law must not be thought of in terms of actions only. Thoughts, motives, and desires are equally important.

The law of God is concerned as much with what leads to the action as it is with the action itself. Again, it does not mean that the action does not matter; but it does mean very definitely that it is not the action only that is important. This should be an obvious principle.

The scribes and Pharisees were concerned only about the act of adultery or the act of murder. But our Lord was at pains to emphasize to them that it is the desire in man's heart and mind to do these things that are really and ultimately reprehensible in the sight of God. How often He said in this connection that it is out of the heart that evil thoughts and actions come. It is the heart of man that matters.

So we must not think of this law of God and of pleasing God merely in terms of what we do or do not do; it is the inward condition and attitude that God is always observing. "Ye are they which justify yourselves before men; but God knoweth your hearts: for that which is highly esteemed among men is abomination in the sight of God" (Lk. 16:15).

Third Principle

The next principle we can put in this form. The law must be thought of not only in a negative manner but also positively. The ultimate purpose of the law is not merely to prevent our doing certain things that are wrong; its real object is to lead us positively, not only to do that which is right but also to love it. Here again, is something that comes out clearly in these six illustrations.

The whole Jewish conception of the law was a negative one. I must not commit adultery, I must not commit murder, and so on. But our Lord emphasizes all along that what God is really concerned about is that we should be lovers of righteousness. We should be hungering and thirsting after righteousness, not merely negatively avoiding that which is evil.

It is surely unnecessary that I should turn aside to show the practical relevance of each one of these points to our present condition. Alas, there are still people who seem to think of holiness and sanctification in this purely mechanical manner. They think that, as long as they are not guilty of drinking, gambling, or going to theatres and cinemas, all is well. Their attitude is purely negative. It does not seem to matter if you are jealous, envious, and spiteful. The fact that you are full of the pride of life seems to be of no account as long as you do not do certain things. That was the whole trouble with the scribes and Pharisees who perverted the law of God by regarding it purely in a negative manner.

Fourth Principle

The fourth principle is that the purpose of the law as expounded by Christ is not to keep us in a state of obedience to oppressive rules but to promote the free development of our spiritual character. This is vitally important. We must not think of the holy life as something hard and grievous, which puts us into a state of servitude. Not at all.

The glorious possibility that is offered us by the gospel of Christ is development as children of God and growing "unto the measure of the stature of the fullness of Christ." "His commandments," says John in his first Epistle, "are not grievous." So if you and I regard the ethical teaching of the New Testament as something that cramps us, if we think of it as something narrow and restrictive, it means we have never understood it. The whole purpose of the gospel is to bring us into "the glorious liberty of the children of God," and these special injunctions are simply particular illustrations of how we may arrive at that and enjoy it.

Fifth Principle

That, in turn, brings us to the fifth principle, which is that the law of God, and all these ethical instructions of the Bible, must never be regarded as an end in themselves. We must never think of them as something to which we just have to try to conform.

The ultimate objective of all this teaching is that you and I might come to know God. Now, these Pharisees and scribes (and the apostle Paul said it was true of him, too, before he was truly converted) put, as it were, the Ten Commandments and the moral law on the wall, and having viewed them in this negative, restricted manner said: "Well, now, I am not guilty of these various things; therefore I am all right. I am righteous, and all is well between God and me." You see, they viewed the law as something in and of itself. They codified it in this way, and as long as they kept to that code, they said all was well.

According to our Lord, that is an utterly fallacious view of the law. The one test which you must always apply to yourself is this: "What is my relationship to God? Do I know Him? Am I pleasing Him?" In other words, as you examine yourself before you go to bed, you do not just ask yourself if you have committed murder or adultery, or whether you have been guilty of this or that, and if you have not, thank God that all is well. No. You ask yourself rather, "Has God been supreme in my life today? Have I lived to the glory and the honour of God? Do I know Him better? Have I a zeal for His honour and glory? Has there been anything in me that has been unlike Christ—thoughts, imaginations, desires, impulses?' That is the way. In other words, you examine yourself in the light of a living Person and not merely in terms of a mechanical code of rules and regulations.

And as the law must not be thought of as an end in itself, neither must the Sermon on the Mount. These are simply agencies which are meant to bring us into that true and living relationship with God. We must always be very careful, therefore, lest we do with the Sermon on the Mount what the Pharisees and the scribes had been doing with the old moral law. These six examples chosen by our Lord are nothing but illustrations of principles. It is the spirit, not the letter that matters; it is the intent, object, and purpose that are important. The one thing we have to avoid above everything else in our Christian lives is this fatal tendency to live the Christian life apart from a direct, living, and true relationship to God.

Finally, we can illustrate it like this. Discipline in the Christian life is a good and essential thing. But if your main object and intent are to conform to the discipline that you have set for yourself, it may very well be the greatest danger to your soul. Fasting and prayer are good things, but if you fast twice a week or pray at a particular hour every day merely in order to carry out your discipline, then you have missed the whole object of fasting and praying. There is no point in either of them, or in observing Lent, or in anything else that is meant to be an aid to the spiritual life, unless they bring us into a deeper relationship to God. I may stop smoking, I may stop drinking or gambling during these six weeks or at any other period. But if during that time my poverty of spirit is not greater, my sense of weakness is not deepened, my hunger and thirst after God and righteousness are not greatly increased, then I might just as well not have done it at all. Indeed I would say it would be very much better for me if I had not done it.

All this is the fatal danger of making these things ends in themselves. We can be guilty of the same thing with public worship. If public worship becomes an end in itself, if my sole object in a pulpit is to preach a sermon and not to try to explain the blessed gospel of God that you and I, and all of us, may come to know and love Him better, my preaching is vain, and it may be the thing that will damn my soul. These things are meant to be aids to help us, and illustrations of the Word. God forbid that we should turn them into a religion. "The letter kills, but the Spirit giveth life."

I Want a Principle Within

I want a principle within
Of jealous, godly fear,
A sensibility of sin,
A pain to feel it near.
I want the first approach to feel
Of pride or fond desire,
To catch the wand'ring of my will,
And quench the kindling fire.

From Thee that I no more may part,
No more Thy goodness grieve,
The filial awe, the fleshly heart,
The tender conscience, give.
Quick as the apple of an eye,
O God, my conscience make;
Awake my soul when sin is nigh,
And keep it still awake.

Almighty God of truth and love,
To me Thy pow'r impart;
The mountain from my soul remove,
The hardness from my heart.
Oh, may the least omission pain
My reawakened soul,
And drive me to that blood again,
Which makes the wounded whole.

- Charles Wesley

CHAPTER 25

Choked Channels

S. D. Gordon

S. D. Gordon (1859-1936) was a widely traveled speaker in high demand. A prolific author, he wrote more than 25 devotional books, most with the phrase *Quiet Talks* in the title. His quiet manner, simplicity, and gentle spirit won for him and his Lord a great following wherever he ministered. *Quiet Talks on Power* was his first book, published in 1901, and sold five hundred thousand copies in its first 40 years. Gordon never became an ordained minister and graciously declined to receive honorary doctor's degrees. One who knew him well, said of Gordon: "He never called himself a preacher, preferring the title of "Lecturer." In a real sense, he was unique; his manner of speaking, never dull, always illustrated by parabolic stories, had gripping power to hold the attention and stir the heart."

The following article is adapted from *Quiet Talks on Power* by S. D. Gordon, © copyright 2003, Mercy Place.

A FEW YEARS AGO, I was making a brief tour among the colleges of Missouri. I remember one morning in a certain college village going over from the hotel to take breakfast with some of the boys, and coming back with one of the fellows whom I had just met. As we walked along, chatting away, I asked him quietly, "Are you a Christian, sir?" He turned quickly and looked at me with an odd, surprised expression in his eye and then, turning his face away, said: "Well, I'm a member of a church, but I don't believe I'm very much of a Christian."

Then I looked at him, and he frankly volunteered a little information. Not very much. He did not need to say much. You can see a large field through a chink in the fence. And I saw enough to let me know that he was right in the criticism he had made upon himself. We talked a bit and parted. But his remark set me to thinking.

A week later, in another town, speaking one morning to the students of a young ladies' seminary, I said afterward to one of the teachers as we were talking: "I suppose your young women here are all Christians." That same quizzical look came into her eye as she said: "I think they are all members of a church, but I do not think they are all Christians with real power in their lives." There was that same odd distinction.

Perhaps it was a month or so later, in one of the mining towns down in the zinc belt of southwestern Missouri, I was to speak to a meeting of men. There were probably five or six hundred gathered in a Methodist Church. They were strangers to me. I was in doubt what best to say to them. One dislikes to fire ammunition at people that are absent. So stepping down to a front pew where several ministers were seated, I asked one of them to run his eye over the house and tell me what sort of a congregation it was, so far as he knew them.

He did so, and presently replied: "I think fully two-thirds of these men are members of our churches"—and then, with that same quizzical, half-laughing look, he added, "but you know, sir, as well as I do, that not half of them are Christians worth counting." "Well," I said to myself, astonished, "this is a mining camp; this certainly is not anything like the condition of affairs in the country generally."

The Night Visitor

After that trip I became much interested in discovering in John's Gospel some striking pictorial illustrations of these two kinds of Christians, namely, those who have power in their lives for Jesus Christ and those who have not. Let me speak of only a few of these. The first is sketched briefly in the third chapter, with added touches in the seventh and nineteenth chapters. There is a little descriptive phrase used each time—"the man who came to Jesus by night."

That comes to be in John's mind the most graphic and sure way of identifying this man. A good deal of criticism, chiefly among the upper classes, had already been aroused by Jesus' acts and words. This man, Nicodemus, clearly was deeply impressed by the young preacher from up in Galilee. He wants to find out more about him. But he shrank back from exposing himself to criticism by these influential people for his possible friendship with the young radical, as Jesus was regarded.

So one day, he waits until the friendly shadows will conceal his identity, and slipping quietly along the streets, close up to the houses so as to ensure his purpose of not being recognized, he goes up yonder side street where Jesus has lodgings. He knocks timidly. "Does the preacher from up the north way stop here?" "Yes." "Could I see Him?" He steps in and spends an evening in earnest conversation. I think we will all readily agree that Nicodemus believed Jesus after that night's interview, however, he may have failed to understand all He said. Yes, we can say much more—he loved Him. For after the cruel crucifixion, it is this man that brings a box of very precious spices, weighing as much as a hundred pounds, worth, without question, a large sum of money, with which to embalm the dead body of his friend. Ah! He loved Him. No one may question that.

But turn now to the seventh chapter of John. There is being held a special session of the Jewish Senate in Jerusalem for the express purpose of determining how to silence Jesus—to get rid of Him. This man is a member of that body and is present. Yonder he sits with the others, listening while his friend Jesus is being discussed and His removal—by force if need be—is being plotted. What does he do? What would you expect of a friend of Jesus under such circumstances? I wonder what you and I would have done? I wonder what we do? Does he say modestly, but plainly, "I spent a whole evening with this man, questioning Him, talking with Him, listening to Him. I feel quite sure that He is our promised Messiah, and I have decided to accept Him as such."

Did he say that? That would have been the simple truth. But such a remark plainly would have aroused a storm of criticism, and he dreaded that. Yet he felt that something should be said. So, lawyer-like, he puts the case abstractly. "Hmm—does our law judge a man without giving him a fair hearing?" That sounds fair, though it does seem rather feeble in the face of their determined opposition. But nearby sits a burly Pharisee, who turns sharply around and, glaring savagely at Nicodemus, says sneeringly: "Who are you? Do you come from Galilee, too? Look and see! No prophet comes out of Galilee"—with the most intense contempt in the tone with which he pronounces the word Galilee.

And poor Nicodemus seems to shrink back into half his former size and has not another word to say, though all the facts, easily ascertainable, were upon his side of the case. He loved Jesus without doubt, but he had no power for Him among men because of his timidity. Shall I use a plainer, though uglier, word—his cowardice? That is not a pleasant word to apply to a man. But is it not the true word here?

He was so afraid of what they would think and say! Is that the sort of Christian you are? Believing Jesus, trusting Him, saved by Him, loving Him, but shrinking back from speaking out for Him, tactfully, plainly, when an opportunity presents or can be made. A Christian, but without positive power for

Him among men because of cowardice!

The Master's Ideal

There is another kind of Christian, an utterly different kind, spoken of and illustrated in this same Gospel of John, and I doubt not many of them also are here. It is Jesus' ideal of what I, a Christian, should be. Have you sometimes wished you could have a few minutes of quiet talk with Jesus? I mean face to face, as two of us might sit and talk together. You have thought you would ask Him to say very simply and plainly just what He expects of you.

Well, I believe He would answer in words something like those of this seventh chapter of John. It was at the time of the Feast of Tabernacles. There was a vast multitude of Jews there from all parts of the world. It was like an immense convention, but larger than any convention we know. The people were not entertained in the homes but lived for seven days in leafy booths made of branches of trees. It was the last day of the feast. There was a large concourse of people gathered in one of the temple areas, not women, but men, not sitting, but standing.

Up yonder stand the priests, pouring water out of large jars, to symbolize the outpouring of the Holy Spirit upon the nation of Israel. Just then, Jesus speaks, and amid the silence of the intently watching throng His voice rings out: "If any man thirsts let him come unto Me and drink; he that believeth on Me, as the Scripture saith, out of his belly shall flow rivers of living water." Mark that significant closing clause. That packs into a sentence Jesus' ideal of what a true Christian down in this world should be, and may be. Every word is full of meaning.

The heart of the sentence is in the last word—"water." Water is an essential of life. The absence of water means suffering and sickness, dearth and death. Plenty of good water means life. All the history of the world clusters about the watercourses; study the history of the rivers, the seashores, and lake edges, and you know the history of the earth. Those men who heard Jesus speak would instinctively think of the Jordan. It was their river.

Now plainly Jesus is talking of something that may, through us, exert as decided an influence upon the lives of those we touch as water has exerted, and still exerts, on the history of the earth, and as this Jordan did in that wonderful, historic Palestine. Mark the quantity of water—"rivers."

Not a Jordan merely, that would be wonderful enough, but Jordans—a Jordan, and a Nile, and a Euphrates, a Yang Tse Kiang, and an Olga and a Rhine, a Seine and a Thames, and a Hudson and an Ohio—"rivers."

Notice, too, the kind of water. Like this racing, turbulent, muddy Jordan? No, no! "Rivers of living water," "water of life, clear as crystal."

You remember in Ezekiel's vision which we read together that the waters constantly increased in depth, and that everywhere they went there was healing, and abundant life, and prosperity, and beauty, and food, and a continual harvest the year-round, and all because of the waters of the river. They were veritable waters of life.

Now mark that little, but very significant, phrase—"out of"—not into, but "out of." All the difference in the lives of men lies in the difference between these two expressions. "Into" is the world's preposition. Every stream turns in, and that means a dead sea. Many a man's life is simply the coastline of a dead sea. "Out of" is the Master's word. His thought is of others.

The stream must flow in and must flow through if it is to flow out, but it is judged by its direction, and Jesus would turn it outward. There must be good connections upward, and a clear channel inward, but the objective point is outward toward a parched earth. But before it can flow out it must fill up. And outflow, in this case, means an overflow.

There must be a flooding inside before there can be a flowing out. And let the fact be carefully marked that it is only the overflow from the fullness within our own lives that brings refreshing to anyone else. A man praying at a conference in England for the outpouring of the Holy Spirit said: "O, Lord, we can't hold much, but we can overflow lots." That is exactly the Master's thought. "Out of his belly shall flow rivers of living water."

A Clogged Channel

Out in Colorado, they tell of a little town nestled down at the foot of some hills—a sleepy-hollow village. You remember the rainfall is very slight out there, and they depend much upon irrigation. But some enterprising citizens ran a pipe up the hills to a lake of clear, sweet water.

As a result, the town enjoyed a bountiful supply of water the year-round without being dependent upon the doubtful rainfall. And the population increased, and the place had quite a western boom. One morning the housewives turned the water spigots, but no water came. There was some sputtering. There is apt to be noise when there is nothing else. The men climbed the hill. There was the lake full as ever. They examined around the pipes as well as possible, but could find no break.

One day one of the town officials received a note. It was poorly written, with bad spelling and grammar, but he never cared less about writing or grammar than just then. It said in effect: "Ef you'll jes pull the plug out of the pipe about eight inches from the top, you'll get all the water you want."

Up they started for the top of the hill, and examining the pipe, found the plug which some vicious tramp had inserted. Not a very big plug—just big enough to fill the pipe. It is surprising how large a reservoir of water can be held back by how small a plug. Out came the plug; down came the water freely; by and by back came prosperity again.

Why is there such a lack of power in our lives? The answer is very plain. You know why. There is a plug in the pipe. How shall we have power, abundant, life-giving, sweetening our own lives, and changing those we touch? The answer is easy for me to give—it will be much harder for us all to do—pull out the plug. Get out the thing that you know is hindering.

I am going to ask everyone who will, to offer this simple prayer: "Lord Jesus, show me what there is in my life that is displeasing to Thee; what there is Thou wouldst change." You may be sure He will. He is faithful. He will put His finger on that tender spot very surely. Then add a second clause to that prayer—"By Thy grace helping me, I will pull it out, whatever it may cost or wherever it may cut."

My Body, Soul, and Spirit

My body, soul and spirit,
Jesus, I give to thee,
A consecrated offering,
Thine evermore to be.

O Jesus, mighty Saviour,
I trust in thy great name;
I look for thy salvation,
Thy promise now I claim.

O let the fire, descending
Just now upon my soul,
Consume my humble offering,
And cleanse and make me whole!

I'm thine, O blessèd Jesus,
Washed by thy precious blood;
Now seal me by thy Spirit
A sacrifice to God.

- Mary D. James

CHAPTER 26

Step by Step

J. Gregory Mantle

J. Gregory Mantle (1852-1925) was born in England and ministered as pastor of the Norfolk Road Church, Brighton, and as superintendent of the West London Mission, St. James's Hall, Piccadilly; he also served as editor of the *Illustrated Missionary News*. Early in the 20th century, Dr. Mantle left England for the United States and taught at the Missionary Training Institute at Nyack-on-the-Hudson (now Nyack College), New York. During his lifetime, Mantle wrote many books, including *According to the Pattern* and *The Way of the Cross* (also known as *Beyond Humiliation*). Friend of F. B. Meyer and G. Campbell Morgan, he is not as well known as these famous preachers, but his writings are still fresh and fragrant with the Spirit of Christ, which appears to have characterized his life.

The following article appeared in *Prairie Overcomer*, September 1985.

BISHOP HANDLEY MOULE, in his valuable work, *Veni Creator,* reminds us that there is a "specialty of phrase in the Greek word rendered "walk" in Galatians 5:25. He translates the verse, "If we live by the Spirit, let us also *take step by step by the Spirit.*" Conybeare's translation is equally suggestive: "If we live by the Spirit, let our steps be guided by the Spirit."

It is one thing to "live by the Spirit," to know that we have life by His power; it is another thing, in the minutest details of daily life, to yield to the authority and guidance of our Life-giver. Andrew Murray thinks these words suggest to us very clearly the difference between the sickly and the healthy Christian life. "In the former, the Christian is content to 'live by the Spirit'; he is satisfied with knowing that he has the new life, but he does not walk by the Spirit. The true believer, on the contrary, is not content without having his whole walk and behavior in the power of the Spirit."

Why is the position so often taken in those large gatherings of Christian people now so common, not more generally maintained? How many, in a supreme moment, under the mighty power of God, throw open every avenue of their being to the incoming of the Holy Spirit! And we dare not doubt that He floods the entire being with His energy when it is thus surrendered to Him. But the experience is often transitory, as set forth in the following lines:

> *There have been moments pure,*
> *When I have seen Thy face and felt Thy power;*
> *Then evil lost its grasp, and passion hushed*
> *Owned the divine enchantment of the hour.*
> *These were but seasons beautiful and rare.*

Why "season beautiful and *rare*"! Because those who thus surrender themselves, do not go away to "take step by step by the Spirit." In an unguarded moment, *self* has been allowed to regain the supremacy, and some portions of the life have been given over to its control. Steps have been taken, not by the Spirit, but by the flesh. For a little moment, perhaps only in what seemed a trifling detail, the reins, which were unconditionally placed in the hands of the Spirit of God, were snatched out of His grasp. A grieved Spirit, and a life and work from which the power had departed, are the result.

Carelessness

In many cases, this is more the result of carelessness than anything else. Hence the need for clearer teaching on the subject. The Christian worker has said, like Samson, "I will go out as at other times and shake myself. And he wist not that the Lord was departed from him" (Judges 16:20). He finds, to his sorrow, that some subtle evil has shorn him of his strength, that some little rift within the lute has made the music mute, but how or why he scarcely knows.

John Wesley, knowing how much higher an experience it was to take step by step by the Spirit than simply to live by the Spirit, refused to recognize the Christian perfectness of some of his converts, because they were wanting, he said, in the evidence.

> They do not steadily use that kind and degree of food which they know, or might know, would most conduce to the health, strength, and vigor of the body; or they are not temperate in sleep; they do not rigorously adhere to what is best for body and mind; otherwise they would constantly go to bed and rise early, and at a fixed hour; or they sup late, which is neither good for body nor soul; or they use neither fasting nor abstinence; or they prefer (which are so many forms of intemperance) that preaching, reading, or

conversation which gives them transient joy and comfort, before that which brings godly sorrow or instruction in righteousness.

Many Christians have yet to learn the meaning of that word, "Whether therefore ye eat or drink, or whatsoever ye do, do *all* to the glory of God," for to take step by step by the Spirit means that our meat and drink, and everything that touches the domain of our senses, must ever be placed under a sacred discipline. The same discipline is equally indispensable for the life of our affections and thoughts; for our reading, for our recreation, for our literary and artistic pursuits. To ignore the guidance of the Holy Spirit in any of these departments of life is to cause Him grief, and to forfeit the spiritual power of which He would have us to be the unfailing aqueducts to a dying world.

Unfailing Joy

Lest anyone should imagine that a life which is thus lived step by step by the Holy Spirit is an irksome one, let us say that unfailing obedience always produces unfailing joy and peace. A joyless Christian is almost invariably a disobedient Christian. "A life of self-renouncing love is a life of liberty," for where the Spirit of the Lord is—where He is recognized and obeyed in the minutiae of life—"there is liberty."

"Step by step" is the secret of a life which is never perturbed, never surprised by sudden assaults of the evil one, never shorn of its spiritual strength. With returning consciousness, there is, in such a life, a resolute determination to take no step in the untrodden pathway of the day but by the Spirit. His guidance is sought, and His will consulted in the choice of food. Anything that has been known to dull the spiritual vision, and unfit the body for the sacred uses for which it is designed, will be avoided. "What effect will this book have upon my spiritual life? Will it increase or diminish my relish for the Word of God?" are questions we shall ask when opportunities for reading are afforded us.

"I never spend a penny," said a poor widow one day to the writer, "without asking that I may be guided how to spend it." She was seeking to take step by step by the Spirit. We need not particularize further. Here is the principle by which our life is to be governed, and to follow it will fill our life with such joy and power as we never dreamed of before.

The two realms, which men have designated secular and sacred, will "melt into each other as the roseate streaks of dawn melt into the splendors of the morning" as we take step by step by the Spirit, for when the Spirit of Christ breathes through our life the meanest occupation becomes divine. Nothing is little or great with regard to the things of God. Everything that bears the impress of His will is great, however trifling it may appear. It is this alone which gives value to the duties of our life, and nothing can be regarded as small or insignificant that is the object of His desire. A natural tendency to untidiness is easily overcome if, for His sake, and that we may please Him in everything, we keep the room or the papers in order....

Triumphs in the Trifles

Our life is made up of these little steps. We fancy we could be heroic on some great occasion. We could die for Christ, we think, if called upon to lay down our life for Him. It is questionable, however, if we could, unless we have cultivated the martyr spirit hour by hour, for if our strength and desire to please God have failed in the trifles of our life, how can we be sure of them in the great testing time? It is far harder to live for Christ moment by moment than it is to die once for Him. If we wait for great occasions in which to display our fidelity, we shall find that our life has slipped away, and with it, the opportunities which each hour has brought of proving our love to our Lord, by being faithful in that which is least.

We understand that if the earth were dependent upon the sun alone for heat, it would not keep existence in animal and vegetable life upon its surface. The stars furnish heat enough in the course of the year to melt a great crust of ice, almost as much as is supplied by the sun. This seems strange when we consider how immeasurably small must be the amount of heat received from any of these distant bodies. But the surprise vanishes when we remember that the whole firmament is so thickly strewn with stars, that in some places thousands are crowded together with a space no greater than that occupied by the full moon. This illustrates the truth we have been seeking to enforce. It is to the thousands of little acts, which have been made bright because the Spirit of Christ has come into them all, that the true child of God owes the light and heat and beauty of his life.

We cannot do better than close with the following striking words of Pastor Stockmayer:

> When sin or our selfishness, at any distance whatever, shows itself in our horizon, when we notice something in the wind so that our moral sky, our spiritual atmosphere, is not altogether clear, let us know that it is His grace which signals the danger, His Spirit who awakens our attention. Let us stop at once; let us hasten to our refuge under the shadow of His wings; let us renewedly tighten the bonds that unite us to Him, until the light of His countenance has driven away the last vestige of the cloud, and the at-

mosphere has again become luminous.

Be not discouraged, if at the first attempt you fail to realize this life. Though thy communion with God be a hundred times, yea, a thousand times interrupted, do not suffer thyself to be paralyzed by these sad experiences. It is true that the wrong done to thy soul by even one momentary separation from God, such as one sin can occasion, a sin by thought, or word, or deed, is far more disastrous than you can know. Nevertheless, there may be something worse, something which adds evil to evil, namely, permitting yourself to be discouraged instead of returning immediately to God, in order to find in Him pardon and renewing of life.

"If we live by the Spirit, let us also take step by step by the Spirit."

Come Near to God

Come near to God.
* How can that be?*
I've sinned,
* the Law I've broken—*
*   there's no hope for me.*

Come near to God.
* The way is now open:*
Jesus has died,
* the Lord crucified—*
*   the veil has been torn.*

Come near to God.
* With a heart sincere,*
Faith fully assured
* and heart made clean—*
*   the conscience now clear.*

Come near to God.
* Your Priest intercedes,*
Your Father's arms open,
* Your need brings you near—*
*   The Spirit with you pleads.*

                - Ralph I. Tilley

CHAPTER 27

What to Do When You Stumble

W. E. Sangster

Never taken to a place of worship for the first eight years of his life, W. E. Sangster (1900-1960) found his way into an inner-city London Methodist mission where he attended Sunday School for years. When he was 12, a sensitive teacher gently asked him if he wanted to become a disciple of Jesus Christ. "I spluttered out my little prayer," he wrote years later. "It had one merit. I meant it." The outbreak of World War II found him senior minister at Westminster Central Hall, the "cathedral" of Methodism. The sanctuary, seating 3000, was full morning and evening for the next 16 years.

In 1949, Sangster was elected president of the Methodist Conference of Great Britain. He knew that while the Spirit alone ultimately brings people to faith in Jesus Christ, the witness of men and women is always the context of the Spirit's activity. He coveted for his people a whole-souled, self-oblivious, horizon-filling immersion in the depths of God and in the suffering of their neighbors. The following article is taken from *Can I Know God?* by W. E. Sangster.

PAUL IS GIVING pastoral advice in this part of his letter to the Galatians. He is telling his readers how they should treat one of their own number who stumbles in the way. There is to be no spiritual pride and superiority, no contempt for the one who had fallen, no forgetfulness that temptation is the lot of us all. "Thrust your shoulder," he says in effect, "under the burden of that man's shame and so fulfill the law of Christ."

My friends, I don't believe you are failing in that ministry. I believe you are tender not only to the tempted but to those who yield to temptation. It is another—and related word—of which I have reason to believe you stand in need.

How do you deal with yourself when you have been overtaken in a fault? All of us stumble at times. Some of us crash. Others may, or may not, know about it, but we know, and God knows! How do we handle ourselves in an hour like that? We may be tempted to wallow in the evil and deny that it is sin at all. We may make restitution and feel, falsely, that restitution (important and necessary as it is when possible) has canceled out the sin. We may be so engulfed in shame that we just give up.

Let me see, as one sinner talking to others if I can help you at that very point. First, don't minimize the sin. Don't let yourself off lightly. If, indeed, it was a moral mishap, don't say that it doesn't matter. Never say about sin, "It isn't important." That is a lie and a lie with awful penalties for your own soul. The Bible says plainly, "The wages of sin is death." The first thing, therefore, is to recognize the sin as a sin, repent the wrong you have done; claim forgiveness from God, and hate the evil for the loathsome thing it is.

Now, there are three common ways in which our guilty souls seek to avoid the admission of guilt. Sometimes we tamper with the labels. Sometimes we plead that the circumstances were peculiar. Sometimes we argue that times have changed. All of them are efforts to deny or minimize the guilt, and they are all perilous because the first thing we have to do is to recognize it quite clearly, admit it to ourselves, and confess before God the evil that we have done.

Let us glance at those three traps in turn.

1. *Don't tamper with the labels.* Don't call a serious thing by a light name and try to sneak it past your moral guard. We began that practice in childhood. We called a lie a "fib," but it was still a lie. We did it (some of us) in the army. We called stealing "scrounging," but it was still stealing. Some people are doing it on buses and trains today. They aim to avoid paying their fare. It is robbery, but they call it "being smart." It isn't smart; it is plain thieving. Some people live a loose sexual life and call it "love." It isn't love; it is lust.

Years ago, I attended a joint meeting of doctors, psychiatrists, and ministers to discover ways in which we could work together. There was a great deal of talk at that meeting about "pre-marital and extra-marital sexual relationships." I knew, of course, what they were meaning by all that, but there was one old rural parson present who was confused by the terms and couldn't keep his feet in the conversation. Finally, he said, "Pre-marital and extra-marital sexual relationships? Do you mean fornication and adultery?" I can recall now the astonishment of those plain and biblical words created in that assembly. We like to gloss things over with less challenging names, and that is one of the ways in which we grease the path to sin.

Now, that is the first trap to avoid if you would never minimize the sinfulness of sin; don't tamper with the labels. You don't make a deadly thing innocuous by employing a light name. Cancer is still cancer, even when you call it "a bit of indigestion."

2. *Don't deceive yourself into supposing that sin is ever justified by circumstances.* How did you get into that guilty relationship, through loneliness—just through loneliness? "The Lord knoweth," says the Bible, "how to deliver the godly out of temptation."

Other people are lonely and don't get into that. The loneliness was only a factor. The lack of a firm moral principle was the real cause, a failure to claim and use the help of God.

How did you come to pass on that slander? Somebody told you? But people often tell untruths. Did you not scrutinize it? Did you not first inquire whether it had any foundation in fact? No, you were eager to pass it on. Why? Because you did not like the person about whom that slander was made. Jealousy gave it currency. You wanted to believe it.

Oh, don't excuse yourself in these things on the ground of circumstances! Admit the sin. There is nothing so healthy, nothing so disposing to spiritual healing than to drop all evasions and admit the fault.

Two or three weeks ago, I crossed Holland. It was all done on a fast train in a couple of hours. What a little country Holland is! What a poor country, too, in some ways! A waterlogged swamp, much of it below sea level. What circumstances!

And in that mold of ugly circumstances, one of the great peoples of the world grew up and contributed to art, to navigation, and to explore some of the world's greatest men.

If people wanted to make an excuse for circumstances, the Dutch had it, but they turned the circumstances into triumph.

3. *Don't persuade yourself that morality varies from age to age.* Among the many stupid phrases which people use to excuse their moral faults is to say of the severer ethical code of an earlier day, "Oh, that's Victorian!"

Listen! We are not dealing with the Victorian, the Edwardian, or the Georgian. Nor, for that matter, with the new Elizabethan. In morality, we are dealing with the eternal God. When God gave the Ten Commandments, he didn't give them just for a few Semitic tribes and for one era in the long history of our race. He gave them to the Israelites, but, through them, to all humanity and for all time. They were meant to be the basis of all morality.

Engraved as in eternal brass,
Thy mighty promise shines;

Nor can the powers of darkness 'rase
Those everlasting lines.

And not the promise only, the Ten Commandments also:

Engraved as in eternal brass,
The Ten Commandments shine;
Nor can the powers of darkness 'rase
One everlasting line.

Time makes no difference to the moral counsels of God. It is for the Negro and for the Eskimo, this side of the "iron curtain" and that, for kings and commoners, and for every era of time. Customs may change but not the decrees of God. What chances to be in vogue may alter, like the shape of women's hats, but not the fiat of the mighty God.

Be on your guard against these traps, and you are not likely to fail in the first of our injunctions. Beware of the danger of tampering with the labels. Beware of the danger of making an excuse for circumstances. Beware of the danger of pleading that customs can affect God's moral demands.

Then you will not minimize your fault. Then you will see sin for the loathsome thing it is, and you will cry from the heart, "Have mercy upon me, O God, according to thy lovingkindness: according to the multitude of thy tender mercies blot out my transgressions."

Having accepted the forgiveness of God, don't brood over the past.

There are many people in the family of God who do not doubt God's forgiveness, but they never seem able to forgive themselves. The memory of their sin lacerates them. It is hardly ever out of their minds. So far from being able, as some are, to forgive themselves lightly, they seem unable to forgive themselves at all. Just like some unhealed wound in the body, this unhealed wound in the spirit drains their strength, hinders their progress, pours pus into the bloodstream, and keeps them in a state of spiritual invalidism.

Let me talk to that need because I know that some of you are in it. God has forgiven you; forgive yourself. Who are you to have superior moral values to the almighty God?

Here are two things which will help you to forgive yourself.

1. *Can't you see that your unwillingness to forgive yourself is a form of spiritual pride?* What you are really saying, at some deep level of your mental and emotional life, is this: "How could I ever have done that?" (Note the stress on the "I," the undue stress). "Me? A spiritual giant like me? A person who has

had all the advantages that I have had? How I hate myself."

Now, look! That self-hate is doing you no good. It is, indeed, at that stage, doing you harm. It wakens the self-destructive principle in your nature. It is like poison injected into your veins. Accept the forgiveness. You cannot undo the past. God has forgiven it and, if God has forgiven you, who can justly accuse you?

That is the first thing: forgive yourself.

2. *In some mysterious way, beyond our human fathoming, God can use sin.* I know it is mysterious, for sin is God's one intolerance, but the God who is mighty in creation is mighty also in transformation.

I point you to the Cross again. The Cross was the foulest thing our race ever did; it was the most sublime thing God ever did. The Cross was our worst, it was God's best. The Cross was our nadir; it was (if we dare use such a word of the All Holy) God's zenith.

Think now! You say you cannot forgive yourself? If you will really take that sin to God—really take it to him and not hug it to yourself—he will make something of it, something of your sin. Not by encouraging you, I think, to talk much about it, but to use it to drive the engine of your will, to quicken all your compassion to sinners, to show God's tender heart to the fallen, when other professing Christians might give the false impression that God is hard and unforgiving.

Have you ever wondered how Paul could toil on at his work as he did, year in and year out, in labors abundant and stripes above measure? What drove him on? The memory, among other things, of his sin. The recollection of the persecutions, the imprisonments, and the stonings he had inflicted on others. You might even suspect at times (though this would be a false inference, I think) that Paul had not forgiven himself! The poet puts these words on his lips as Paul thinks of the saints he had ill-used:

Saints, did I say? with your remembered faces,
Dear men and women, whom I sought and slew!
Ah when we mingle in the heavenly places
How will I weep to Stephen and to you!

Finally, I would say this: Don't fail to claim a perfect cure. What do I mean by that? I mean that sin isn't necessary. "Ah, but," you say, "everybody sins."

I still say that "sin isn't necessary." The Bible promises that God will, with temptation, "make a way to escape."

Our spiritual fathers had a simple technique for convincing people that sin isn't necessary. They would say to those who seemed to argue that we must sin, "Can you live without sin for a minute? Yes? Can you live without sin for five minutes, for an hour ... ?" You see how their simple logic worked. They did not argue that anybody but our Lord had ever lived without sin, and they didn't consider enough the state of sinfulness apart from separate sins. They just insisted that sin in a redeemed man isn't necessary.

Put nothing beyond the grace of God. You have no right to say that God never has and never will keep a redeemed man or woman without sin. Sin (we have said) is God's one intolerance. All the resources of heaven are engaged against sin. It is the purpose of God that you be holy. Charles Wesley sang:

He wills that I should holy be;
That holiness I long to feel,
That full divine conformity
To all my Saviour's righteous will.

Charles Wesley sang also about the miracles of life, the things which never could be and, yet, which God would sometime bring to pass, and he said:

The most impossible of all
Is, that I e'er from sin should cease;
Yet shall it be, I know it shall:
Jesus, look to Thy faithfulness!
If nothing is too hard for Thee,
All things are possible to me.

Don't fail to claim a perfect cure. Don't live in the mental state of those whose subconscious thinking runs like this: "All people sin. I must too." Paul answered that false reasoning when he said, "Make not provision for the flesh, to fulfill the lusts thereof." If you feel that only in eternity could God do this wonderful thing and that perhaps all eternity's too short to transform a nature like yours, think more on the power of grace. Is anything too hard for the Almighty? Have faith for holiness, even though the more you have of it, the less you realize that it is growing within.

Some of the greatest saints had been some of the foulest sinners.

I was reading recently the life of a woman who had been for years anybody's "pick-up," and today she is raised to the altar, entitled "saint," and receives the veneration of vast multitudes.

The God who took the foul-mouthed Peter, the bloodstained Paul, the lustful Augustine, and a million lost and undone sinners and made them not just "highly respectable" but made them saints will not deny his grace to you—transforming grace!

Claim a perfect cure. However impossible this will seem to you (and however difficult the balanced theological statement of this truth undoubtedly is!), you must ever hold before you your true goal.

Have you been overtaken in a fault? A serious fault? A "sin" you would call it, rather than a fault?

It is time for great care.

Don't minimize your sin; go to God, and get forgiven.

Don't brood on the past.

Don't fail to claim a perfect cure.

God, Be Merciful to Me (Psalm 51)

God, be merciful to me,
On Thy grace I rest my plea;
Plenteous in compassion Thou,
Blot out my transgressions now;
Wash me, make me pure within,
Cleanse, O cleanse me from my sin.

My transgressions I confess,
Grief and guilt my soul oppress;
I have sinned against Thy grace
And provoked Thee to Thy face;
I confess Thy judgment just,
Speechless, I Thy mercy trust.

Broken, humbled to the dust
By Thy wrath and judgment just,
Let my contrite heart rejoice
And in gladness hear Thy voice;
From my sins O hide Thy face,
Blot them out in boundless grace.

Gracious God, my heart renew,
Make my spirit right and true;
Cast me not away from Thee,
Let Thy Spirit dwell in me;
Thy salvation's joy impart,
Steadfast make my willing heart.

- Scottish Psalter

CHAPTER 28

Breathe on Me, Breath of God

Ralph I. Tilley

Ralph I. Tilley served as a pastor (38 years), professor of New Testament Studies, founding editor of *Life in the Spirit Journal* for 20 years, and continues to serve as the online editor of *Life in the Spirit*; he is presently engaged in writing, publishing, and teaching ministries. He holds degrees from God's Bible School & College (Th.B.), Andrews University (M.A.), and Trinity Theological Seminary (D.R.S.). Since 2008, Ralph has served as a visiting lecturer at West Africa Theological Seminary, Lagos, Nigeria.

Ralph and his wife Emily reside in Sellersburg, Indiana; they have two married daughters and three grandchildren.

FOR ALL THOSE who were filled with the Holy Spirit on the day of Pentecost (as well as those who experienced a similar filling of the Spirit afterward who were not present at Pentecost), for those who enjoyed subsequent fillings of the Spirit, and for all of those who experienced the fullness of the Spirit as a way of life—each of these was clearly empowered with an ability to cultivate and express a passionate love for Christ, which would have been otherwise impossible. It is the unhindered fullness of the Spirit's indwelling presence, which is the great energizer for loving Christ with all one's heart, soul, mind and strength, and loving our neighbor as ourselves. The fullness of the Spirit makes passionate love for Christ possible.

> [1]*When the day of Pentecost came, they were all together in on place.* [2]*Suddenly a sound like the blowing of a violent wind came from heaven and filled the whole house where they were sitting.* [3]*They saw what seemed to be tongues of fire that separated and came to rest on each of them.* [4]*All of them were filled with the Holy Spirit and began to speak in other*

tongues as the Spirit enabled them (Acts 2:1-4).

Then Peter, filled with the Holy Spirit, said to them ... (Acts 4:8).

After they prayed, the place where they were meeting was shaken. And they were all filled with the Holy Spirit and spoke the word of God boldly (Acts 4:31).[1]

What else can explain Peter's transformed life apart from the fullness of the Spirit's presence in his life and ministry? After the cleansing and filling of the Holy Spirit, Peter was no longer afflicted with a plethora of inner spiritual inadequacies which had long dogged his every step. While facing difficult odds, he became a courageous herald of the good news of Jesus Christ. He was transformed into a faithful, devoted disciple of Jesus, a defender of the faith, and a loving shepherd and a teacher of the flock of Christ. His spiritual poise, disciplined life, loving service, wise leadership, humble example, evangelistic zeal, steadfast spirit, joyful heart, catholic attitude—can all be attributed to the abiding fullness of the Helper at work in and through him.

It is impossible to cultivate and express a faithful, passionate love for Christ apart from the Spirit's fullness pervading the hearts of Christ's disciples. The Spirit's fullness is a divine prerequisite. As Gordon Fee has said, "All truly Christian behavior is the result of being Spirit people, people filled with the Spirit of God, who live by the Spirit and walk by the Spirit."[2] To try to practice the spiritual disciplines, to attempt to know, love, and serve Christ as one should—cannot be done without experiencing the Spirit's help and fullness. This is why the filling of the Spirit should be considered as foundational to cultivating and expressing a passionate love for Jesus Christ and people.

While many scholars would contest his view on this subject, English Anglican preacher and scholar H. C. G. Moule (1841-1920) believed that this filling "is always seen as taking place where there is already present the New Birth; and the possession of that Birth is thus the occasion for a holy desire and longing to possess in some sense the Filling."[3] I could not agree more.

Because of every follower of Christ's significant personal inner needs, and because of the great mission to which Christ's disciples are called, the prayer of Charles Wesley (1707-1788) is appropriate when contemplating this vital subject:

O Thou Who camest from above,
The pure celestial fire to impart,
Kindle a flame of sacred love

Upon the mean altar of my heart.

There let it for Thy glory burn
With inextinguishable blaze,
And trembling to its source return,
In humble prayer and fervent praise.

Jesus, confirm my heart's desire
To work and speak and think for Thee;
Still let me guard the holy fire,
And still stir up Thy gift in me.

Ready for all Thy perfect will,
My acts of faith and love repeat,
Till death Thy endless mercies seal,
And make my sacrifice complete.[4]

It has been the desire of every earnest follower of the Lord Jesus these last two millennia, to have "a flame of sacred love" kindled upon the altar of their needy and unworthy heart. As Christ's disciples seek to cultivate and express their love for him, they are empowered from above as they "guard the holy fire" within, being continually filled with the Spirit to be all God intended them to be, and to perform what he has called them to do.

The Church's Great Need

The church's decline in every age can be attributed to her lack of the Holy Spirit. The same can be said of every Christian's decline. When believers fail to be continually filled with the Spirit, walk in the Spirit, worship in the Spirit, conduct the business of the church in the Spirit, and be led by the Spirit, they will end in grieving the Holy Spirit; they will be substantially ineffective in their service for the Lord Jesus.

What discerning Christian among us is not heartbroken when considering the instability, immaturity, and the powerlessness of so many believers—believers that should be living better than they are.

Too often God's people are acting in the flesh instead of walking in the Spirit's fullness. Thus, we have Christians who are losing their tempers, succumbing to fleshly addictions, materialistic, easily offended, intemperate in controlling their natural passions and affections, indolent, lacking a passionate love for the Lord Jesus and the things of God, listless in prayer, more selfish than selfless, and on we could go.

The church needs the Spirit's fullness! Every follower of Christ needs to be filled—and continually filled—with the Holy Spirit. If we are not filled with the Spirit, we will be filled with self and act in the flesh. It is the Spirit's unhindered control in the believer that brings great honor to our heavenly Father and glory to the Lord Jesus Christ. Without his fullness, we glorify self and parade the flesh.

Like a Dove

The Holy Spirit desires to rest like a dove upon every receptive believer, just as the Spirit came like a dove at Christ's baptism and rested upon him. But he will not remain upon those who refuse to confess their corruption, their need.

At this point, I want to draw from the wisdom of a God-shaped and anointed man, A. W. Tozer (1897-1963). One of the symbols of the Holy Spirit in Scripture is that of a dove. Tozer appeals to the Flood narrative in Genesis to make a point about the Spirit's fullness, the Spirit's resting upon God's people. He writes,

> The Holy Spirit is in some measure resident in the breast of everyone that is converted. Otherwise, there wouldn't be conversion. The Holy Spirit doesn't stand outside a man and regenerate him; He comes in to regenerate him. That is one thing, and we're glad and grateful for that, but it's quite another thing for the Holy Spirit to come down with His wings outspread, uninhibited, free and pleased to fill lives, and to fill churches, and to fill denominations. That's quite another thing. That some measure of the Spirit is in the breast of every converted man is good and right and real. It is also true that the Holy Spirit wants to come down, as the dove wanted to land on the dry ground and could find no place for the sole of her foot. In our day, too, the Spirit seeks a resting place for His feet."[5]

What Should We Do?

If you are a follower of Christ and your life is not characterized by the Holy Spirit's fullness, what should you do? Let me encourage you to fall on your face before God. Allow the Spirit to search your heart as you prayerfully meditate upon the Word of God. As the Spirit reveals to you and convicts you of your failures, your sins, confess those sins and take them to the Cross for forgiveness. Ask the Lord to give you a total cleansing, a renewed heart. Ask him to fill you with his holy love. Ask the Lord to grant you his promised fullness. Do not seek the gift of tongues or any other gift. Seek Christ, look to Christ—always look to Christ.

On the last day of the feast, the great day, Jesus stood up and cried out, "If anyone thirsts, let him come to me and drink. Whoever believes in me, as the Scripture has said, "Out of his heart will flow rivers of living water." Now this he said about the Spirit, whom those who believed in him were to receive, for as yet the Spirit had not been given, because Jesus was not yet glorified (Jn. 7:37-39).

The only prerequisite required for a seeking heart to be filled and purified—and continually filled and purified—with the Spirit, is a strong appetite for God, a deep thirst for God, a complete consecration of ourselves to God. Pray with Elwood H. Stokes (1815-1895):

Hover o'er me, Holy Spirit,
Bathe my trembling heart and brow;
Fill me with Thy hallow'd presence,
Come, O come and fill me now.

Thou canst fill me, gracious Spirit,
Though I cannot tell Thee how;
But I need Thee, greatly need Thee,
Come, O come and fill me now.

I am weakness, full of weakness,
At Thy sacred feet I bow;
Blest, divine, eternal Spirit,
Fill with pow'r, and fill me now.[6]

Remember, God forgives what we confess; he sanctifies what we offer; he fills what he sanctifies; he uses what he fills.

Breath of God

"If we are going to be the children of God," to quote Tozer once more, "we must have the Spirit of the Father to breathe into our hearts and breathe through us. That is why we must have the Spirit of God. That is why the Church must have the Spirit of Christ."[7]

What breath is to our body, the Holy Spirit is to the believer and Christ's Church. In the Hebrew language, in which the Old Testament was originally written, the word for breath, breathe, wind, and spirit are all the same word—*ruakh*.

In the Genesis creation account, man did not become a living being until he experienced the inbreathed breath of God: "the Lord God formed the man of dust from the ground and *breathed* into his nostrils the *breath* of life, and the man became a living creature" (Gen. 2:7).

When God called the prophet Ezekiel to prophesy to the valley of dry bones (a symbol of God's lifeless people), these hardened structures were only restored to life the moment the breath of God entered them: "Thus says the Lord God to these bones: Behold, I will cause *breath* to enter you, and you shall live" (Ezek. 37:5). What was once a hopeless graveyard became a mighty army, energized by the Spirit of God—as soon as the breath of God entered lifeless bones: "So I prophesied as he commanded me, and the *breath* came into them, and they lived and stood on their feet, an exceedingly great army" (Ezek. 37:10). So that they and we would not miss the message of this vivid illustration, God said to the people through the prophet: "And I will put my *Spirit* within you, and you shall live" (Ezek. 37:14).

Now let us turn to the New Testament. It was Sunday evening following Christ's resurrection that very morning. Because of fear of what the authorities might do to them, all the apostles, except Thomas, who was absent, were meeting behind locked doors. Jesus suddenly entered the room. Following his pronouncement of peace, Jesus did an amazing thing. He "breathed on them and said to them, 'Receive the Holy Spirit'" (Jn. 20:22), thus speaking and acting in anticipation of the coming Pentecost event, which would occur a few weeks later.

Furthermore, on the day of the promised outpouring of the Holy Spirit, the "breath" language continues: "And suddenly there came from heaven a sound like a mighty rushing *wind* [breath], and it filled the house where they were sitting" (Acts 2:2). The Greek word translated "wind" in most versions, could just as accurately be translated "breath" (the word is translated "breath" in Acts 17:25).[8]

Christians and churches are in great need of experiencing the manifest presence and power of God. And the church can only experience God's presence and power if individual believers are living in a dynamic, intimate relationship with the Lord Jesus Christ, made possible by the inbreathed Spirit.

The Spirit of God indwells all true believers, but not all believers are always fully surrendered to Christ and walking in the fullness of the Spirit. We need the Holy Spirit—the forgotten member of the Triune God! We need the Breath of fresh air!

Writing over a century ago, while serving as a Baptist pastor in the city of Boston, Dr. A. J. Gordon (1836-1895), noted:

> The Spirit is the breath of God in the body of his church. While that divine body survives and must, multitudes of churches have so shut out the Spirit

from rule and authority and supremacy in the midst of them that the ascended Lord can only say to them: 'Thou hast a name to live and art dead' (Rev. 3:1). In a word, so vital and indispensable is the ministry of the Spirit, that without it nothing else will avail.... The body may be as to its organs perfect and entire, lacking nothing; but simply because the Spirit has been withdrawn from it, it has passed from a church into a corpse.[9]

Less than fifty years after Gordon, the Methodist president of Cliff College, England, Samuel Chadwick (1860-1932), wrote:

> The church that is man-managed instead of God-governed is doomed to failure. A ministry that is college-trained but not Spirit-filled works no miracles. The church that multiplies committees and neglects prayer may be fussy, noisy, enterprising, but it labours in vain and spends its strength for nought. It is possible to excel in mechanics and fail in dynamics. There is a superabundance of machinery; what is lacking is power. To run an organization needs no God. Man can supply the energy, enterprise, and enthusiasm for things human. The real work of a church depends upon the power of the Spirit.[10]

Lamenting the desperate lack of the manifest presence of the Holy Spirit in our midst, while unwittingly depending on human resources, present-day minister and writer Frances Chan observes: "The church becomes irrelevant when it becomes a purely human creation. We are not all we were meant to be when everything in our lives and churches can be explained apart from the work and presence of the Spirit of God."[13]

Yes, we need the Breath of God!

Full-of-the-Spirit Baptist pastor, Charles Spurgeon (1834-1892), was mightily used of God as he witnessed thousands of conversions under his ministry, as well as seeing multitudes of his parishioners mature in Christ (this is not to suggest that all Spirit-filled people will witness great, observable success). Spurgeon lived and ministered in the power of the Holy Spirit because he believed the Spirit to be more than dry ink on a creedal statement of faith.

There were fifteen steps up and into the pulpit (one literally walked into those old pulpits) of the London Metropolitan Tabernacle, steps which Spurgeon climbed twice each Lord's Day. At each step, the great evangelical preacher would quietly affirm with full conviction, "I believe in the Holy Ghost!" Fifteen times: "I believe in the Holy Ghost!"

Do you, dear reader? Do you really believe in the Holy Spirit as Christ's gift to you? Is he a living reality in your heart and life?

THE SPIRIT OF HOLINESS & POWER

We are speaking about experiencing the Holy Spirit and living a life of holiness—all to the glory of God with our eyes fixed on Jesus. We have not prescribed any "magic formula" or "three easy steps" in living a victorious Christian life. With the Spirit's help, what I hope will occur as you read these pages is a renewed hunger for reality—an authentic Christian life, a holy life—a full life lived in the power of the Holy Spirit.

Too many Christians are living defeated lives; they have settled down to live a defeated Christian life without experiencing the reality presented in Romans 8. If that is the case with you, I pray you will meet God in a deepening, in-breathing encounter, repenting of your sin, lukewarmness, and shallowness.

Call it the baptism with the Holy Spirit, the infilling of the Spirit, entire sanctification, total consecration, second blessing, anointing of the Holy Spirit, etc.—I will not quibble with the terminology. The questions we might ask are: Am I living a life of holiness and power? Am I consistently overcoming willful sin? Is my life characterized by love, joy, and peace? Am I living a selfless, generous lifestyle? Am I fully surrendered to Christ? If my answers to the questions are not in the affirmative, I need to earnestly pray for God to perform a further, deep work of the Holy Spirit in my heart, and then, daily live my life keeping in step with the Spirit, walking in love, and keeping short accounts with God when I have failed.

It is God who is working in us to accomplish his purposes. We must work out what God works in. To walk with God is to cooperate with God; this is the Christian life. Allow the grace of the Lord Jesus Christ to produce in you his holy character, that you may glorify God and be a blessing to others.

As we conclude this article and book, please join me in praying this prayer, written by the English Anglican minister, professor, and hymn writer, Edwin Hatch (1835-1889).

Breathe on me, Breath of God,
Fill me with life anew,
That I may love what thou dost love,
And do what thou wouldst do.

Breathe on me, Breath of God,
Until my heart is pure,
Until with thee I will one will,
To do and to endure.

Breathe on me, Breath of God,
Till I am wholly thine,

Till all this earthly part of me
Glows with thy fire divine.[14]

---

1. Unless otherwise indicated, all Scripture quotations in this article are taken from the *English Standard Version*.
2. Gordon D. Fee, *God's Empowering Presence: The Holy Spirit in the Letters of Paul* (Peabody, MA: Hendrickson Publishers, 1994), 721.
3. H. C. G. Moule, Veni *Creator: Thoughts on the Person and Work of the Holy Spirit*, reprint (London: Hodder and Stroughton, 1890), 211.
4. Charles Wesley, "O Thou Who Camest from Above."
5. A. W. Tozer, *Life in the Spirit* (Peabody, MA: Hendricksen Publishers, 2009), 166-167.
6. Elwood H. Stokes, "Fill Me Now."
7. A. W. Tozer, *The Counselor,* Gerald B. Smith, ed. (Camp Hill, PA: Christian Publications, 1993), 63.
8. See George R. Berry, *The Interlinear Literal Translation of the Greek New Testament* (Grand Rapids: Zondervan, n. d.), 313.
9. A. J. Gordon, *The Ministry of the Spirit* (Philadelphia: American Baptist Publication Society, 1896), 141-142.
10. Samuel Chadwick, *The Way to Pentecost* (Berne, IN: Light and Hope Publications, 1937), 12.
11. Francis Chan, (2009) *The Forgotten God* [Kindle iPad version]. Retrieved from http://www.amazon.com.
12. Edwin Hatch, "Breathe on Me, Breath of God."

Descend Upon Our Hearts

You who long ago descended
*   upon a seeking, waiting host,*
Descend upon our hearts today—
*   the Father's promised Holy Ghost.*

O illuminating Spirit,
*   O Light to darkened, blinded eyes,*
Enable us to see Jesus—
*   Heaven's exalted, risen Prize.*

O fiery Spirit of burning,
*   consume in us all that is dross;*
Come and cleanse your prepared temples,
*   as we gaze upon God's own Cross.*

While bending low before the Throne,
*   all self-rule we boldly renounce.*

THE SPIRIT OF HOLINESS & POWER

"Jesus is Lord," you help us pray;
  this we most joyfully announce.

O Wind of God, breathe within us,
  filling everyone's yielded heart;
Renew in us Christ's holy love,
  leaving no inner, untouched part.

O Spirit of God, now send us
  to serve others in Jesus' name,
Humbly walking before our God,
  spreading abroad Christ's worthy name.

- Ralph I. Tilley

BOOKS BY RALPH I. TILLEY
(available in paperback and Kindle)

Authored

Thirsting for God: Poetry, Meditations, Prayers

Letters from Noah *(historical fiction)*

Breath of God: Experiencing Life in the Spirit

A Passion for Christ: A Devotional Journey into Christlikeness

Christ in You: Living the Christ-Life

Renewed by the Spirit: 365 Daily Meditations *(also available in Spanish)*

Wellspring: 365 Devotional Readings

All about Jesus: 365 Daily Meditations

Anthologies Compiled & Edited

The Christian's Vital Breath: An Anthology on Prayer

How Christ Came to Church: An Anthology of the Works of A. J. Gordon

Called to Be Saints: An Anthology on Holiness

The Spirit of Holiness & Power: An Anthology on the Holy Spirit

Edited and Reprinted

The Mind of Christ / *John D. MacDuff*

The Bow in the Cloud / *John D. MacDuff*

In the Footprints of the Lamb / *George Steinberger*

Not Peace But a Sword: How Revival Came to Riverby Memorial Church / *Vance Havner*

Convicted & Transformed: The Christian's Relationship to the Holy Spirit / *Myron S. Augsburger*

Evangelical Saints: 47 Biographical Sketches / *Ernest Gordon*

The Master's Way / *Frank Mangs*

(go to litsjournal.org or Amazon.com)

www.ingramcontent.com/pod-product-compliance
Lightning Source LLC
Chambersburg PA
CBHW071454040426
42444CB00008B/1337